ANNEVILLE

A Memoir of the Great Depression

Thomas G. Robinson

authorHOUSE®

AuthorHouse™
1663 Liberty Drive, Suite 200
Bloomington, IN 47403
www.authorhouse.com
Phone: 1-800-839-8640

First published by AuthorHouse   4/3/2009

ISBN: 978-1-4389-7008-0 (sc)

Library of Congress Control Number: 2009902815

Printed in the United States of America
Bloomington, Indiana

This book is printed on acid-free paper.

This book is dedicated with gratitude and love to

my brother,

Joseph D. Robinson

Acknowledgements

This book, of course, could not have been produced without the help of many people. I dearly wish I had the time, space, and memory to thank every single person who helped me, but that is impossible; so I will try to name some of those who were especially essential to getting this book published.

First I must thank my wife, Patricia, who for 52 years has been my partner and best friend. I must also thank my siblings, all of whom were the inspiration and the subject matter of Anneville. Thank you, Jim Heiner for your diligence and skill you so generously expended in proofreading and correcting my manuscript. Thank you Mary Ann Robinson for working so hard on the graphics and editing prior to submitting the manuscript to the publisher. I cannot tell you how much I appreciate your generosity in helping to get this book published. I must also thank my good friend, John Smith, who had enough faith in my book to keep pestering me to get it published. I want to thank all those who read the manuscript and encouraged me with their kind words about my work. Here are some of them:

Rosemary Johnston, Mark Masterson, Roger Devenyns, Rosemary Devenyns, Lorra Laven, Russell Lomperis, Jill Tucker, Shandel Gamer, Kathy Bogomaz, Rob Smith of Iowa, Mary Soares, and Trudi Fletcher.

Finally, I want to thank my daughter, Alana Millard, my granddaughter, Erin Millard, and my grandson, Tommy Millard. Their love, and their faith in me gave me strength and comfort whenever I lost hope in my work.

Preface

Tuesday, the 29th of October, 1929, "Black Tuesday," is considered by most people to be the seminal event in the decade-long disaster that has come to be known as The Great Depression. In the early months of 1929, some economists were warning that the financial structures of America, and indeed of most of the industrialized world, were heading for a massive breakdown; but very few investors heeded these warnings and no one foresaw the full magnitude of the calamity that was about to occur.

Statistics alone cannot fully illustrate how bad things became after the crash, but they are useful to some extent, and so they are presented here for what they are worth.

On Black Tuesday over sixteen million shares were traded -- a record that lasted for 30 years. In only two weeks the market had lost 26 billion dollars, one third of the value recorded in September, 1929 -- money that could never be recovered. How much that 26 billion would be worth in today's dollars is inestimable; how much human suffering this loss caused can only be imagined.

Businesses began to fail at an alarming rate. By the end of 1930, there had been a record-breaking 26,255 business failures, and the Gross National Product was down 12.6 per cent. Agriculture, which had been in trouble all through the twenties, was now in even deeper trouble. Farm foreclosures reached epidemic proportions. The miseries of those impacted by the Dust Bowl have been brilliantly described by John Steinbeck in his *The Grapes of Wrath*, but similar miseries were inflicted on farmers all over the country.

In Iowa groups of farmers had to resort to armed violence to try to keep their farms from being taken away from them by the banks. Farmers who managed to keep their farms were unable to sell their products, and it was not uncommon to see crops rotting in the fields and live stock dying on the hoof for want of markets.

People who had bank savings lost their money too.

The banking system began to collapse. In 1930, 1,352 banks suspended operations forever, wiping out the savings of all of their depositors. A pathetic example of one of these failures might help to illustrate how devastating these were to ordinary folks:

On December 11, 1931, New York City's Bank of the United States failed, and 400,000 depositors lost all of their savings permanently. Most of the depositors had been immigrants -- small businessmen and wage earners who had labored long and hard to set aside money that would tide them over during hard times. It would be a long time before these folks would ever trust an American bank again.

The shrinking buying power of the public resulting from the losses in the stock market and banks created a chain reaction that ravaged our entire economy. Business and industry were forced to lay off more and more workers, and these unemployed workers were unable to buy goods, which caused businesses and factories to lay off even more and more workers. By December, 1930, 4 million workers had lost their jobs. By the end of 1931, unemployment had soared to 8 million; and by November, 1934, unemployment had reached 13 million.

Those who had lost their savings in the stock market or in bank failures became completely destitute once they lost their jobs. The few public, private, and religious relief agencies that had existed before the crash became hopelessly overwhelmed. The federal government was restricted by law from assisting local and state relief authorities; so these agencies became overwhelmed also.

Those who depended on pensions for income soon found their income reduced drastically and, in many cases, completely cut off.

For the first time in the history of the country the tide of immigration was reversed: hundreds of thousands of people left our shores to try to find a better life some place else. Many American citizens of Mexican heritage headed for south of the border. In California illegal Mexican farm laborers were packed into boxcars like cattle and shipped back to Mexico. The catalogue of grim statistics goes on and on.

Hunger, privation, and malnutrition became widespread. In some areas people, especially children, died of famine. A reporter wrote about the terrible plight of a small band of unemployed coal miners in Appalachia. One worker told the reporter: "The winter is the worse. That's when we begin to lose the children. Seven have died already -- you ain't seen anything really bad until you see one of your little ones shrivel up and die cause you don't have enough food to keep 'em alive."

Such tragic anecdotes are not isolated examples: they are all too familiar.

But the allotment of human misery is never evenly distributed, and the severity of the suffering in those days varied widely from region to region.

Not everyone was personally affected by the economic woes of the times. Some even prospered, and there are those alive today who say that the reports of wide-scale suffering during The Depression are exaggerated. Some even claim that if a person had enough intelligence and determination, he would have had little trouble making a living during the thirties. It's impossible to fully refute such charges, but we do know that many people of high intelligence and boundless determination were destroyed by The Depression. Regarding the extent of the suffering, there is no way to quantify human misery; there is no Richter scale to measure the magnitude of such disasters, but all evidence indicates that The Great Depression was the worst economic upheaval in our history, and that it caused extreme poverty, squalor, unhappiness, and despair to untold millions of Americans and other people of the world.

Demagogues, religious extremists, and crackpots of all stripes try to use the hard times of the thirties to prove the efficacy of their various beliefs; but there seems to be no clear answers as to what actually caused The Depression and what can be done to prevent it from ever happening again. All we can do is to continue to study such events carefully, and, if we find we have made mistakes, avoid making them again.

This novel does not try to examine the causes of the Depression; it only tries to examine a few stitches in a vast tapestry. It tells the story of the Robinson family--eight souls out of the tens of millions of people who suffered through those grim times.

The suffering of the Robinson family was certainly not as great as that of someother families, but it was bad enough. Their story is true. The names of most of the people and places have been changed, and the dialogue and sequence of events have been presented only as accurately as the memory of the author has permitted; therefore this book is called a novel rather than a memoir or autobiography. It has often been said, and is probably true, that most nonfiction contains some fiction; and that all good fiction contains much truth. Whether this book is good fiction or not is up to the reader to decide, but the author has taken great pains to be as truthful as is humanly possible.

CHAPTER 1

Brother, can you spare a dime?"
__Popular song of 1932__

ON A BLEAK, BITTERLY cold morning in early January, 1932, the small town of Anneville in southeastern Massachusetts, is hunkering down for the second winter of The Great Depression. Thos Robinson, who will be five years old on January 21, three weeks away, has no conception of the economic catastrophe that has befallen his country; but he knows full well that something is horribly wrong in his home. Mother and Daddy are often shrieking at one another; the baby, Regis, is constantly crying; he and his brothers and sisters are always hungry; and many pieces of furniture have been hauled away by strange men in large trucks.

There is a knock on the door. When Daddy opens it, a stocky, dark-haired man is standing there. He is wearing a hat with a shiny bill, and a dark gray zipper jacket with the name of the Acme Furniture Company prominently displayed on the left side of his broad chest. He holds an invoice in his hand.

"This is 112 Slocum Street, right?" The man asks.

"That's right," Daddy says belligerently.

The man ignores the belligerence. "You Mister Robinson? James Robinson?"

"I am!" Daddy says firmly, then his voice becomes sarcastic. "If you're selling anything, Buddy, you've sure knocked on the wrong door."

1

The man becomes impatient. "Look, Mr. Robinson, You know why I'm here. I'm repossessing a linoleum rug. That one you're standing on, I believe."

The man is pointing to a nine-by-twelve foot rectangle of linoleum which has been manufactured to simulate a cheap woolen rug. James Robinson does not budge. "Move aside, Sir, I gotta job to do," the man says

"I've already made three payments on this rug. I've lost my job, Mister. I'll make the rest of the payments as soon as I get another. I'm out every day looking. . ."

The man interrupts. "Get serious, Brother! Everybody in this freaking country is looking for a job!"

James begins to shout. "Goddamn it! You can't pull a rug out from under an honest man's feet while his kid is looking on! I'm tired of you bastards taking back stuff I've practically already paid for!" His voice is shaking now. "You take one step inside my house, and I swear I'll knock you down!"

The man is silent for a moment. He takes a deep breath. "Don't be stupid, Mac. I hate this job. It's a stinking, rotten job; yet there were hundreds of guys begging for this one. The only reason they chose me is because I used to be a professional fighter--you might'a heard of me--Earthquake Quigley they called me. Hell, of course you've never heard of me! I guess nobody's ever heard of me. But I hadda punch that could've felled a horse. I don't want to have to hit you here in front of your kid. Get out of the way man! If I don't get this rug back soon, I'll be looking for a job-same as you."

As the man rolls up the linoleum and hauls it out to the truck, Daddy looks helplessly on; then he stands on the bare boards of the kitchen floor. His shoulders sag, and he hangs his head.

Mother comes in carrying Baby Regis in her arms. "You let him take the linoleum, didn't you!" she says bitterly.

"What could I do, Mary? The guy had the Law on his side, and he outweighed me by a hundred pounds. He was a prize fighter for cripes sakes!"

Regis starts crying.

"You're weak, Jim! You just let everybody walk all over you. We've got seven hungry kids, for God's sake! You need more gumption! Start fighting back! There must be jobs out there somewhere! Are you just going to stand there feeling sorry for yourself while we all starve or freeze to death!"

"As God is my witness, Mary, I'm doing the best I can. There's no work anywhere--everybody knows that!"

"They are advertising in the paper. I've seen the ads . . ."

"Sure! *Wonderful opportunity for men willing to work. Make big money!* I've applied for every one of them--bloody crooks! Hundreds of guys fill out the forms and wait in long lines for interviews. Then you find out the scam. They want you to buy, with your own money, some product that's not worth half of what they charge you. Then they tell you that you can go door-to-door and sell it at a profit. Hell, you can't even give the stuff away!. The crooks will never buy the junk back for any price, and you're stuck. I'm dumb, but not that dumb! Let's face it, Mary; we've hit bottom. None of the charities can help us. They're all swamped with poor people—even our parish can't help us. Sure, the churches are packed now, but nobody has any dough to put in the collections. There's some talk about the government setting up a relief system, but that'll take years or, at best, many months before that would do us any good. What am I supposed to do now, Woman?"

"One thing we've got to do is get back to Philadelphia. At least we have relatives and some friends there. I should have never let you talk me into coming up here to this Godforsaken hole in the first place. 'It's an opportunity,' you said. 'I'll be foreman,' you said."

"It was good while it lasted. Wasn't it Mary? I had a good salary, we had money in the bank, a good stock portfolio. I was planning to get a car, put a down payment on a home. Then the goddamned Crash comes! I lose my job, my savings, and all my stocks are worthless! Hell! Can I help it if the whole freaking country suddenly falls apart? We've been over this before. There's no way we can get back to Philly. We're totally broke. Nobody will lend us enough dough to get us out of this town. If it were just us two, we could hitch-hike back. But with seven kids. . ."

"I suppose it's my fault we've got seven kids?" She pauses, and her voice becomes ice. "I'll tell you one thing, James Andrew Robinson! I'm not having any more!"

3

Daddy's voice is different now. He is close to tears. "Mary, it's nobody's fault that we're in this fix. I just can't think of anything else to do but put the kids in St. Mary's. Then we can thumb our way down to Philly and try to get to where we can afford to come back for them."

"I'll never put my children in an orphanage! Never!" she screams.

Regis begins wailing. Thos leaves and joins Lorraine, young James, Patricia, Joe, and Rosebud in the front room. They cluster together wide-eyed, wondering what will happen to them all.

The next morning when Thos wakes, the bedroom window is thick with frost. He pulls his clothes on over his flannel pajamas, puts on his shoes, wraps a blanket around himself, and goes downstairs. Mother is sitting at the kitchen table hunched over a mug of coffee, holding it with both hands as though trying to keep herself warm. Her hair, which is usually carefully brushed, is bedraggled, her face is haggard, and her lovely blue eyes hollow and bloodshot. She stares at him and says slowly, "Daddy is gone, Thos. I don't think we're going to see him again for a very long time."

CHAPTER 2

"Having been poor is no shame,
But being ashamed of it, is."
-Benjamin Franklin-

January 23, 1932

WRAPPED IN THEIR WARMEST clothes, but still shivering against the bitter New England cold, the four youngest of the Robinson children: Joe, seven; Thos, five; Rosebud; four; and Regis, two; sat at the bottom of the unpainted cellar stairs. The cellar was dusty, dank, moody, and cob-webbed.

Upstairs the children could hear people bustling around, and someone pounding on the pipes.

"Why did Mother put us down here?" Thos asked, and each of his words was accompanied by a puff of frosted breath.

"This is the warmest place in the house now that they've turned off the gas and electricity," Joe said.

"I don't like the cellar. It's dark and it smells funny and there's spiders down here," whimpered Rosebud.

"Don't worry, there are no spiders dumb enough to be out in this cold," Joe said. "And besides, we won't be here long." He paused, trying to think of something cheerful to say. Mother had told him that since he was the oldest of this little band, he'd have to keep the others from crying. Then he continued. "We're going to get to ride in a truck, and we'll go to a place where we'll be warm, and there'll be plenty of food."

Rosebud, who had a cold, wiped her nose with her mittened right hand, and sniffled, "I heard Lizzie Horton tell Patricia that we're being sent to St. Mary's home where the nuns whack you with rulers, and you have to eat oatmeal with lumps in it."

Regis began to cry, and Joe put his arm around his baby brother. "Stop crying, Regis, It's going to be all right. Mother said that Lizzie is a Calamity Jane—a trouble maker who's always trying to scare kids. Mother told me that the nuns at St. Mary's love children, and the food is good there--fresh milk from bottles and toasted bread with butter--even oranges."

"Will Mother and Lorraine and Patricia and James come with us?" Rosebud asked.

"No, but Mother said that she and the rest of them will come to visit us often," Joe said.

The door at the top of the stairs opened and Lorraine, the eldest of the children, said cheerfully, "Come on upstairs, kids. Joe, you take Regis's hand."

Lorraine, at fourteen, was tall and pretty with lovely green eyes. She held the cellar door as the four waifs moved past her into the hall. Mother ushered them into the warm kitchen. The heat was coming from the gas stove whose four burners were all lit, and the smell of burning methane gas was heavy in the air.

"I've got good news: the gas is back on," Mother said. "Come in and thaw your poor little bones. Be careful, children, don't get too close to the flames."

Lorraine came in and stood next to a teen-aged boy, Alex Wallington. He was skinny and had an enormous Adam's apple, but he had a shock of sandy hair and a twinkle in his blue eyes that gave him a pleasant, friendly air.

"Alex here, God bless him, fixed the gas and electricity. The company turned them off because we couldn't pay the bill, so I asked Alex to jimmy the meters. He did it for his own family--learned how to do it in vocational school. Normally it's wrong to do this, but it's almost zero in this house, and I'm not going to let us all freeze to death! I hope God will forgive me this time, and if the company finds out, I'll take responsibility for it. It's my fault and not Alex's."

Alex, still holding a large monkey wrench, appeared embarrassed and stared down at the worn wooden floorboards.

Mother turned to James, her oldest son-- a sturdy lad of twelve.

"James, you stand by the window. The minute you see the truck pull up, go out there and tell the driver that your mother is sorry that he had to come all the way out here for nothing, but there are no orphans in this house yet." James quickly took his post at the window, and Mother continued." Lorraine, you go to Gabrowski's. Tell them you want a soup bone, and don't let them charge you a cent for that; they throw most of them in the garbage, anyway. Get four potatoes, two carrots, and two onions. That's not much so they should let you put it on our bill."

"But, Mother," Loraine said respectfully, "Mr. Foquette told me to tell you, you can't charge anything more until you pay for what you owe."

"You tell that weasel Fourchette that Mr. Gabrowski said that I could buy some food if it was a real emergency--this is an emergency. And tell Fourchette he better not make me come up there to get it myself, if he knows what's good for him!"

Then she turned to Alex and her voice was much kinder now. "Alex, you can go with her; just leave the wrench here on the table on top of the newspaper."

She waited until Lorraine and Alex had left, then she began: "Now all of you, listen carefully, and if you know what's good for you, do <u>exactly</u> what I tell you to do from now on. Remember, it is a mortal sin to disobey your mother! What goes on in this house is our business, and our business only. If anybody ever asks you any questions about our business, you tell them you don't know. If they ask you where your father is, you don't know. If they ask you if you have gas or electricity, you don't know. Any questions they ask you--about anything—you don't know. This is very important, children, do you understand?"

All the children nodded affirmatively, although the only thing they really understood was that from now on, the only answer to any question from anyone but the family would be: "I don't know;" for there was no way they ever wanted to incur the wrath of Almighty God and Mother at the same time!

Mother paused until her commandments had sunk in, then she continued: "Children, I know you're frightened and confused--hungry and cold. You don't understand the bad things that are happening to us. I don't understand it all myself. I do know this though: I know things will get better. This horrible cold won't last forever, we'll have some warm food soon, and I'll tell you something very important. Each and every one of you is very precious to me--my flesh and my blood. I will never let anyone take you away—never!"

Then Mother's eyes began to glow more brightly. She clenched her jaw, and she began to speak as though the children were no longer there. "The Selectmen of this town told me that I would have to put the four youngest of you in the orphanage. They said that I'm only a woman--that there's no way I can take care of you without a man to support me. Huh! I don't know how I'm going to do it. I'll need God's help, of course, but I'm going to show those old fools! They'll find out what the poet really meant when he said, 'Hell hath no fury like a woman scorned!'"

Finally she simmered down and spoke more gently. "But you have to help me. It's going to be tough on me, but it may be even tougher on you. I've been praying to the Blessed Mother to help me. You may be cold sometimes, but I won't let you freeze to death. You may be hungry, but I won't let you starve. When Lorraine gets back, I'll start making some hot, delicious soup. Patricia, you fill the teakettle and put it on the burner. Be careful. I've got flour and baking powder, so I'll start making some biscuits. You'll be surprised how quickly I can make them. You kids can stay in the kitchen until you're good and warm."

The warmth of the kitchen, and the promise that they would finally get some food in their pinched bellies was good news indeed to the three youngest of the children, but Thos was disappointed. He was looking forward to the ride in the truck, and the thought that the nuns liked kids and would keep them warm and well fed sounded a lot better to him than what had been happening around this house ever since Daddy had left. He watched dejectedly as the truck drove away.

Mary Robinson also felt dejected. She was no fool, and she understood very well the difficulties of the task that lay ahead of her. She was only 34 years old—still young and vivacious—a shapely, blue-eyed, auburn-haired beauty. Though she had never finished grammar school, she read omnivorously; and her speech was often peppered with literary and Biblical allusions. But all of these qualities would do her little good now. She would have to forget about herself, and, like so many other mothers, devote the coming years to her kids.

Even if she were able to get someone to care for her children, It would be impossible to get a job. There were just none available.

Doing anything unethical or illegal was totally against her nature. She knew of a very decent woman who had to resort to making and selling bootleg whisky in order to feed her children. She admired the woman, but she didn't have the knowledge or the courage to do that. The only recourse left to her was beggary, and to beg was totally repugnant to her proud Irish spirit; but she had no other option. She had to find some kind of public assistance to provide her family with food, clothing, and shelter until she could manage to support them herself.

The only relief available to indigents was to put themselves "on the town." This meant that the unfortunates would have to appear at a public town meeting and plead their case before the Board of Selectmen, who were the guardians of the meager tax revenues of the town. The process was deliberately designed to be humiliating. In those "good old days" the community leaders felt that people who had to ask for public assistance were no better than bums, and a little humiliation might encourage these wretches to try harder to find means of supporting themselves. And so Mother had to swallow her pride and begin her battle to get some kind of regular income for her destitute family.

None of her children ever attended any of the town meetings, but Thos would sometimes overhear Mother talking to Lorraine about the clashes with the three stern-faced men who had been elected to the Board of Selectmen. Occasionally Thos would hear townspeople gossiping about that "nervy Robinson woman mouthing off at the town meetings."

Some of the most vicious gossipers whispered that Mary had used her feminine wiles on one of the selectmen, Giles Brewster, who was one of the wealthiest men in town. The Brewsters were one of the original settlers of Anneville, and many Anneville mothers held hopes of having the handsome bachelor as a son-in-law.

It was true that Giles had taken Mother's side in most of her arguments with the board, but the gossip, of course, was absurd. In a town as small as Anneville there was no way a man as prominent as Giles, and a woman with seven children could secretly manage even the most innocent kind of relationship.

Somehow, though, and Mother admitted that she probably couldn't have done it without Brewster's help, she managed to persuade the Board to award her the small allowance of one dollar a week for each child. Even in those days that wasn't enough money to feed, clothe, and house seven growing children.

So, swallowing her pride again, she sent out letters to every friend and relative she knew asking for "loans" to help her get by. Most of the people she contacted were practically as penniless as she, but occasionally a letter would come with a few dollars in it, and her kids would have butter on their bread, and maybe an orange or two, and sometimes even fresh milk.

Therefore, thanks to the kindness of good people, the Robinsons had some good days, but there were also some very bad days, too.

None of the children had heard anything about Daddy since he had left. Whether Mother had heard from him during that time was not known by the children or probably anyone else in Anneville. Mother's commandment to answer all questions about "family business" with the three words, "I don't know," was rigidly adhered to by all seven of the children.

Once, Thos had heard Lorraine ask Mother, "But where is he, Mother, really?"

"I told you, Lorraine, not to ask that question. As far as you're concerned, he's dead." she said firmly.

But he wasn't dead.

On a cheerless Saturday, late in March, 1932, as James, Joe, and Thos were shooting at tin cans with sling-shots in the back yard, Daddy, looking tired and unkempt, for he had hitch-hiked from a long way off, appeared. He greeted the boys and embraced each one of them. His sons were all so glad to see him, they asked no questions. As James wrapped his strong young arms around his father, Thos heard his brother whisper, "I love you, Daddy."

Daddy was silent, but he held on to his oldest son for some time. Then he took the sling shot from James's hand and said. "Mind if I take a few shots?"

Daddy quickly found some small rocks in the dirt part of the yard, and let fly a few stones at the tin cans. He missed, and said with a grin, "I'm a little out of practice boys."

He handed the sling-shot to Joe. "Here, Joe, see what you can do," he said.

Joe quickly scored three hits in a row. He was well-known among the kids of Anneville as the best shot in town.

Just then Mother appeared at the back door. "What are you doing here?" she said angrily.

"I want to talk to you, Mary, please!"

Mother ignored him and spoke to the boys." James! Joe! and Thos! Come in this house this instant!" She glared at her husband. "You, go to hell!"

The boys hurried into the house, and Mother slammed and locked the back door. Then she hurried to the front door and locked that too. Daddy lifted up the cellar doors and went down into the basement. Then Mother quickly locked the inside cellar door. All the kids stood in shocked silence. Lorraine took both Regis and Rosebud in her arms and hugged them.

They could all hear Daddy coming up the rickety stairs. He began pounding on the door. "Unlock this, Goddamit! I've got a right to talk to my kids! Open up!"

Mother's face was pale, but hard as New England granite. She turned to the children and put her finger to her lips. All seven knew that they'd better be silent.

Daddy pounded vainly on the door; then he went down the cellar stairs. Among a few tools left over from the pre-Depression days was an axe for chopping firewood. He came back up with the axe.

"You open this door, Mary, or by Jupiter I'll chop it down!"

Mother remained resolutely silent.

"I mean it, Mary! Open this Goddamned door!"

Suddenly, to the horror of his children, he began hacking away at the flimsy door. As it started to splinter, Regis and Rosebud began howling in terror.

The pathetic sound of their wails was too much for Daddy. His rage subsided; and sick with despair and helplessness, a man completely broken by The Great Depression, he threw the axe down into the cellar. Then he went back down the stairs, exited the cellar, and left Anneville, never to return again.

The incident left indelible scars on the souls of all the children, but the trauma that was left with them was not caused by fear or terror, at least not in the case of Thos and his older siblings. Not once during all of that ordeal were any of them afraid of their father. The scars that were left on the souls of those children were scars of shame and sadness.

CHAPTER 3

By AUGUST, 1932, DESPITE Hoover's optimistic assurances that the depression was almost over and that "Prosperity was just around the corner," more and more workers were losing their jobs, and for the first time in history more people were leaving America than were immigrating to our promised land.

In Anneville, superstitious people were saying that the coming total eclipse of the sun was just another sign that disaster was about to come upon the world. Lizzie Horton told Thos, Rosebud, and Regis that the moon was going to bump into the earth and everybody would be killed. Mother told the terrified children that Lizzie was always imagining foolish stuff like that, and she wished Patricia would stop having her as a friend.

Mother read the kids some scientific explanations of the eclipse from *The New Bradford Times*, which allayed Thos's fears, but they still awaited the coming event with some uneasiness.

In the early afternoon of August 31, as excitement grew, and after the children had been warned for the tenth time not to watch the eclipse directly, the sun began to fade, people stopped talking, birds stopped singing, and the whole Town of Anneville was enveloped in darkness. Mother told the amazed children that, "This is something that we will remember for the rest of our lives."

Thos was relieved that Lizzie's predictions were groundless, and that he would live to see his first day of school, which was only six days away.

When that great day finally arrived, Thos was filled with a mixture of excitement and anxiety. He had heard his elder siblings talk about it often, but school was still a very confusing concept to him.

The teeth of the comb bit into his scalp as Mother scraped his wet hair to one side, out of his eyes. He was dressed in hand-me-downs from James and Joe--a baggy sweater, a pair of knickers whose elastic was gone so that they drooped down well below his knees, and an enormous newsboy's cap. Thos was painfully aware of how ludicrous he looked, but Mother gave him words of encouragement.

"You look so handsome in your knickers and sweater! I'm very proud of my little man today. Just imagine! Your first day of school. You're going into the first grade already, and you won't be six years old until January. Most kids have to go to kindergarten, but you're so smart, I'm having you skip kindergarten and you'll be with the big kids right away. You will love school, and I know you will do what the teacher tells you to do."

It was only the first week in September, but Autumn had already arrived. The breeze was brisk, and leaves were falling from the oaks, elms, and maples; and the sidewalks were littered with leaves and acorns.

As Thos hurried along with James, his little legs vainly trying to match strides with his older brother's much longer ones, he bent down and scooped up one of the acorns. He liked them--the way they looked nestled in little cups with the knurled edges, and he also remembered that when you were really hungry, they don't taste too bad.

"Don't play with that acorn, Thos. It'll get your hands dirty and the teacher will send you to the basement to wash them."

Thos dropped it quickly. Being sent to the basement sounded pretty awful to him. He didn't know then that "the basement" was simply the name given to what his family called "the bathroom."

At school James greeted some of his pals and explained that he had to keep an eye on his kid brother because it was his first day. His pals glanced at Thos and gave a sympathetic look to James. One of them, a husky, rosy-cheeked boy named Jerry, looked at Thos', and said, "Cripes! Where did he get that outfit?"

The kids milled noisily around the yard for awhile; then the first bell rang. This meant that the students were to line up outside of the front door until the second bell rang, and then they were allowed to march in.

James showed Thos what room he was to be in, wished him luck and walked away.

This was the first time in his life that Thos could remember being with a group of strangers without the support of any of his family, and he was frightened. Everyone except him seemed to know what they were supposed to be doing. They jabbered away at each other as though they all belonged to the same family. They stared at Thos, and he became very conscious that his moth-eaten sweater, his oversized knickers, and his black cotton stockings marked him as someone from outside their tribe.

The only friendly face in the room was that of the teacher, Miss Moore. She seemed to realize that he had not been to kindergarten. She smiled at him, led him to a desk, showed him how there was a small storage shelf under the top containing crayons and a mimeographed picture of a barn with a tree next to it. He had never used crayons before, but Miss Moore was so kind, and looked at him with such beautiful blue eyes that he would do anything to please her. She was the most beautiful creature he had ever seen. Mother, Patricia, Lorraine and Rosebud were beautiful, but Miss Moore was something beyond beautiful! When she came near him, all the humiliation, fear, and uncertainty of the day was gone, and he was filled with happiness.

Recess came and the students hurried out into the crowded, noisy playground. Some kids were eating bananas, apples, oranges, and one kid even had a tangerine. The delicious aroma of the fruit hung in the air around them. Thos noticed that he was not the only one who was staring hungrily at the lucky ones with recess snacks. He remembered that Mother had taught him that it is rude to stare at others when they are eating, and he tried to think about the hot soup that Mother had promised them for lunch. Then he saw something that was totally surprising to him. Three children, a few years older than he, were standing around staring at another kid who was eating an apple. One kid, whose clothes looked even worse than Thos's, said boldly. "I get the core first, if there's anything left after I get it, you two can have it."

Somehow, this scene comforted Thos. His family was not the only poor family at this school!

He looked for Lorraine, or James, or Joe, but the upper grades were separated from the kindergartners and first graders in the playground.

Mercifully, recess was short, and he was soon back in the classroom under the spell of the glorious Miss Moore.

When lunchtime came, James found Thos and they hurried home accompanied by Lorraine and Joe. They asked Thos about his morning, but everyone was talking and slurping down soup, so he had little time for his story. They finished their lunch quickly hurried the few blocks back to school.

The afternoon session was as confusing as the morning, but his growing fascination with the entrancing Miss Moore made him feel much less miserable.

The first grade was let out an hour and a half before the upper grades, so he had to walk home by himself. James had prepared him for this and explained that crossing Main Street was dangerous even though there were very few cars on the road in Anneville.

There was only one place where Thos would have to cross the street as he walked to and from school. This was at the corner of Main Street and South Main, an area that had been known in early times as Parting Ways. The school, the police station, and the town hall were on the southeast corner; a large nineteenth century home, surrounded by a box hedge occupied the southwest corner, a gas station and grocery store were located on the northwest corner, and St. Francis Church was across the street to the northeast. It was at this corner where Thos would have many memorable experiences, but few would make as deep an impression on his memory as his first encounter with motiveless malignity.

He looked carefully in both directions. He saw no cars, but he saw something that filled him with dread: Elmer Sharkey was coming after him with a tightly clenched fist and a very mean look on his face. Thos broke and ran for home with Elmer close on his heels. He took the shortcut down Jean Street and across Horton's yard. He scrambled over his back fence and ran breathlessly into the back door of his house, screaming for Mother.

She hurried out of the bathroom where she had been washing clothes in the bathtub. She took him in her arms and tried to calm him down; and though she smelled of laundry soap, and her hair was bedraggled, he clung to her and buried his head in her shoulder.

When he finally stopped crying , she smoothed his hair and asked gently, "What happened, Thos?"

"A big kid chased me home," He whined.

"Only one kid? Was he from a higher grade?'

"I think he was in my room at school."

By this time Rosebud and little Regis were watching the scene with wide eyes. Mother gave them one of those looks that told them to keep quiet; then she studied Thos carefully.

"Did he hurt you?" she asked kindly.

"No, he couldn't catch me, Mother."

"Well, that's good; but you're going to have to learn how to fight. You can't be letting boys in your own class chase you home. When James comes home, he'll show you how to take care of yourself. If the boy is from a higher grade, or there is more than one, you run, but this is a very tough town and you have to learn to stick up for yourself. If you run from boys your own age, every kid in town will be after you."

She made him blow his nose; then she told him to keep an eye on Regis and Rosebud because she had to get back in the bathroom and finish the laundry. She always washed the clothes in the bathtub; for, of course, they couldn't afford a washing machine, or even a washtub, and the bathtub was the only container large enough to hold the dirty laundry generated by seven growing children. She made the best of it-- heating the water on the stove in her largest kettle, carrying it to the tub, throwing the soap and clothes into water, and agitating the clothes with a sanitized plumber's helper;(which she always called a "posser"), then leaning over and rubbing the clothes on a washboard. Thos often sat on the toilet lid and watched the whole procedure with wonder. When Mother finished and began wringing the water out of the damp clothes, he would always be amazed at the strength of her hands.

After supper James and Joe took Thos out in the back yard, and in the September twilight gave him his first lessons in how to fight. James first showed him how to assume a Jack Dempsey pose: keep the left ready to jab, keep the right cocked for the hard punches.

Joe told him to keep his fists clenched tightly: "It hurts 'em more. Aim for their nose. If you pop 'em there hard enough, their nose will bleed all over the place, and the big guys will stop the fight, and you win."

James gave him some of the fundamentals of fair play: "Don't kick or bite, don't hit below the belt, if they go down, let them get up before you belt them again. Never back away from a fight; this town hates sissies. If the guy is a lot bigger than you, tell him you're my brother. If he still comes after you; run like heck, and when I find out who he is, I'll take care of him."

Joe added some further advice: "Take a good look at the guys in your class. There's always a few that you'd be smarter to run from. Watch out for the husky farm kids; they're the ones that usually smell of cow manure. Most of them are nice guys and won't give you any trouble; but if they come after you, run for it. If they ain't too big, I'll take care of 'em later."

When darkness came, and the lessons were over, Thos felt pretty confident, but he still was not looking forward to seeing Elmer Sharkey the next day.

CHAPTER 4

THE SECOND DAY OF school was mostly a repeat of the first day, except that recess was more miserable. Several of the kids asked him why he was dressed so funny, and why he talked like a sissy. He remembered Mother's orders and simply answered, " I don't know."

"Why are you dressed so funny?" the same kid asked.

"I don't know."

"What's your name?"

Thos knew he was being baited now and said nothing.

Elmer Sharkey suddenly appeared and joined the tormenters. "He doesn't know! he doesn't know his own name!" Elmer chanted.

The recess bell finally rang, and Thos managed to get back to the classroom without enduring further harassment; though as he settled into his seat, he saw Elmer glaring at him and holding up his clenched fist in that gesture which clearly meant that Thos was in for it after school.

When school let out, Thos tried to avoid Elmer, but as he crossed Main Street he saw his enemy waiting for him. Sick with fear, he ran diagonally across the street hoping to get ahead of Elmer, but It was no use. There he stood, his fists doubled up, and glowering like an angry savage, blocking the only way to Thos's house. There was no way out. With heart pounding, Thos stopped and assumed the Jack Dempsey position. He heard Joe's voice in his head, " Aim for his nose!"

Elmer was caught completely by surprise. The look of savagery became a look of terror. He hesitated, then wheeled around and ran with Thos hot on his heels. Thos had no idea what he would have done if Elmer had turned to fight, but for the moment he was caught up in the exhilaration of the predator pursuing the prey, even though this time the prey was more eager to escape than the predator was to capture; so Elmer was soon far ahead, and Thos gave up the chase. But he had learned something terrible about himself: he had found that the act of terrorizing another human being was somehow very exciting.

When he told James and Joe about his triumph, he was lathered with praise for being so "tough." He was soon to learn that being called "tough" was the greatest compliment that could ever be given to a male in the town of Anneville.

"Why did the kids in the schoolyard say I talked like a sissy?" Thos asked James.

James put his hand on Thos's shoulder. "Look, Thos, we all talk a little differently because we come from Pennsylvania and this is Massachusetts. Some kids are so ignorant, they think that having a different way of talking makes you weird--a 'sissy.' You're going to have to learn to ignore stupidity like that. They don't know any better."

"Maybe a good punch in the nose would teach them a lesson," Joe said.

"You can't fight every stupid kid you run into, you'd spend the rest of your life, fighting," James said, and they all went back into the house.

A few days later a bag of used clothing was delivered to the house by a man from the American Legion. Some of it was old and patched, but it was clean and Mother was glad to get it. She distributed the clothes to the children according to size and need.

"I'm not wearing any hand-outs," said Patricia. "it's like we were beggars. It's too embarrassing, Mother!" Patricia said firmly.

"You'll wear what I tell you to wear, Patricia; and that goes for all of you!" Mother said. "The men who collected these clothes and delivered them to us are the same heroes who survived the slaughter of The Great War, which ended only fifteen years ago. Many are still suffering from their wounds or poison gas, and here they are trying to help us. We all ought to get down on our knees and thank God for these men! You're embarrassed! Well I'm embarrassed too that the high and mighty people who run this country are so ungrateful to these men. They treated them like beggars when the poor guys asked for the bonus that was promised them. In Washington D.C the government actually fired on our veterans, gassed them, and burned their shacks. <u>Well, those devils will get theirs in November</u>! We'll throw the whole lot out of there and give this country back to the decent people for a change. But for now we're poor, and we all have to make the best of it; and if I hear any more whining out of any of you, I'll give you something to whine about! "

Thos's portion from the bag of clothes was a beret, a woolen, navy-blue beret with a small tassel sticking out of the top like a piece of navy blue macaroni. It was hate at first sight.

"I can't wear that to school, Mother! They'll call me a sissy! It looks like a girl's hat," he whined.

"Don't be foolish, Thos, it's a man's beret. Lot's of men in France wear them, and you look so darling in it."

"You really look cute in it, Thos," Lorraine chimed in.

"No more arguing, you will wear what I tell you to wear, and that's that!" Mother commanded.

The next day Thos, with the beret planted firmly on his head, walked dejectedly behind James and Joe to school. As he approached the school, he could bear the misery no longer. He took off the hated beret and stuffed it in his jacket pocket. The weather was chilly, but not cold enough for frostbite, so James did not stop him.

"if Mother finds out, you're a dead duck," Joe said. "But we won't rat on you, will we, James."

"No, we won't blab on you Thos, but we won't back you up either. It's your funeral, kid, don't say we didn't warn you."

There were a lot of kids already at school, but Thos was able to find an opportunity to hide the beret under the fire escape. and saunter around bare-headed.

When they went home for lunch, Mother was so busy feeding them, she didn't notice the missing beret, but as Thos was about to leave, she asked where his hat was.

" I -- I must have left it at school," Thos said lamely. He had never lied to Mother before, after all, this was technically a statement of fact.

"Well you better have it when you come back, if you know what's good for you, young man!"

"Let's get back to school, Thos," James said quickly, and Thos headed out the door without saying anything.

During the afternoon session Thos , once again under the spell of the divine Miss Moore, had almost forgotten about the wretched beret; but as Miss Moore was leading the class in a rendition of "This Old Man," the classroom door opened, and in walked one of the eighth-grade boys who had been sent around to all the grades to find out who had lost a hat. The janitor, M. Neezlick, had found the beret under the fire escape. Thos's heart sank, but he remained resolutely silent.

Miss Moore took the beret from the boy, and held it up for all to see. "This is a beautiful beret, children. does anybody know who owns this?"

Fortunately, no one had seen Thos wearing the stupid thing, so for the moment his secret was safe, but Thos spent the rest of the afternoon worrying about what would happen when Patricia or Lorraine saw it.

When he got home, Mother immediately asked him where his hat was.

Thos had prepared an answer for her. He bit his lip and said, "I don't know."

Mother looked at him carefully. Was her sweet little Thos mocking her? But he looked so frightened and miserable, she finally asked gently, "Did you lose it, Dear?"

Thos lowered his head. "I don't know," he repeated.

Mother left him alone after that, but Thos knew that when Patricia and Lorraine came home, he would indeed be a "dead duck."

A miracle occurred though, that saved him: none of his sisters or his brothers said a word.

After supper, when he and Joe and James were playing catch with an old tennis ball in the backyard, James told him what had happened. Both Lorraine and Patricia had realized that Thos had tried to throw the hat away when the boy with the "lost and found" beret had visited their classrooms. On the way home from school they all agreed to save poor Thos from disaster by not telling Mother. Thos felt guilty that he had been the cause of such a conspiracy against Mother, but he also felt not only greatly relieved, but also elated and proud -- almost as if he had just been initiated into a very exclusive secret society.

Two days later Thos came down with a bad cold-- sore throat, fever, head congestion -- HE WAS MISERABLE. Mother said it was because he had walked home from school with his head uncovered. Thos wasn't sure whether she was right or whether he was being punished for lying to Mother.

He had to stay home for two days, and when he went back to school he was bundled up with the warmest clothes Mother could find: which included a bulky, hand-knitted sweater Mother had found in the bag of clothes from the American Legion. At school Thos had to remove his outer jacket and hang it in the cloak room. As he walked to his seat, the kids began to point at him and giggle, especially the girls. Red-faced, Thos tried to figure out what was wrong with his outfit this time. In a few minutes the class was in such an uproar that, for the first time in Thos's memory, Miss Moore had to raise her voice to silence them. Then she went to Thos and led him out in the hall. She leaned down and put her arm around him. It's all right, Thos, we just have to straighten out your sweater."

It was only then that Thos realized the awful truth: his sweater, which Mother had stuck into his knickers was bulging out on his chest to form what looked like two well proportioned breasts! The shame of it brought tears to his eyes.

"Thos, dear, it's okay, it could have happened to anyone. Why don't you just go to the basement and straighten yourself out. And, please, Thos, after school stay and I'll help you with some of the work you missed."

Evidently Miss Moore had talked to the class while Thos was in the basement; for when he came back in, they studiously avoided staring at him.

After school Miss Moore asked Thos to erase the blackboards while she tidied up the room. He knew this was an honor usually bestowed only on the best of students, and he felt very proud. Miss Moore showed him some of the lessons he had missed and helped him to do them. Having her close to him and giving him individual attention made him happier than he ever had been since Daddy had gone away. She was the most beautiful creature he had ever seen, but the effect she had on him was more than just from beauty alone. There was a pleasure in being near her that was almost unbearable. He wanted nothing more than to please her, to show her that he loved her more than anybody else in the world -- even more than he loved Mother and his brothers and sisters. He felt guilty about that, but he couldn't help it. He adored Miss Moore.

Even many years afterwards when Parting Ways School was only a dim memory, he remembered how beautiful she was. The only woman who ever rivaled her in beauty was the movie actress Jean Tierney, and that was because Jean Tierney had the same heavenly eyes, and just that hint of an overbite that made her, like Miss Moore, utterly irresistible.

When they had finished, and Thos was about to leave, Miss Moore said kindly, "Are you happy at school, Thos? Are the other kids mean to you?"

Thos blushed, but could not answer."

"That's all right, Thos, you don't have to say anything, but promise me, if you ever want to talk to me, you just stay after school and I'll try to help you. Okay?"

Thos reached out and put his arms around her. She hugged him back and planted a soft and gentle kiss on his flushed cheek.

It was just then that Thos looked up to see Billy Fortier, one of the other first graders, sitting on the fire escape that went by the classroom window. Billy had been watching the whole thing, and there was a look on his face that made Thos realized he would soon be paying dearly for that incredible kiss from Miss Moore.

Billy Fortier was one of the kids who lived on outlying farms, some distance from school and had to take the bus. The ones in kindergarten and first grade had to wait until the upper grades got out before the bus came. They were allowed to play in the schoolyard, but were cautioned to be quiet as long as school was in session. Billy was one of those husky farm kids that smelled of cow manure. Joe had warned Thos that it was better to run like heck from these types. Thos left the school preparing to run for it, but Billy and his pals were waiting for him far enough away from school so that the noise of what they were prepared to do would not disturb the classes. They surrounded Thos cutting of all escape.

"Teacher-kisser! Teacher kisser!" they chanted.

"Sissy! Sissy!" others cried.

The kids were laughing as though they were having great fun; but the remark that they laughed loudest at was when Billy said, "Go ahead, Thos, show us your tits!"

Thos was frightened and hurt; but these kids were trying to turn the beauty of Miss Moore's kiss into something ugly, and his fear suddenly turned to rage. He stood his ground and assumed the Jack Dempsey position. "All right, you buggers! You call me a sissy, but if you weren't ganging up on me, I'd beat the snot out of each of you rats one at a time."

The kids were startled and three of them moved back a little, but Billy stuck his face close to Thos. "You think you can take me, you skinny little puke!"

Thos's stomach became filled with ice, but it was too late to back down now. He stared right back at Billy. "I can whip you're butt any day of the week and twice on Sundays, you stinking clod-hopper!" he said, trying to sound a lot tougher than he felt.

Every kid in Anneville, no matter how young, knew the protocol for a good fight.

They moved back to give the combatants room. Several of the kids even offered to hold Thos's jacket. Billy handed his coat to a pal of his. One of the kids found a twig and placed it on Thos's shoulder. "The minute Billy knocks it off, you can start swinging," he told Thos.

At first Billy was puzzled by Thos's left jabs, and Thos got in several rights that surprised Billy, but soon Billy's weight advantage began to batter down Thos's defenses and the farm boy landed some punches that hurt Thos's face. Thos lowered his head and protected his face with his arms. Then he lowered his head even more and charged Billy. Billy, who evidently had been in fights before, caught Thos with a vicious uppercut that smashed into Thos's nose, making him dizzy, and splattering blood everywhere. By then school had let out and several of the big boys stopped the fight and made the little gladiators shake hands. James came running up. He held a handkerchief to Thos's nose to stem the bleeding. Then he and one of the other big boys made a kind of portable chair with their arms and carried Thos triumphantly home .

"They said you put up quite a fight, I'm sorry I missed it" Joe said.

James stopped the nosebleed and cleaned Thos up. "They tell me the Fortier kid caught you with an uppercut. I'm sorry I didn't warn you about that one. I'm real proud of you, Thos." James said, giving Thos a pat on the back.

After making sure that he was all right, Mother hugged him. "Well, it sounds like you showed those Anneville kids that we Irish are not afraid to fight. That's my little man!" she said.

CHAPTER 5

ON NOVEMBER 4, 1932, Franklin Delano Roosevelt was elected by a landslide, and the hopes of the poverty-stricken folks of Anneville were lifted; but Mother knew that it would take some time, probably many months, before Roosevelt's ambitious plans to bring relief to the poor could take effect. At the time of the election Lorraine was in the eighth grade, James in the sixth, Patricia was in the fifth, Joe in the third, Thos was in the first, and Rosebud and Regis were still toddling around the house.

Mother was constantly worried about how much longer she could continue to care for all of her kids on the meager income she was receiving from the town of Anneville, but a more immediate concern was how much longer would it be before the gas and electric company found out that she was using their services without paying for them.

One day after school, Thos and Joe were in their front yard playing catch with an old baseball. A Chevrolet pulled up, parked, and a man in a snap brimmed hat got out of the car and walked up to the fence.

"Hi boys!" He gave them a friendly smile. "I see you're playing catch. You both look like you have pretty good arms. I guess the Red Sox could use a couple of good pitchers next year." He laughed, but the boys just stared at him. He tried again. "Haven't you been listening to the games on the radio this season?"

Both of the boys moved away from the fence, and prepared to run for it if this guy turned out to be one of the strange men they had been warned about.

The man sensed their fear and moved back away from them. "Don't worry boys, I won't come near you. I work for the gas and electric company. You have gas and electricity, right ?"

Thos didn't answer, but Joe said, "I don't know, Mister."

The man looked at him for a second, and understood. "It's okay son. Could you ask your mother to come out? I'd like to talk to her."

Just then Mother opened the front door, and spoke to the man. "What do you want, Mister!" she said.

He reached in his pocket took out an identification card and held it up. "I'm Bill Jarvis, with the gas and electric company. I'd like to come in and talk to you for a few minutes."

Mother eyed him carefully. You can't come in," she said. "But if you go around to the back porch, we can talk there."

By the time the man walked around to the back of the house Mother was standing just outside the kitchen door. Though there were two old, straight-back chairs nearby, she did not ask Jarvis to sit down, and he stood respectfully at the top of the porch stairs.

Bill Jarvis was not a villain, but he had a job to do. He took out a small notebook from his shirt pocket, thumbed a few pages and glanced at them quickly. "You are Mrs. Mary Robinson, and you live at this residence?"

"Yes," Mother said firmly.

Jarvis knew people well, and he could tell that this Robinson woman would not scare easily, but he thought he would give it a try. "You've been stealing gas and electricity from our company now for many months, and we are prepared to take legal action against you." He waited for a reply, but Mother only stared at him calmly. Then he continued. "However, Mrs. Robinson, we'd like to avoid any unpleasantness; so we are prepared to make you the following offer: If you will pay for the services you have received, and give us the name of the person who illegally connected our services to your home."

Mother did not bat an eye. She remained absolutely motionless and silent.

Jarvis had never encountered such a response. He cleared his throat. "Of course, we will not charge you for the entire seven months you have been stealing our services—we would let you get away with only paying for three. . ."

Mother cut him off, and in a surprisingly sweet voice said, "Mr. Jarvis, please don't take this personally, but you are talking nonsense. You have not established that we've been stealing anything from you, or that anyone has done anything illegal. Besides, even if anything you say is true, we both know that you can't get blood out of a turnip. Now, if you can't say anything more sensible, this conversation is over."

Jarvis closed his little book and put it back in his pocket. "All right lady! You want to play hard ball? Tomorrow, a man will come here and fix it so than no one will ever be able to by-pass the meters again. And, if you try to harass him in any way, we will call the State Troopers!"

He left without another word, and Mother waited until his car had driven away before she began to cry softly.

She went quickly into her bedroom and dried her eyes, but she was still very frightened and discouraged. Jarvis had made her face the harsh reality of her situation. She had been breaking the law, and setting a bad example for her children, and she had been encouraging others to break the law for her. Life once had seemed so simple. Now it seemed that whatever she did, things just got more miserable.

Oh well, this was no time to moan and groan about how things used to be—there was just too much to take care of right now.

Winter was coming fast and without gas or electricity she would have no means of cooking food, lighting the house, or keeping her family from literally freezing to death.

She had a furnace in the cellar which could heat the house, and an old cast-iron wood stove in the kitchen which would allow her to do the cooking; but she needed fuel—coal for the furnace, wood for the stove, and there was no way she could afford any kind of fuel.

As much as she hated the thought of it, she knew that she would once again have to attend a town meeting and, in the presence of the townspeople, beg the selectmen for help.

When the selectmen heard her plea, Mr. Taber, the chairman-pro tem, reminded her that when she had refused to put her children into the orphanage: and when, despite that, they had awarded her the seven dollars a week; and when they had told her they could not possibly afford to give her any more of the taxpayer's money, she said she understood. Why was she now back here whining for more?

Most of the people attending the meeting murmured with satisfaction. This was the kind of stuff they came for. Some of them were descended from the Puritans who settled this town in the seventeenth century. The town hall now occupied the plot of ground where the pillory, the whipping post, and the hanging tree once stood.

Mother's face burned with shame and anger. She could feel the crowd waiting eagerly for her to start groveling. But she remained silent. It was hard enough for her to beg: she would not grovel!

Mercifully, Giles Brewster came once more to her rescue.

"Gentlemen, he said. We have a problem here, but we were elected to solve problems. I suggest that we table this matter for the present; and if one of you will volunteer to help me investigate the situation, and try to find a humane solution, I'm sure we can be of some help to this good woman."

A few days later Giles and Mr. Taber came out to the Robinson home, and after some haggling, they agreed that the town would pay to have the old wood stove converted to burn kerosene, and they would pay for enough kerosene to keep the stove going during cold weather so that the house would at least be warm enough to prevent the family from dying of hypothermia. They could not, at present, supply fuel for the furnace; but when the weather got colder they would see what they could do. For lighting, the selectmen would try to find some old oil lamps, and Mother could use the kerosene supply to keep these lamps burning when needed.

The Selectmen found, and delivered a number of second hand lamps which Mother had James and Joe clean up and ready for use. A large 50 gallon drum of kerosene was set on a sawhorse at the far end of the backyard to provide fuel for the lamps and the stove. All of the kids were instructed carefully in the fire danger. She had a fire drill and instructed the kids how to escape if the downstairs was on fire. She and Lorraine would take care of the two younger ones, and James would be in charge of the rest. They would all go to the front bedrooms, open the windows and crawl out onto the roof of the front porch. From there it would not be too difficult to get down to the ground.

The danger was very real. Converting the old wood stove to kerosene had made it much more convenient to use, but the stove would have never passed the Fire Underwriter's safety code. The stove was fueled by a ten gallon bottle of kerosene which stood upside-down on a rack next to the stove. A copper tube gravity-fed fuel to the burners. There was no automatic shut-off; so if anything happened to cause a fuel leak; or if the burners malfunctioned, the stove could explode and the resulting inferno could be very deadly.

In several places around Anneville there were the burned out remains of homes where converted kerosene stoves had blown up, and the resulting fire had destroyed the home, and in several cases trapped sleeping families in the upper floors and burned them alive.

Somehow, though, the Robinson family managed to get along without anything really bad happening, and sometimes they were even able to smile at their bleak situation.

One Saturday a door-to-door salesman appeared, selling electric vacuum cleaners. This was not to be one of this poor devil's better days. Mother should have explained right away that, since their power had been cut off, they could not possibly use an electric anything: but she felt sorry for the poor guy, invited him in for a cup of tea, and began to explain her pitiful predicament. Before she was through with him he had agreed to buy, out of his own almost empty pockets, an old Hoover vacuum cleaner which Mother and Daddy had bought during better times.

A glitch in the deal, though, occurred, when the man discovered that there was an accessory missing -- a hard rubber tube, and he could not buy the Hoover without that tube.

Mother immediately called all her kids away from their Saturday chores. "Children!" she said. "This is an emergency. There is a piece missing from this vacuum cleaner, and we have to have it right this instant. If we find it, I will not try to figure out which one of you took it for whatever reason; but if we don't find it, and I find out who took it, so help me, you'll wish you were never born!"

The kids scattered, and the house was searched as no house had ever been searched before, but the missing tube could not be found. Mother flew into such a rage it caused Rosebud and Regis to begin crying, and the hapless salesman quickly gave Mother the three bucks they had agreed upon. "You just gotta promise me one thing lady," he said seriously. "You gotta swear that you won't murder the poor kid who was responsible for losing that damned tube. Then he hurried away carrying the old vacuum cleaner and the newer model he had used for demonstration.

All agreed that the man was a "good egg," and they felt sorry for him, and hoped he might make some profit on the old vacuum cleaner. But, in the grim months ahead, that pathetic incident provided them with some much needed laughter.

Chapter 6

On the Monday before Thanksgiving, an American Legion truck showed up and dropped off a basket full of groceries, which included a turkey with all the trimmings. The turkey had been cleaned, but had not been plucked; so Mother assigned James the job of removing all the feathers -- a daunting task for anyone unfamiliar with the techniques of the business. He enlisted Joe and Thos in the project, and finally the last pin feather was plucked.

Without a refrigerator or ice box, keeping the bird cool was a challenge. Luckily the weather was cold -- almost always below cold storage temperature. Mother assigned one of the smaller rooms in the house as the cooler, and she kept the door to that room always closed so that no heat from the kerosene stove could warm the turkey and cause enough bacteria growth to poison them all.

Mother, who never was the greatest cook in the world, still prepared quite a Thanksgiving Day feast, and as she put it: "You kids certainly stuffed yourselves. In fact you are now stuffed a lot more than that turkey ever was!"

All in all, Thanksgiving was a pretty good day, but it was nothing compared to Christmas. The anticipation of this glorious holiday began right after Thanksgiving with the little notice on the front page of The *New Bradford Times*, which announced the number of shopping days left to Christmas.

Mother, even in the most penurious days of the Depression, was able to find the eighteen cents a week needed to have the paper delivered to her door. She would sometimes explain that "food for the mind is as necessary as food for the body."

At Parting Ways School the teachers put forward a great effort to prepare for Christmas. Carols were sung every day, art projects all had a Christmas theme, and each class planned a Christmas party. There were strict orders given that no flammable decorations be allowed in the classrooms of the old wooden school, but the blackboards and windows were gaily adorned.

Thos, who normally did not like attending school despite his continuing infatuation with Miss Moore, looked forward to class during this season.

There was one little custom that almost spoiled the school Christmas spirit for Thos. Miss Moore announced that they would all exchange names so that at the party each child would receive a gift from one of their classmates. Then she added, with a twinkle in her pretty eyes, "And if you children are all very good, Santa may also have a little surprise for each of you."

The problem was that each kid would also have to buy one gift for the student whose name he or she drew at random. They were told that this gift was not to cost more than ten cents in any case.

Thos knew that in no case would he be able to get that kind of money. When he explained the problem to Mother, she told him, "You just tell Miss Moore that your mother said you can't afford the ten cents, and she will handle that for you. Just give her the name of the kid you picked and she'll see that the kid will get a gift and never know it didn't come from you; and you'll get a gift too from the kid that picked your name."

"But I can't do that, Mother! I just can't do that!"

"Be quiet, Thos! You can, and you will do it, if you know what's good for you, you hear me!" Then Mother's face softened. She looked away from Thos. "Those teachers are saints," she said.

Thos hurried out to the backyard where no one would see him cry. Lorraine came out and put her arm around him. "Thos, dear, I know how you feel. We all have to do that thing about the ten cents--tell our teachers how poor we are, and we all hate it. I hate it more than anybody. Sometimes I think that being poor is like being constantly poked with a pitchfork. All of the prongs on that fork are sharp--two of the sharpest are cold and hunger, but the sharpest of all is humiliation."

She wiped his nose with a handkerchief that smelled of lilies of the valley.

Christmas was on Friday that year, and the class party was on the preceding Friday. Thos had gotten over his embarrassment about having to beg from Miss Moore, and the party was marvelous. His gift from his classmate was a tin whistle which had a slide on it to change pitch, and the "little gift from Santa" turned out to be a small box of Christmas rock candy. Later James told him that all the teachers at Parting Ways school did this every Christmas, and he asked Thos to remember how much this cost them out of their pitifully small salary. Under the circumstances that box of candy was like the "Gift of the Magi" to Thos.

Having two weeks vacation was also an exciting gift. The weather was cold, but there was no snow. Mother allowed Thos to go into the woods with James and Joe to search for a Christmas tree.

In the cellar where Daddy had found the infamous axe was also a hatchet. James stuck this into his belt, and they plodded through the sweet-smelling pines searching for the perfect specimen. Many were inspected and rejected before they found the tree of their dreams. After James had cut about halfway through the trunk, he handed the hatchet to Joe, who continued chopping. Then James took the hatchet from Joe. He ceremoniously held it out to Thos. "Now Thos, this is a very dangerous tool, but you're growing up and you'll soon be a man. I'm going to show you some very important safety tips, and I want you to pay close attention, because I'm going to let you take a few whacks at this tree."

After Thos had hit the tree with a couple of blows, James took the hatchet back and finished the job. Then he tied a small length of clothesline to the prize, and all three of them dragged it proudly home. "Man alive!" Thos said. "Ain't Christmas swell?"

James set up the tree in the parlor, but it was a family custom not to trim the tree until Christmas Eve (so that Santa Claus could help with the trimming). The parlor, of course, was a special place, not to be entered by the children unless they were dressed in their best clothes.

The week before Christmas was a time of hard work and preparation. All the children, except for the toddlers, Rosebud and Regis, were put to work preparing the house and yard for "Jesus' birthday." It was understood that there was to be no merriment or feasting until Christmas Day itself. The box of rock candy provided by the teachers could be consumed, but no other special treats were allowed. The rock candy did not survive the weekend; so the kids watched hungrily as the food for the Christmas feast began to appear. Several baskets were delivered to the Robinson home: one from the faithful American Legion, one from the Salvation Army, and one from the Welfare League of New Bradford. There were oranges, tangerines, mixed nuts, cans of cranberry sauce, onions, celery, one fruit cake, a can of plum pudding, and several turkeys. Thos catalogued each wonderful item as they were put away in the pantry, or in the case of the turkeys, in the small room used for cold storage. Luckily, this time the turkeys were already cleaned and plucked.

Excitement grew to a fever pitch as the great day drew near, and by Christmas Eve, the Christmas spirit was almost unbearable.

This was the first Christmas that Thos had realized that Santa Claus was no more than a nice story for little children. He had suspected this last Christmas, but he kept the faith until logic and the big mouth of Lizzie Horton confirmed the sober truth. When he saw the mail truck deliver a huge cardboard box to the house three days before Christmas he understood where the presents had come from on the previous Christmas. Lizzie Horton had warned Thos not to let grown-ups know that you knew that Santa was "just a big lie," for they would then stop giving you presents.

On Christmas Eve Mother informed Regis, Rosebud, Thos, and Joe that they must go to bed early, and that Santa would never come until they were all asleep, and that they better not ever come down stairs if they knew what was good for them!

After this warning, Thos finally asked James what Mother meant by, "if you know what's good for you."

"Look, kid," James said, "Trust me, you never want to find out!"

Of course, it was almost impossible for the kids to carry out Mother's Christmas Eve commands, but they finally all fell asleep.

Christmas morning at four A. M., Lorraine, James, and Patricia scurried around awakening their younger siblings. Mother and the older children had been up all night preparing the home for the celebration of the birthday of the Prince of Peace. The kids were cautioned that they could look at but not touch the wonderful things prepared for them. The first thing they must do, Mother said, was to attend five o'clock mass at St. Francis Xavier Church. "This is the least we can do," she said, "for our Savior, who gave so much to us all."

As the children hurried to get dressed, they looked around at what was waiting for them on the return from church.

At the bottom of their beds each child had a stocking crammed with goodies. In the parlor they could see the tree, gloriously decorated; and under its aromatic branches were piled beautifully wrapped gifts. There were Christmas decorations everywhere, and a wreath that had been fashioned out of fresh pine boughs and red ribbon was hanging above the fireplace.

As the Robinson family trudged through the icy pre-dawn air on their way to church, the stars glittered so magnificently above them, Thos imagined that God himself had decorated the heavens especially for this holy night, and that the Heavenly Choir was singing Christmas carols.

Mass was interminably long, and the incense hung too heavily in the air, but the choir music, with Mother's strong, beautiful voice leading the sopranos, was thrilling. Most of the choir, as well as the congregation, was made up of French Canadians. Mother always said that the French Canadians were even better at singing than they were at ice hockey. "In fact," she added seriously, "they're almost as good as the Irish."

The family trooped home wild with excitement; and Mother, totally exhausted by the all night marathon, retired to her room in order to get a few hours sleep before she would have to begin getting ready for the cooking of the Christmas dinner. She put Lorraine in charge of breakfast and the gift opening.

Lorraine, who preferred democracy to dictatorship, allowed the children to vote on whether they wanted to open the gifts first or wait until after breakfast. The vote was unanimous: "Open the presents!"

They made so much noise, James, obviously second in command, cautioned them to be quiet so that Mother could get some sleep.

There were two gifts for each child -- one from Grandmother Flanagan, Daddy's mother, and one from Mother. Somehow she had been able to beg or borrow enough money to buy a small gift for each of her kids. Of course the younger kids were told that all the presents came from Santa, but Thos knew that at least some of the gifts had come via the giant cardboard box which he had seen being delivered to their home earlier in the week.

Evidently Grandmother had been corresponding with Mother, because she knew what would be appropriate for each of her grandchildren: a toy dump truck for Regis, a doll for Rosebud, a steam shovel for Thos with string-operated controls that would allow him to pick up and drop dirt, a pop-gun for Joe which shot bottle corks, a copy of *Anne of Green Gables* for Patricia, a pretty blue sweater with matching hat for Lorraine, and a football for James. Mother had bought a game for each child--tiddley-winks for Regis, jacks for Rosebud, quoits for Thos, dominoes for Joe, a set of paper dolls for Patricia, a game of checkers for James, and a Parcheesi game for Lorraine.

Those gifts may not seem like much, but for youngsters who had not been given one single present since the previous Christmas, these were magnificent treasures.

The stockings, which each kid got, were also received very gratefully. They weren't your ordinary Christmas stocking: they were Mother's castaway silk stockings—old and useless, but immaculately clean. They contained no little gifts, but they were crammed full with fruit -- oranges, apples, tangerines, and dried apricots. There were also little packets of candies, dates, nuts, and chocolates. These 'stockings" were as welcomed by the kids as the gifts under the tree.

That Christmas, the Christmas of '32, in the blackest days of the Depression, was the most exciting of Thos's entire life. During the next 364 days there was not one hour in which he didn't think about how long would it be until next Christmas.

New Year's day was almost anti-climactic, but it was still fun. Mother invited a few of her friends over to celebrate the coming of 1933, and the kids were allowed to stay up to bring the New Year in. Dressed in freshly laundered pajamas and arranged on the stairs like a children's choir, they sang Christmas carols, and then, as the clock and the noise from the neighbors indicated that 1933 was arriving, they joined in the singing of "Auld Lang Syne." Then, Mother carried out an old family tradition. she led a parade of the whole company out the back door of the house around to the front door. The exit out the back door signifying the year 1932, and the entrance through the front door representing the year 1933. The following Monday it was back to school and grim reality for Thos and all of the Robinsons.

The first day back from vacation in Miss Moore's classroom was especially grim. Lionel Pelletier, one of the few boys in the class who had never given Thos a bad time, and had even helped him occasionally with his schoolwork, was not present. Miss Moore, fighting back tears, announced that Lionel had died three days after Christmas of a ruptured appendix. His empty desk was a conspicuous reminder to Thos that there were worse things in this world than humiliation, hunger and cold.

CHAPTER 7

THE JOY AND THE glory of Christmas faded quickly as the New England winter set in with a vengeance. Very cold weather is not pleasant for anyone, and there are many places in our country and all over the world where people suffer more from the cold than they do in costal New England, but Anneville is certainly up there on the list of miserable places to spend a winter. Any place is miserable when one is poorly fed, clothed and housed, but it is better to live in a warm climate if you are unfortunate enough to have poverty thrust upon you.

One of the unusual things about the children of Anneville, but perhaps it is true of all young people who live in bitterly cold places, is that there was some unspoken rule that it was forbidden to complain about the cold. "Sissy" was only one of the epithets hurled at any boy who spoke openly about how much he hated the cold.

No matter how low the temperature, the teachers of Parting Ways School, who were usually models of kindliness, would order their charges out onto the frozen ground of the schoolyard. "It'll make your cheeks rosy!" they said.

On the really cold days the students would huddle like sheep, their frosty breath blowing from their mouths, their hats pulled down over their ears, and their hands jammed into their pockets, most of them waiting silently for the bell to ring so that they could hurry back into the warm classrooms. There were a few hardy souls though who still prowled around the schoolyard looking for mischief. Maybe there was something about the extreme cold that brought out the meanness in them, for It was at such times that some small moaning kid would be found with his tongue frozen to the steel framework of the playground swings. The custodian, kindly Mr. Neezlick, would be called upon to free the sufferer with warm water and some choice Polish curses for the sadists who could perpetrate such cruelty.

All the kids, except for the farm kids who took the bus, walked to and from school on the coldest days. it was unheard of to have any student driven to or from school, even in the worst weather. Of course, it must be said that in those days no parent ever had to be worried about anyone harming a child on the streets.

January 21, Thos and Regis's birthday, like all of the birthdays of the Robinson children, went uncelebrated. At dinner that evening as they slurped their soup, now thinner and containing more cabbage because of the scarcity of fresh vegetables at that time of the year, Mother reminisced about giving birth to the two boys: "Thos, you were born at home, and you were easy -- bald as a peeled egg, but a cute little face . . ." She became wrapped up in her recollections, and seemed to be unaware that the subjects of her remarks were sitting right there and listening to every word. "Regis, you were a breach birth, and delivered in that shack they call the Anneville hospital. That quack who delivered you was nothing but a horse doctor. Giving birth to you almost killed me!"

Regis, just turned three, looked very uncomfortable. He said nothing out loud, but his face was saying, "Gee, Mother, I couldn't help it! I'm sorry!"

There was no cake or candles, of course, and none was expected.

* * *

In many native American tribes of the Northeast, February was known as the Hunger Moon, and rightly so. The winter stores were running low and food was almost impossible to obtain anywhere in the woods or fields or icebound lakes, and the stormy coastal waters prevented them from gathering seafood.

So it was with the poor people of Anneville. Mother managed to put enough food on the table to prevent starvation, but it was rough fare -- nourishing but unappetizing -- cabbage, carrots, beets, onions, sometimes carrots and potatoes mashed together. She made oatmeal in the morning, which with canned milk and a sprinkling of sugar wasn't too bad. She also made cocoa with canned milk, which was very pleasant on cold mornings; but the cocoa and oatmeal together could cause some disgusting belching if one didn't let it digest a little before exercising.

There was usually enough food available to prevent malnourishment, but the kids were often very hungry. Thos, though, was cursed with a very finicky stomach, and would not eat some of the roughest fare unless he was absolutely ravenous, and, even then there were certain foods he could not force down -- boiled onions, turnips, and his culinary nemesis: dried pea soup. As a result of this "champagne taste on a beer income" (Mother's term), he became skinny and undernourished. Nothing Mother tried could get Thos to consume some items. Sometimes when she was able to force him to swallow something he hated, he would vomit it up in an involuntary, but revolting display of his unhappy stomach. As a result he would occasionally become very weak.

One day after class let out, he was walking listlessly along the box hedges that lined the walkway leading to the street. He became faint, tottered, then collapsed into the box hedge. He awoke, surrounded by Lorraine, James, Miss Moore, and the principal, the strong and indomitable Mrs. Philips.

Dr. Simpson was sent for; but by the time he arrived, Thos was fully conscious and sipping some tea from Mrs. Philips' Thermos bottle, and munching on some cookies left over from Miss Moore's lunch.

Dr. Simpson assessed the situation, and asked some questions. Then he told Mrs. Phillips that he wanted to talk to her and Thos somewhere in private. Mrs. Phillips took them into her office, and, after he had examined Thos, he asked him," Are you getting enough to eat at home, son?"

Thos, remembering Mother's admonition, looked down at his shoes. "I don't know, Doctor," he said.

"Do you get fresh milk? Fruit? What kind of meat do you get?"

Thos did not answer.

"Doctor, the Robinson family is very poor. I don't think this boy is getting proper nourishment."

Thos tried to fight back tears of humiliation.

"It's all right, Thos," Mrs. Phillips said kindly. Then she turned to Dr. Simpson. "If you're through with the examination, is it all right for this boy to go home with his siblings? I'd like to discuss this case with you after he's gone."

After this incident Thos was treated a little differently than his brothers and sisters. Mother made sure that he ate everything on his plate. He was forced to swallow tablespoonfuls of cod-liver oil daily. Bottles of the nourishing, but foul-tasting extract were provided by some public health agency.

Reluctantly, Thos cooperated with these measures, partly because he had been frightened and embarrassed by the concern and fuss made about his collapse, but mostly because of Mother's stern warning of what she would do to him if he ever failed to carry out her instructions on this matter.

The most painful, yet heart-warming result of his fainting spell involved Miss Moore. She told him, making sure that some of his classmates heard her, that he would have to stay in with her during recess because he needed to do "extra work."

When he reported to her during recess, she smiled at him. "Thos, I'm sorry that I told that fib about extra work. I just felt you wouldn't want the other children to know what we're doing during recess. It will be our little secret." Then she went to her closet and handed him a small bottle of fresh milk and some oatmeal cookies. "For a while, Thos, I want us to have our recess snack together."

Thos had never known such a feeling before: a feeling that was a confusing mixture of love, gratitude, and humiliation.

Another consequence of Thos's black-out was that Mother decided to get more bread available for her table by buying old stale bread at the Daisy Company's Thrift Store. This shop was in New Bradford, almost two miles away from the Robinson home.

The job of getting this bread fell to Joe. It meant that he would have to trudge all the way to the shop pulling a steel red wagon which was one of the vestigial remains of the pre-depression days. Every kid in Anneville could see him pulling the wagon filled with Daisy stale bread for the poor Robinson family.

The bread was frequently many days old, and often it would become moldy before it was open. Mother learned that the mold was not poisonous, but she told the kids to cut off the moldy portion of the bread before they ate it.

One day she told the unfortunate Joe that he was to tell the man who sold him the bread that, "Your Mother is fed up with paying for bread that's so stale it turns moldy before we can get it on the table."

The man who sold the bread must have read Dickens's *Oliver Twist* because when Joe delivered Mother's message, the man flew into a rage and practically reenacted the famous, "May I have some more?" scene from the novel.

He thundered down at Joe, "What! Are you telling me that your old lady thinks I'm cheating you?" He heaved a loaf against the wall, and as though God was trying to demonstrate the truth of Mother's accusation, the stale, hard bread thudded against the wall with such force, it chipped off some of the plaster.

As the outraged man handed the loaves to Joe and rang up his money he railed, "The Goddamned nerve of these poor people! Just because Roosevelt's in, they think they can take over this country!"

Ever after that, when Joe went into the thrift shop, he was treated with rudeness and silent contempt by this jerk.

Another incident occurred during the "Hunger Moon" that involved bread and Joe that was very disturbing to Thos.

Joe had a pal named Vasco who was also a victim of The Great Depression. Vasco's father had been a fisherman, and during the prosperous days of the Twenties he had made enough money for a down payment on a farm. When the crash came, Vasco's father was wiped out and he lost everything. The blow was too much for this hardworking man; and before turning his beloved farm over to the bank, he hanged himself from a rafter in his cow barn, leaving his widow without a penny to rear her nine fatherless children by herself.

One bitterly cold Saturday, Vasco asked Joe and Thos to join him in an old garage next to an empty house near where the Robinsons lived. He closed the door and secured the latch from the inside. Then he opened his coat and pulled out a loaf of bread. But this was not a loaf from the Daisy Bread Thrift Shop. This was a fresh, sweet-smelling loaf of delicious raisin bread which he had just stolen from Gabrowski's grocery store.

Of course Joe and Thos knew they would be committing a mortal sin by sharing in these ill--gotten goods. They would never have reported the theft; the code of never squealing on a friend was deeply ingrained in every boy in Anneville, but they knew they should have walked away from Vasco and left him to devour the bread by himself. But it was not only a question of good and evil. Vasco had obtained his prize at considerable risk, and he was now willing to share it with his friends. And then, of course, this was raisin bread! Fresh, un-sliced raisin bread that could be torn apart and eaten with great gusto! And that's exactly what they did until there was not a crumb left!

Neither Joe nor Thos ever mentioned the incident again, and no one ever found out; but the guilt of it remained with them for a very long time.

The incident was especially troubling to Thos. It reminded him of the recess sessions with Miss Moore, even though there were many differences. Devouring the raisin bread, like drinking the milk and munching Miss Moore's cookies had satisfied his hunger, renewed his energy and made it easier to endure the cold; but both events had left him uneasy. The experiences of having to accept Miss Moore's kindness and generosity had embarrassed him, and participating in the wild and animal-like tearing and consuming the stolen raisin bread had left him with a sense of shame and guilt that would haunt him for a long time.

During the Washington's Birthday holiday Joe, and Lorraine came down with sore throats and fevers. That night their throats became so sore they had trouble swallowing. In the morning there was ugly swelling on both sides of their throats, and they were burning up with fever. Mother kept them home from school, and when the other kids came home for lunch, Joe and Lorraine were much worse.

Mother, grim-faced, told Patricia that she would have to feed the younger kids their lunch. Then she ordered James to go next door and ask Mrs. Horton to phone Dr. Simpson.

Thos came home after school to find a car parked in front of his house and a large red sign nailed to one of the pillars of the front porch. In huge letters it read: "Quarantine!" James came out to meet him. "Go into the back yard, Thos, and wait there. Dr. Simpson is here, and Joe and Lorraine are very sick. I'll come out soon and tell you more about what's going on."

Another car stopped in front of the house, and the Public Health nurse, Miss Martin, got out and hurried in.

As soon as Thos got into the backyard, Rosebud and Regis, looking very frightened, came out. Rosebud was clutching her Christmas doll, and Regis carried his dump truck with him. "Keep an eye on them," James told Thos.

Patricia had walked home with Lizzie Horton. When Lizzie saw the quarantine sign, she squealed and ran into her house. Patricia saw the kids in the back yard and joined them.

A few minutes later James came out and, ignoring the younger children, began talking to Patricia and Thos. James sometimes forgot that not all kids were as smart as he was, and he would explain things in greater detail than his listeners could understand. This inclination of his had earned him the affectionate nickname of "Professor." Now he began to give one of his lectures: "Dr. Simpson says that Joe and Lorraine have a disease called diphtheria; it's very bad. It's caused by a germ that invades the body and begins to make a poison that gets into the bloodstream. It also causes a thin kind of skin called a membrane to grow in the throat. This membrane can block the throat so people can't eat, and the air passages so that people can't breathe. The doctor says there's a chance he can counteract the poison if it hasn't gone too far. Mother says we all have to pray that he's gotten here in time."

As soon as James went back into the house, Lizzie Horton's head appeared above the back fence. She had gotten all the news from her mother, who had overheard the phone calls of Dr. Simpson, and Miss Martin. Lizzie, bug-eyed with excitement, began to blab away. "Ain't it awful! Lorraine and Joe have diphtheria! Mother said that in this country over fifty thousand people died from it in 1921. Joe and Lorraine are goners for sure. They're gonna' die just like Lionel Pelletier. He had a ruptured appendix: this stuff is much worse. Ma said the rest of you will probably catch it too. She says I'm not to go near any of you. You all are gonna' have to be immunized! (she mouthed this as though she had just heard the word and wanted to be sure she got it right.) They take this big, sharp, steel needle and stick it right into your spine!"

Thos was stunned by Lizzie's outburst. Up to that moment he had been in a daze—unable to grasp the full horror of this disaster. Now terror took hold of him: *Joe and Lorraine, dead like Lionel? No! God, please!!*

45

Then Miss Martin opened the back door and told all the children to come in.

Lizzie lowered her voice. "She's going to stick you with the big needle! Your best bet is to run for it, kids!"

Patricia moved obediently towards the kitchen, but the others panicked, and scattered like chickens. Rosebud and Regis were quickly collared, but Thos tried to scramble over the fence. Miss Martin caught him by the legs, pulled him off the fence and carried him struggling wildly into the house.

Dr. Simpson, assisted by Miss Martin and Mother and James, administered the dreaded shots to Patricia, Thos, Rosebud and Regis.

"This should protect them from the pathogens unless, of course, they already have been infected. When we get more help from the county, we'll take throat cultures from all of you and that will tell us if anybody else has contracted the disease."

Then he took Mother into the parlor, where they could not be overheard, and said, "I've given antitoxin to Joe and Lorraine. It's all I can do. If I got it to them in time, they will have a good chance of recovering." He took Mother by the hand, and looked into her eyes. "I think they're going to make it, but I can't promise anything."

Mother bit her lip. "I'm Catholic, you know. Should I call my priest to administer extreme unction, Doctor?"

The doctor could not look at Mother now. "If it makes you feel better, go ahead. I wish I could tell you that there's no chance they will die, but we won't know until morning."

Father Reynold was sent for and administered the last rites to the unconscious Lorraine and Joe.

That night, by the light of two candles, Mother knelt and led her five children in the Sorrowful Mysteries of the Rosary.

Whether it was the prayers or the anti-toxin, or a combination of the two, no one knew; but when Dr. Simpson examined them the next morning, he told the family that it now looked like Lorraine and Joe would recover. They recuperated rapidly, the quarantine was lifted, and the Robinson kids were allowed to go back to school. Dr. Simpson, with the help of the County Board of Health, had been able to confine the diphtheria outbreak to only a few cases, and most of the young people in Anneville (including a terrified Lizzie Horton) had been vaccinated to prevent any further outbreaks of the deadly disease.

Mother did not mention the ordeal again except on one occasion when she was heard to say: "Some day, so help me, I'm going to wring that Lizzie Horton's neck."

CHAPTER 8

BY THE END OF February the Robinson family and the rest of Anneville began looking forward to the end of the winter. There was hope in the air because Roosevelt would soon be sworn into office, and spring was on its way. But there was still a long way to go before The Depression would be over and the country could get back to normal. The people of Anneville were too engrossed in their own troubles to worry about what was happening in the rest of the world.

There were events taking place overseas, though, that would, in a few years, drastically affect the lives of the Robinson family and most of the people of the world. The Empire of Japan was tightening its grip on Manchuria, Adolph Hitler was bullying his way into complete control of Germany; and the strutting megalomaniac, Mussolini, was turning Italy from a nation devoted to beauty and "La dulce vita' to a pack of fascist dogs fawning at the heels of Hitler. But in Anneville people continued on with their everyday activities.

One Thursday in early April Mother was doing her ironing. The four older children were at school. Thos, Rosebud, and Regis were playing in the side yard. Mother had said they could play outside as long as they kept in sight of the living room window where Mother had her ironing board set up. Someone knocked on the door, and when Mother opened it, she saw a well-dressed, attractive woman standing there. Though Mother had never met her, she recognized the woman as Mrs. Elizabeth Standish, wife of a wealthy Anneville farmer.

"Mrs. Robinson, I'm Beth Standish," she said. "I'm sorry to break in on you like this, but I was in the neighborhood, and I'd like to visit with you, if it's all right."

The woman tried not to stare. As a member of the Methodist Women's Welfare Society, she had visited the homes of poor families before, but this was different. It was cheerful and neat. There were curtains on the windows, and though there was no covering over the slightly worn floor boards, they were spotlessly clean.

The only noticeable odor was of kerosene and stove polish that came from the massive, chrome-trimmed wood stove which had been converted to burn kerosene. The ten gallon kerosene bottle that was strapped to an iron pole next to the stove gave out a loud gurgle at regular intervals as blue flames consumed the fuel.

Mrs. Standish noticed the ironing board and the large basket full of clothes. "Oh dear! I see that you're busy. Perhaps I could come back at a more convenient time . . ."

"Don't be silly, come on in and sit a while. I don't have to start lunch for another hour, and we can chat while I finish the ironing." She noticed that Beth was looking at the huge load of clothes. "Oh, don't worry, I only have to do a few of the things for my school kids. It won't take a minute. I have some water on for tea. Maybe you'd be kind enough to join me."

As Mother worked on the ironing, her guest watched with wonder as Mother deftly wielded an old-fashioned stove heated flat iron. Three irons were on the top of the stove, and Mother, using a clamp with a sturdy wooden handle, dropped a cold iron on the stove top, seized a hot one and ironed away on the clothes until its heat was dissipated, returned that one; then repeated the process.

She finished the ironing, made the tea, set up a tray with two cups, spoons, sugar, and a small pitcher of evaporated milk.

Why don't we go into the parlor, Mrs. Standish? I can still watch the children from there."

Mrs. Standish followed her into the parlor and sat in the Morris chair proffered by Mother. They both took a sip of tea.

"These are lovely cups – Belleek, aren't they?" Mrs. Standish began.

"Yes, they are. They are leftovers--like that wool rug and the Morris chair -- from better times," Mother said.

Mrs. Standish took another sip of tea and set the cup and saucer carefully down on the table next to her. "First of all, Mrs. Robinson, could you please call me Beth?"

"Of course, Beth, if you like, and if you will call me Mary."

"Mary, what I have to say is very, very difficult. You've heard of my boy, Leveret, of course?"

"No, I'm sorry, but I've not, Does he go to Parting Ways?"

"Yes, he's in the second grade. Your boys have never talked about him?" She paused, and took out a lace handkerchief. "You have five children at Parting Ways, Mrs. -- Mary, none of them have ever mentioned my son? Some kids call him Looney Leveret." Now she dabbed her eyes with the elegant handkerchief.

"Beth," Mother said firmly, "If any of my children were ever cruel enough to call another child a name like that, I'd be ashamed of them and they know that. But, Beth, some of the kids in this town are very mean. If any child is the least bit different, the little barbarians think of some cruel name: lemon-head, Flagpole Dubois, Bird-legs Laplant -- I sometimes wonder if the children realize how cruel they are. The old saying, sticks and stones can break your bones, but names can never hurt you is nonsense, in my opinion!"

"If it were just name-calling -- but it goes way beyond that. Poor Leveret!" She began to cry. "I know he's different, but he's not retarded or anything. He gets good grades, and his teachers like him; but he's very gentle and sensitive, and this makes him different I guess, and some kids are threatened by anyone different. The little bastards, I'm sorry Mary, to use vulgar language in your home, but that's what they are--rotten little bastards! Poor Leveret! Sometimes he comes home with his toes black and blue. They come up to him and say, 'Hey, Looney Leveret! I wrote a letter and forgot to stamp it.' Then they stomp on his toes with their heavy shoes. anything they ask him to do, he does it. In the first grade they talked him into putting his tongue on a steel bar and his tongue froze solid. She paused and tried to get her composure. "Mary, I'm at my wits' end. The teachers try to protect him, but that just makes matters worse. 'Teacher's pet' they call him. I want to move away from this rat hole they call a town, but my husband's family has lived in this place for almost 300 years. He'll never move; he's almost proud of how 'tough' this town is. He says it will do Leveret good to have it tough for a while. It'll make a man of him. Men! Mary, sometimes I get furious. They gave us the vote only twelve years ago, but they still treat us like indentured servants. I've seen you at the town meetings Mary, I really admire you, the way you don't let them push you around--"

Mother looked at her kindly. "Beth, what can I possibly do to help you? You know I'm 'on the town,' and dirt poor. You're --"

"Mary, I know some people in this town think I'm rich. I'm not, my husband is. This may sound phony, but in some ways--you're richer than I am. Those kids you have at Parting Ways--I've been told that James is the finest boy they've seen at that school, Patricia is definitely the prettiest girl in town, and I hear that Lorraine will be valedictorian this year."

"Thank you very much, Beth, but I don't think you came here just to praise my kids. Let's get down to brass tacks. Why did you come?"

Mrs. Standish was silent. She stared at the floor: then she continued. "Your boys have a reputation for being able to fight and take care of themselves. They never bully anyone, but the schoolyard bullies give them a wide birth. I'd like to plead with you, Mary, to get your boys to keep an eye on Leveret. I can't expect your boys to prevent the name-calling, but, for pity's sake, could you get your sons to stop the little rats from physically abusing him? I can't do much for you in return. My husband is tighter than the bark on a hickory tree, and I have no money of my own, but I'll be eternally grateful if you can help me."

"Of course, I'll help you, Dear, but when you insinuate that I would expect anything for getting my boys to do something that any half-way decent human being should do, you insult me. I know you don't mean to insult me, and maybe I'm too sensitive, but my boys will see that Leveret will not be picked on at school anymore; but please don't patronize me. "

"I'm truly sorry for that, Mary. I realized as soon as I said it that it was a dumb thing to say. I do hope we can be friends , though."

Mother got up and gave Beth a warm Irish hug. "This little chat will be our secret. We won't mention it again, Dear. And don't you worry about Leveret. He's a lucky boy to have a mother like you."

That night Mother held a council of war with James and Joe. James enlisted the aid of his baseball teammates in the protection of Leveret, and from then on the schoolyard terrorists found other grist for their mill.

* * *

Although the ground hog had not seen his shadow on February 2, which was supposed to indicate an early spring, the icy grip of winter held on well into March. Finally, though, the first welcome signs of spring began to appear, and by March 21, the Vernal Equinox, there was no doubt that spring was on schedule.

Spring is a thrilling time in any place that has severe winters, and it was especially so in Anneville and at Parting Ways School. A huge chart was hung in the vestibule of the school upon which was listed all the wild flowers that grew in that region. Next to the flower was a place for the name of the student who found and brought in the first example of that flower found in Anneville that spring. A prize would be given to the student whose name appeared most frequently on that list by May 31. Even the roughest and toughest of the students would scour the fields and woods of Anneville for newly arrived blossoms, and more than one fist fight broke out over who was the first guy to bring in a violet or daisy.

Miss Gillette, the Art and Nature teacher, was in charge of the flower contest, and it was she who made the final decision on who received credit for finding each flower.

There were also many other activities that were part of the rites of spring at Parting Ways School. Poetry, for instance, was an important part of the curriculum at this time. The beloved New England poets: Longfellow, Whittier, Bryant, Frost, Dickinson, and others were studied, but so also were many British masters, such as Wordsworth, Byron, Shelley, and Keats.

The students were asked to memorize many poems. Modern educators doubt the value of emphasizing the memorizing of poems, but in the New England schools of the thirties there was almost unanimous agreement that poetry was an essential part of a child's education. For the Robinson children it was definitely the most enjoyable part of their schoolwork. All of them found memorization easy, and the Robinson home rang with stanzas from some of the best loved poems of the day.

Lorraine, James, and Patricia were excellent students in every subject, and they were popular with their teachers and classmates. James, in addition to being the most intelligent of the family, was a natural athlete, and a starting player of the Parting Ways baseball team. Baseball, like poetry, was considered an important part of the public schools even in the grimmest part of The Depression. The baseball games between Parting Ways and schools from the neighboring towns were almost as important to the residents of Anneville as the Red Sox games at Fenway Park. None of the Robinson family ever missed one of James's games if it could be helped.

The successful school performances of James, and Lorraine raised the prestige of the Robinson family among the citizens of Anneville, but many of the important old time residents would never let the Robinsons forget that they were "on the town," and they better not get too "uppity."

In early April, Parting Ways School began an annual fund-raising campaign by enlisting all the students in the selling of flower seeds. Every kid was expected to take a certain quota of seed packets and go door-to-door selling seeds to their neighbors. It was during this activity that Thos became painfully aware that people 'on the town' were not fully accepted as respectable citizens of Anneville. No matter how many doors he knocked on, the response was always the same: a cold stare and a blunt refusal. Perhaps his natural lack of good sales techniques contributed to his failure, but not once during any of his dogged attempts to sell seeds did he sell one packet. Many times before the refusal was made, it was preceded by the comment, "Oh, you're one of Mrs. Robinson's kids, aren't you?"

These unsuccessful sales forays were made more unpleasant by the unusual number of vicious dogs favored by the townspeople. Often the only thing that kept Thos from being torn apart by these curs was that the dog owners would open the door only a crack to tell Thos they didn't want to buy anything. Thos would have given up his futile attempts after seeing his first snarling dog through a partially opened door if it hadn't been for Mother's insistence that a good salesman must always remember that even if they make only one sale out of twenty tries, they can still be successful, and a good salesman could always get a job.

Nothing, though, could diminish the tremendous excitement that Thos felt at the coming of spring. There were so many things to look forward to: the weather was becoming warmer, the bleak dark branches of the trees were bursting with buds, food would become more plentiful, birds and butterflies and grasshoppers would soon be everywhere; and, joy of joys, there would be two glorious months of freedom from school.

By the first of April, there were still two and a half months of time to be served before school let out.

Lorraine, though, seemed to be enjoying every minute of her last months of grammar School. She was very popular with everyone, and especially the boys. she had no special boyfriend, and her relationship with them was more friendship than romance. She was pretty, with rich dark hair, high cheekbones, classically sculptured nose, impish smile, and warm hazel eyes. She was tall and slender, but she had a full compliment of girlish curves.

When boys came over to the house, she loved to play pranks, some very startling, on them. The more she liked the boy, the more mischievous would be the prank. Once she gave a boy a piece of chocolate candy laced with pepper. One of her most infamous pranks involved the use of a "posser,' a plumber's plunger. The device had never been used for its designated purpose; it was only used by mother as an agitator when she washed clothes in the bathtub, so it was very clean. Trevor Pendleton, her victim of the day, had evidently never seen a posser. Mother had left it sitting next to her laundry basket in the kitchen where Lorraine, Trevor, and some of the Robinson kids were sitting around talking.

"What's that thing?" he asked.

Lorraine's imagination sprung quickly into action. "Oh, that? That's something we use to strengthen our teeth. It helps to give you a great smile."

"Really?" said Trevor. "Does it work?"

Lorraine gave him her most dazzling smile. "What do you think?"

"How does it work?"

"Of course we always wash it off before we use it, but then we just bite on it on the rubber a few times. I always bite it five times."

"Gee! Can I try it?"

Lorraine hesitated for only a fraction of a second. "Well, why in the heck not. I'll wash it off."

With the most devilish of all her impish grins she rinsed it off carefully and handed it to poor Trevor. He held it like and ice cream cone and gave it a good bite. When the kids exploded with laughter, Trevor realized he'd -- been had. He was a good sport, though, and joined in the merriment.

He left soon after that, and all the kids, but especially Loraine, hoped against hope that he never would find out the real use of that disgusting object.

Lorraine swore them to secrecy about the incident with Trevor. she said it would be cruel to let the other kids hear about it. He evidently forgave her, for a few days later he was walking home from school carrying her books.

* * *

Mrs. Phillips, who was not only principal but also taught the eighth grade, was a firm believer in tradition; so despite The Depression, she still insisted that the graduating seniors be allowed to have a Senior Prom. There would be no dating--the girls and boys would simply attend to dance and socialize. The school had no hall, so the Town Hall, in the same block as the school, was decorated for the occasion. The music would be supplied by Mrs. Phillips herself playing the piano. This Prom may seem pathetic by today's standards, but for the eighth graders of Parting Ways School, especially the girls, it was the most important event of their young lives, and they looked forward to it eagerly. Lorraine was very apprehensive about how she could ever get a dress fit for the occasion, but Mother assured her that she would make her eldest daughter a dress that would make all the other girls of Anneville green with envy.

One of Mother's most treasured possessions left over from happier times was a sewing machine powered by a foot treadle. She very seldom had spare time, but for this project she found the time and had a beautiful blue organdy dress finished well before the early May date of the happy occasion. Lorraine evidently was, to use a cliché' of the time, "the belle of the ball." The affair was the main topic of conversation in the Robinson home for many days afterward.

The most important of the rites of spring, though, was the Decoration Day observances held on the school lawn. This lawn was a special place-- a plot of carefully tended ground surrounded by a perfectly trimmed box hedge. No student was ever allowed in that place except on the last school day of May when the memory of all the brave men who had died for their country was honored.

The preparations for this event began shortly after Easter. The teachers, using only a pitch pipe to keep the kids on key and waving their arms to keep time, practiced songs appropriate for the occasion: songs from the Civil War such as "Tenting Tonight," and "Just Before the Battle, Mother;" and songs of World War One, such as "The Yanks Are Coming."

Only the top students from each class were selected to present short orations or poems appropriate for the occasion. Mother was very proud that every one of her five children was chosen for this honor. Thos's first performance was a stanza from "In Flanders Fields." Although, at the time, he barely understood the words, he never forgot them:

"To you from failing hands we throw
The torch; be yours to hold it high.
If you break faith with us who die
We shall not sleep, though poppies grow
In Flanders fields."

A large crowd gathered that day to honor the heroes and to see their children perform. Mrs. Phillips' production stirred the hearts of even the most cynical and hard-hearted of the townspeople.

One of the most solemn moments of that celebration occurred when an 86 year old veteran of the Civil War, a survivor of the G A R, the Grand Army of the Republic, rose unsteadily to his feet to receive the respect and acclaim of every person there.

The Decoration Day ceremonies marked the end of the most rigorous part of the curriculum of the school. The atmosphere in the classes after that was much more relaxed.

For Thos the year that had begun with such fear and humiliation was ending with much excitement and even some satisfaction, for he was proud of the fact that his siblings were so highly respected by the faculty and most of the students in the school. His relationship with

Miss Moore, of course, had been the most pleasurable part of the year, and he would sorely miss her during the summer.

The graduation (or "commencement" as Mrs. Phillips called it) was especially pleasant because Lorraine was clearly a campus favorite, and when Lorraine arose to make her speech, the applause was loud and long. Mother and her children cheered longer and louder than anyone. It was the happiest moment in Thos's life since Christmas.

CHAPTER 9

The woods are lovely, dark and deep,
*- Robert Frost_*

ON THE FIRST DAY of summer vacation, Mother presented Joe and Thos each with a pair of bib overalls. How she ever managed to get these, (they were brand-new), was a mystery to both the boys; but they were gloriously happy. Denim overalls were the uniform of the summer for all lads in Anneville. They were comfortable, durable, easy to put on or take off, and endowed with almost as many pockets as a guy would need.

Mother told them they were not allowed to go barefoot, because there was too much danger of stepping on broken glass, or, even worse, a rusty nail. In farm areas lockjaw (tetanus) was believed to be an ever present threat, and the kids were warned that they might never make it through summer vacation alive because of that deadly disease.

There were other dangers too, for kids wandering the fields and woods, but Mother knew that her boys were familiar with most of the hazards, and she allowed them an amazing amount of freedom to explore and discover the countryside. Joe took Thos on his first, wonderful excursion into the woods. In the past James led the way, and Thos was too young to go, but this summer James had been offered fifteen cents an hour to work on the Standish farm four hours a day, five days a week. This meant that three dollars a week would be added to the family budget--too good an offer to turn down; so only Thos and Joe would be free to wander the woods this year.

After they left the houses and the paved roads of Anneville, they had to cross several stone walls. Then they had to get through a barbed wire fence before they could enter the lovely darkness of the woods. The stone walls, which seemed to form the border of every piece of undeveloped land in New England, were almost a pleasure to climb over. The technique of crossing a stone wall was quickly learned. Joe explained some of the fundamentals of stepping on the boulders without getting hurt, and without disturbing the architecture of these venerable structures. Both safety, and respect for the old stones could be obtained by understanding the rules of balance and gravity. One learned to judge which boulders could be stepped upon without tipping them or slipping off of them. Once a kid learned to get over a stone wall properly, the experience became a challenging and pleasurable game.

The stone walls that bordered the woods were a haven for most of the small creatures of the countryside: every variety of crawling insect, mice, rats, chipmunks, squirrels, snakes, rabbits, foxes, woodchucks, skunks, and birds of all varieties. The stone wall was also a great place for every kind of vine, creeper, or bramble to grow. Joe had learned all of this and passed the knowledge on to Thos. He warned Thos about poison ivy and poison oak, about copperhead snakes, about bees, hornets, and wasps. He showed Thos how to keep mosquito bites and the stinging of bees and horseflies down to a minimum. All of this lore was absorbed quickly, and Thos enjoyed learning about it almost as much as he enjoyed the freshness and beauty and the wonder of the woods.

Thos had never known anything like the contentment and peace he felt in the dark recesses of this mini-wilderness. It stirred something in him even more profound than that which he felt during early morning Christmas Mass at St. Francis Xavier Church.

As they went deeper into the woods, Joe stopped talking. They were walking on a path that appeared to be well worn, but it hadn't been walked upon for many months, probably since last autumn. Above them was a canopy of hardwood trees -- maples, oaks, chestnuts, beeches, and elms -- and the air was filled with birdsongs.

Joe stopped, and held up his hand. "Listen!" he whispered, "that's a scarlet tanager! If you look, you might get a peek at him. There! Up in that maple!"

Thos saw the flash of scarlet, but not much more.

"Keep your eyes pealed! I heard an oriole, and a bluebird too."

When they came to a small stream that crossed the path, Joe stopped again. "This is fed from a crystal spring which bubbles out of the ground about fifty yards through the tangle wood up that slope. The water is the best I've ever tasted. You can drink from it by cupping your hands like this, but I like to drink by lying on my belly and sucking it right out of the stream. Have to be careful not to suck in a bug, and you get a little mud on your overalls, but it tastes better that way. If you get mud on your clothes, don't try to rub it off; just wait till it dries, then you can dust it off."

The stream was only a preview of a greater wonder to come. About a quarter mile on they broke out of the tangled woods to the banks of the upper reaches of the Anneville River. The water was pristine--purified by the heavy spring rains and miles of filtration through wetlands, trees, and thick underbrush.

There was a small clearing at the place where the path met the river. "This is Martel's. It's where we swim," Joe said.

The river, which normally ran south, made a turn to the east here, toward the sea; and over the years, had cut a little cove into the bank, which made a good place to enter the water. Joe let himself down the bank to the edge of the stream, and dipped in his fingers. "It's still chilly, he said, but if the weather's sunny again tomorrow, we might take a dip."

"It looks like it's over my head; I can't swim," said Thos.

"Right here at the cove, it's shallow, you'll be okay. Up there towards the log, it gets deeper."

About fifty yards upstream from the cove, an old tree trunk had fallen across the river, forming a picturesque natural bridge. "When you learn how to swim, that's a great place to dive from," he said.

Thos was taking in the whole scene, marveling at how perfect he thought it was, when he saw a snake swimming across the river less than ten yards from where Joe stood.

A shiver of fear ran through Thos. "Yikes!" he said," Look at that! You're never getting me to go in that water!"

Joe laughed. "I gotta' admit, they scare the heck out of you when they swim near you; but they're just water snakes, they can't hurt you.

They come from that swampy area over to the right. There's a lot of other good things in there like frogs, turtles, and muskrats. But I'll tell you what I hate -- blood suckers! Yuck!"

"Blood suckers?" Thos said, "You didn't tell me about them. What are they?"

Joe examined the shallow water close to the edge of the cove. "Thos, take off your shoes, and come down here near the water. I'll show you some."

"Not me," said Thos.

"Come on down, you sissy. They can't jump out and get you."

Thos obeyed, and Joe crouched down. "See 'em there? They look like black worms swimming around."

It took Thos a minute or two, and then following where Joe pointed, he saw an ugly black worm swimming with an undulating motion.

"They look kind'a long and skinny now, but once they latch on to you, they make a hole in your skin, become a blob, and start sucking until they get so fat with blood, they fall off."

"You're just making that up to scare me," Thos said.

"Word of honor!" said Joe, and when Joe or Jim said that, Thos knew it was the absolute truth.

"That does it," Thos said, "I'm not even going to get close to that water," and he backed away up the bank.

"Listen Thos," Joe said, " James and I and most of the Anneville kids swim in here and never get one of those things on us. The secret is to keep moving--either wading or swimming. If you don't stop they can't get on you. I've never got one on me in my life. The city bums-- no kid in Anneville will ever tell them the secret, so they get them on all the time. some of them start screaming and stuff. They try to pull them off, but the bloodsuckers become like rubber bands; and if you pull them hard enough, they snap off and take a piece of skin with them when they come off. Most of the Anneville kids just stand around laughing, but James and some of the nicer big kids show the city bums how to touch the blobs with a lighted cigarette or a quickly extinguished match head."

Joe suddenly stopped. "Somebody's coming!" he said.

Thos could hear the voices of some boys coming down the path. He noticed Joe looked apprehensive.

"Nothing to worry about" Joe said, with more bravado than certainty.

When they came into view, Thos was relieved to recognize them as friends of James, Ziggy Pinkowski and Ray Le Blanc. "Where's your brother Jim?" they asked Joe.

"He's working. He's got a job on the Standish farm."

"Jeez!" said Ray; then he looked around. "Seen any city bums?"

"Ain't seen nobody," Joe said.

"How's the water?" Ziggy asked.

"Still chilly," said Joe, "but I think I'll go in tomorrow."

Ziggy came down to the edge of the cove and dipped his fingers in the water. "Hell, it ain't bad," he said. "Wanna take a dip, Ray?"

"Sure," Ray said, and began peeling off his clothes and stacking them on the ground up on the bank.

Ray did the same thing. Both their naked bodies were winter white, but very muscular. Ziggy waded right in and began swimming out towards the log. "Wow!" he hollered. "This is swell!"

Ray, dipped his fingers in the water and made the sign of the cross, as all French kids did before they entered the water; then he began swimming after Ziggy.

Thos looked at Joe. "They're bare ass! What happens if a girl comes?"

"Girls never come here, you dope! One time a couple girls from New Bradford came and the boys started giving them 'moon shots,' and they ran away screaming."

As they walked back home through the woods, Thos wasn't quite sure he was going to like swimming at Martel's or not. As they were nearing the stone wall at the edge of the woods, he finally asked a question that had been bothering him. "What are city bums and why do we hate them?"

"They're kids from New Bradford that cross the river at King Phillips' bridge and come up into our swimming places."

"Why do we hate them?"

"Some of them don't have any respect for the woods and the places where we swim."

"What do they do?"

"They leave trash around, sometimes they break bottles in the water, they bend down small birches, shoot birds with BB guns--I hate 'em"

"I hate 'em too," said Thos.

The next day was warm and sunny. Thos and Joe were the first kids at Martel's. Shortly after they got there Vasco, Joe's friend, arrived. Vasco and Joe were quickly in the water. Vasco's swarthy, muscular frame contrasted markedly with Joe's scrawny, white body; and Vasco could swim much faster and hold his breath much longer underwater than Joe, but Joe tried gamely to keep up with his pal.

Thos stood on the bank watching, telling his brother that he would get in the water later. When Vasco finally came out, he shook himself like a dog, and stood around naked letting the sun dry him off, and Joe quickly followed. While they were standing around, three kids that Thos had never seen before came out of the woods from a different path. "City bums!" Vasco muttered to Joe.

The city kids looked at Joe and Vasco. "How's the water?" they said nervously.

Vasco and Joe stared silently ahead. The oldest one, a boy about ten, went down to the water and checked it." It's still cold, but I'm going in anyway. He went to another part of the clearing, followed by the other two and began stripping down. He and the other two stacked their clothes neatly near one another, and went into the water.

Vasco looked at Joe; then sauntered over to the city kids' clothes. The kids were too busy swimming to notice Vasco take several of the kids' shirts and walk to the edge of the river a few yards downstream from the cove. He soaked the shirts in the water, then he carefully tied knots in each and pulled the knots very tight with his powerful arms.

It wasn't until he was returning the dripping shirts to the stack of clothes that one of the kids saw what he was doing.

"Hey!" One kid shouted, "Look what that guy's doing!"

All three scrambled out of the water and ran over to their clothes. "What the hell you think you're doing?"

Vasco feigned surprise. "Your clothes were dirty, I was washing them," he said.

It was a terrible scene: They were like young savages standing there naked, bristling with rage, ready to do battle-- all they needed were spears and war clubs. There was no doubt who was the superior animal here. Vasco's muscular, athletic body was more than a match for all three of the others.

The older boy was terrified, but game. "Why are you doing this?" he demanded.

"You don't belong here, you're city bums," Vasco sneered.

"You don't own this river! What right do you have to . . .?"

Vasco hit him in the gut with a hard punch. "There's my right," he snarled.

The boy panicked, "Please! Don't hit me again! I've got a bad heart," he pleaded.

Vasco back-handed him viciously across the face. "That won't hurt your heart," he snapped.

The two younger boys grabbed their clothes and ran down the path they had come with the older boy close behind them.

Vasco was laughing triumphantly, and Joe was smiling weakly. They both went back into the water and swam to the log. Thos felt sick.

When Vasco and Joe swam back to the cove, Thos said, "I've got to go home, Joe."

"Come on in and take a swim first," Joe said, "I don't want to leave yet."

"I'm going home right now," Thos insisted." I can find my way by myself if you don't want to go with me."

Joe got out of the water. As he dressed, he told Vasco, "Mother will kill me if I let him go by himself."

On the way back Joe didn't say anything for a while, then he said, "What's the matter with you, Thos?"

"Nothing."

"You sick?"

"Kind'a,'" said Thos.

Joe shot him a quick look. "You're not going to tell Mother what went on back there?"

"I'm not a squealer."

"Good," said Joe, and they walked silently home.

CHAPTER 10

WITH THE EXTRA MONEY from James's farm job, Mother was able to buy more food. The usual diet at the Robinson's home did not include much meat, but now that she could afford it, Mother would occasionally buy a picnic ham and serve ham and cabbage for Sunday dinner. The remnants of the ham would augment Monday's supper, and the bone made for good soup, or gave flavor to a delicious meal of lima beans.

She was also able to make a larger batch of baking powder biscuits with raisins in them. The kids loved these delicious biscuits and Mother let the hungry children have their fill as long as they ate their vegetables first.

The biscuits became stale quickly, but they were still edible for days. Joe and Thos found them very useful for taking as nourishment on their trips into the woods. They would wrap the biscuits with whatever clean paper they could find and stuff them into the large pockets of their overalls. Both of them were still hungry all the time, but the biscuits gave them enough energy to stay in the woods until late in the afternoon.

Joe showed Thos many wonderful places. The swimming place called Martel's, where the a log bridged the river was not the only place that the kids could enter the water easily: there was a spot where the river was split by a small, muddy islet which the kids called "Coney Island." There was also a place upstream where the water had a red color caused by the iron content of the soil it moved through; this place was known as "blood's hole." Further downstream from Martel's was a deep part of the river where the branch of on old oak tree stretched out twenty feet above the river. This place was called "Trout Hole," and was a favorite spot for the more intrepid boys who liked to jump to the moving current below.

All of these places were at least a mile away from any road or house or any sign of human habitation. When Thos was at such places he was completely free of the anxieties that plagued him everywhere else -- the misery caused by what Lorraine called "the pitchfork of poverty;" for In the deep woods he did not feel like a poor kid, or like a person "on the town."

Joe shared Thos's feelings about the woods, and he would sometimes quote lines from poems he had studied at school: "One impulse from a vernal wood, can teach us more of man,/ Of goodness, beauty and of God/ than all the sages can."

Thos felt that almost everything in the woods was perfect -- but not everything. He could understand the briars, the mosquitoes, the horse flies, the no-see-ums, he even understood bloodsuckers--all of these things were part of Nature--but he could not understand Vasco.

Vasco seldom came with them any more, but when he did, he usually did something that disturbed Thos -- sometimes deeply disturbed him. Once Vasco found a nest of wood rats full of squirming, hairless little baby rats. Vasco held the nest up, set fire to it and watched while the helpless creatures were incinerated. "I hate rats," he said.

One day Vasco was leading Joe and Thos in a pathless part of the woods when he held up his hand and pointed at a cottontail standing motionless in a small glade. Whether it was frozen with fear, or hoping to escape notice by this ruse, was not clear to Thos. Joe readied his slingshot, took a small rock from his pocket, and was about to aim, when Vasco held up his hand. Slowly Vasco bent down, picked up a stone the size of a grapefruit and hurled it accurately and fatally at the terrified rodent. He gave the rabbit a quick kick to be sure that it had been killed; then he went into action as though he had been doing such things all his life. Carrying his prize by its hind legs he continued on through the woods until he found a suitable place by a brook, then he had Joe hold the rabbit while he filled his cupped hands with water and began washing a nearby rock the size of a small table. He took the rabbit back from Joe and told him to gather wood, make a circle of stones for a fire ring and light a fire. This Joe, assisted by Thos, did quickly, for in the New England woods there is never a shortage of stones or firewood.

While the fire was being readied, Vasco opened his jack-knife and skinned and cleaned the rabbit. Then he cut the meat into small succulent pieces.

He cleaned the knife in the brook, and handed it to Joe. "Cut some sticks and sharpen them -- like you do for hot dogs." Things were happening so quickly, Thos was confused; but he made up his mind that whatever happened, he would not eat part of that poor rabbit. He might go so far as to roast some of the meat over the fire -- but he would not even taste it.

That was his intention; but as the meat began to sizzle and the juices started to sputter and pop in the fire, the smell became tantalizing; and his hunger was so great, all his good intentions went for naught.

The boys hung pieces of the flesh on their roasting sticks; and as soon as a piece was browned, they blew on it and gobbled it down. While they were eating, Vasco placed those bones which still had meat on them atop the fire-ring stones closest to where the breeze was blowing the flames so that these morsels could get roasted too.

The rabbit had not been large, and soon anything that was fit to eat was gone, but the boys remained squatted around the fire, their hands and faces greasy, still gnawing on the bones.

It was quiet there except for the sound of the brook, the song of a thrush, and the twitter of a yellow warbler. all three of the boys seemed to be thinking of faraway things. Thos felt a strong sense of de'ja vu. He had been here before, sometime in the distant past, and this thought was powerful and deep-rooted. The boys sat silently around the fire until it burned out. Then they soaked the embers with brook water, buried the little that remained of the rabbit, and went on their way.

* * *

There were other occasions when Vasco's behavior was also incomprehensible to Thos.

Vasco always went barefoot. Whether he was on dirt roads, cinder paths, or in the thorny woods, he was barefoot. No surface seemed to be able to hurt his leathery feet. Thos had felt at first that this was a matter of choice with Vasco, but Joe had explained that Vasco's family simply could not afford shoes for him. Surprising as it might seem there were many families who were poorer than the Robinsons.

There were many reasons why Thos was bothered by the thought of going barefoot in the woods , but what bothered him most was the idea of stepping on a snake. They had never seen any venomous snakes. Some people said that copperheads had been seen in that part of the country, but even a garter snake gave Thos a slight shiver. They had often been startled by a black snake racing across their path. There was something about the power and speed of these creatures that brought out some atavistic dread in Thos. Vasco, though, was no more disturbed by any kind of snake than he would be by an earth worm.

Once when they were exploring the woods north of Blood's Hole, they heard a bird calling excitedly in the distance. "It's a robin!" Joe said. "It sound's like something's raiding its nest!" and he began to run, followed by Vasco and Thos. Joe stopped and pointed up at the branches of a large chestnut tree.

They saw a huge black snake up on a branch moving rapidly towards a robin's nest. They could hear the nestlings squealing with terror while their mother flew frantically about trying to distract the snake.

Vasco sprung into action. Grabbing a stick, he put it between his teeth, clambered up the tree and began attacking the snake. He was not in time to save one of the chicks, but two others owed their lives to Vasco, and the snake died with one partially digested baby robin in its terrible maw.

The nuances of the argument that the snake was hungry and was only doing its natural thing, just as Vasco was doing with the rabbit, never occurred to either Joe or Vasco, and the savagery of the incident gave Thos an image that woke him up in the night on more than one occasion.

The most violent of Vasco's exploits, though, began at the Martel's swimming place. Thos, Joe, and Vasco came there early one morning to find a boy of about Vasco's age swimming out to the log. The boy was not as husky as Vasco, but he was wiry, and his arms were thick and sinewy. It was obvious from the way he swam that he was a fine athlete. Vasco, assuming the lad was a city bum, took the boy's jeans, soaked them in swamp water, and began tying them in knots -- big mistake!

"What the hell do you think you're doing?" you portagee bastard!"

"What's it to you, you pansy frog!"

The boy was Canadian French, and proud of it; and he was no city bum. He lived on a farm in the northeastern part of Anneville. This meant that once the ethnic slurs had been hurled, no power on earth could have prevented these two young bucks from trial by combat. All that remained now was to agree on the rules of the battle. This Anneville tradition of conducting a fight within certain rules was long-standing, and probably not unique to the region. No one knew or seemed to care how and why it had evolved.

It was decided that Leo, the Frenchman, and Vasco would move their fight to another place where the combatants would have more room to maneuver. They both knew of a pine grove where the trees were far apart, and the only ground cover was pine needles and a few small princess pines. Leo's rage had turned into a smoldering fury, and Vasco's eagerness to show his manhood was now focused on the tactics he would employ to defeat what he now realized was a formidable foe. They agreed that this would be a standard fist fight -- no "rough and tumble," no biting, hitting below the belt, or kicking in the nuts. They both agreed on these conditions. Leo sized up Joe and Thos, and seemed convinced that they would be fair, or, if they weren't, he could dispatch both of them with a couple of quick punches.

The contest would begin with the old "twig on the shoulder" manner.

Leo made a quick sign of the cross and said, "Let the little guy put the twig on my left shoulder and we can begin punching as soon as you knock it off," Leo told Vasco.

Thos placed the twig on Leo's shoulder and scuttled quickly out of the way. Vasco knocked the twig off with a left jab and pounded Leo with a right to the ribs and the fight was on.

Leo was not as strong as Vasco but he was quick and tough. Their bare fists made a sickening thud as they smacked into each other's bare flesh. soon both of their faces were covered with cuts, and their knuckles were raw and bloody. The fight had begun as an exchange of heavy blows, but it finally settled into a prolonged defensive struggle. Both boys were in excellent condition and it was some time before their breathing became labored, but neither seemed ready to yield.

Thos, who at first felt sorry for Leo, figuring he would soon be lying on the ground, now began to feel sorry for both of them; and he became more and more puzzled about the need for this mayhem. What sense was there in this? This was ugly, and obscene! They were polluting this beautiful place with this senselessness as surely as did the city bums did with their trash and vandalism.

The contest had become a stalemate, and the boys were rapidly becoming exhausted. Finally they moved apart, and as though by mutual agreement, they flopped on the ground, sweaty, bloody, and gasping for air.

When they finally got their breath back, they sat up. Leo was the first to speak. "You're one tough Portagee son of a bitch," he said.

"My name's Vasco, puddle jumper. What's yours?"

"They call me Leo," the Frenchman said.

"Well, Leo I gotta' say, you're one tough Canuck bastard."

The fight was over, and it was obvious they were settling for a draw. They walked wearily away in opposite directions, battered and bruised, not triumphant but not defeated either.

As they walked out of the woods, Vasco did not answer when Joe said, without too much conviction, "You sure kicked his butt, didn't you, Vasco?"

Thos did not know what to say.

A few days later they found out that Vasco had gotten a job mucking out cow barns on a dairy farm. He would only earn ten cents an hour, but he would get all the milk he could drink, and he could take home a gallon of milk every day for his family. Thos wasn't sure whether he was happy or sad that Vasco would not be able to accompany him and Joe to the woods for a while.

CHAPTER 11

THE FOURTH OF JULY holiday was second only to Christmas as a cause for celebration in the town of Anneville. There was a parade, and a picnic. Every family that wasn't completely destitute would hold its own fireworks display out in front of their house. There would be Roman candles, sparklers, firecrackers, sky rockets, and a variety of other cheap pyrotechnics known collectively as "fireworks." Many people were maimed or even killed, and property was burned, but this could not deter the citizens from celebrating the "birthday" of their beloved country.

This day also reminded people that the year was now more than half over, and some of the kids, especially Thos and Joe, realized that there were now only 174 days to Christmas.

There was some hope in the air. In his inaugural speech on March 4, Roosevelt had announced: "The only thing we have to fear is fear itself!" It was a soul-stirring epigram, but like most popular epigrams, it was woefully simplistic.

In the first 100 days of his administration, Roosevelt had done much to halt the downward slide of the economy, but there was still a long way to go before any honest person could say The Depression was over.

In Europe and Asia there were ominous events happening that were about to bring the people of this planet to the brink of total destruction. Imperial Japan, ignoring the protests of the United States and the League of Nations, was continuing to devour China and other nations in the Far East. In Germany Adolph Hitler, who had become Dictator and had already taken control of the press, was encouraging book

71

burning in great public bonfires, and had begun his hideous campaign of genocide against the Jews.

In America and even in Anneville, some voices were raised to warn people of the coming catastrophe, but most good folks were too concerned with their own problems to think about foreign affairs.

The only news they seemed to be interested in was about sports or the movies -- "King Kong" was coming to the screen, Charlie Chaplin was marrying Paulette Goddard, and Primo Canera had knocked out Jack Sharkey to become heavyweight champion of the world.

Thos and Joe, at least during the time that they were traipsing the woods, were having a marvelous summer, but the struggles of the Robinson family continued. James slaved away on the farm, and was so exhausted by the work in the fields and the two mile walk to and from work, he didn't have the energy to play his beloved baseball in the long twilight hours. Lorraine had a job working in Hyannis helping one of Mother's friends run a summer bed and breakfast place. She only came home on weekends (Hyannis was about thirty miles from Anneville), but she enjoyed being away from Anneville for a while. Always an avid celebrity hound, she would dramatically describe her sightings of the Kennedy children being escorted by their governess as they walked around the environs of the Kennedy's' famous Hyannis compound. James (maybe a bit jealous) would sneer, "What's the big deal? I've seen them -- they're just a bunch of scrawny, spoiled rich kids; they'll never amount to anything.'"

Patricia, who would be twelve in October, was getting prettier every day, and was beginning to attract the attention of the adolescent boys of Anneville. Thos and Joe were sometimes stopped by some of these young swains who would begin the conversation with, "Are you the brothers of Patricia Robinson?"

Patricia, though, in the absence of Lorraine and James, had to spend all of her time helping Mother with the housework. Thos and Joe did not escape these chores entirely. They were assigned the washing and drying of all dishes, the hanging of the wash on the backyard clothesline, and the cleaning up of the cellar and yard on weekends. Rosebud, who had just turned five, and Regis, three, were exempt from chores. They spent their days playing with their meager store of toys and playing games with each other or, occasionally, they would get to play with the next door neighbor's dog, Brownie.

The dogs of Anneville were very important members of the community. Most of them ran free; and though fiercely loyal to their owners, were well--known by most of the grown-ups in town, and personal friends of most of the kids. a few people kept their unhappy wretches chained in the backyard, and others kept their little pooches inside and spoiled them rotten; but most dogs roamed free like most of the chickens in Anneville.

It was an unwritten law that no dog could be allowed to chase or kill any barnyard fowl. Puppies were trained from birth to ignore chickens. This training was severe, often brutal. A puppy was whipped any time it chased a chicken; and, if it killed one, the dead bird was hung about the neck of the pup, and the offender was kept chained until the carcass rotted off. If these measures did not work, the dog had to be destroyed, usually by drowning or shooting.

Dogs that were vicious to children were not allowed to wander the town either.

The kids of the town knew the dogs by their names, not by the names of their owners: it was Rex, or Brownie, or Buster -- never the Taber's dog, or whatever.

The Robinson kids had begged Mother many times for a dog, but the answer was always a variation of the same speech. "I wouldn't make a dog live the way we live, it wouldn't be fair to the dog. You say we could feed it left-overs -- we have no left-overs in this house. Heck, we'd probably end up eating the poor thing. You know some people in the world think dogs are delicious."

Thos and Joe especially longed for a dog. They became friends with the neighbors' dogs, and as they passed by homes on the way to the woods, they would stop and pet those dogs that came out to greet them. They had their favorites--Gondie, a smart, eager to please, black Labrador; Oscar, a foolish but lovable Irish setter; Prince, a powerful, intense German shepherd; but the boys loved any dog in Anneville that didn't try to tear them apart.

Once Joe said to Thos, " Did you ever notice how swell dogs are? Not once, in the whole town of Anneville, did any dog ever look down on us because we're poor."

But their favorite dog was Rover, a beautiful, dignified golden-haired mixed border-collie and retriever.

Rover usually lay in the front yard of his mistress's home. Mrs. Parsons was a small, dark-haired woman who walked with a severe limp. When his mistress was out -- whether tending her flowers, or, as she did several times a week walking to the grocery store--Rover was completely focused on what seemed to be his vocation -- to guide and protect his beloved mistress. He could not be distracted from his duty by anything: not by other dogs, not by children, not even by cats which normally he considered his mission to run up the nearest tree or telephone pole. He never growled or threatened anybody while he was on duty, but there was something about his demeanor at this time that told every living creature in the vicinity, "Don't you even think about harming my lady!"

At first, as long as his lady was not out, Rover would politely wag his tail at the sight of Joe and Thos, then stand with friendly dignity while they petted him or gently scratched behind his ears. On several occasions he followed them for a short distance before returning to his own front yard. As he became friendlier with the two boys he began to follow them farther and farther, until he would follow them to the first barbed wire fence that enclosed the pasture that bordered the woods. At that point Rover would sit down and the boys would say goodbye to him for the day.

Rover would study the faces of his two friends as though he were reading their thoughts. He seemed to understand how much the boys loved him and wanted him to continue on with them. He would lift his muzzle high in the air and breathe deeply of the wonderful smells coming from the woods.

Joe looked at him once and declaimed: "I understand, Rover. 'The woods are lovely, dark and deep, but . . .'"

Then the boys would climb through the fence, and Rover would trot away home.

One day, though, Rover whined as the boys started to leave; then he began to paw at the ground beneath the fence as though he were trying to dig his way under the barbed strands. But he never really did any digging. He was just trying to send them a message, and his intelligent eyes asking them for help.

Thos and Joe got the message: they grabbed the strand in the center of its span and pulled it up as high as they could while Rover bellied under it. Then, with his tail wagging wildly, he barked and took off for his patrol of the woods. For the rest of the day he roamed the woods ahead of the boys, clearing the way of any crawling, flying or burrowing creature. Squirrels, chipmunks, weasels or feral cats were sent clawing up the nearest tree, wood rats; rabbits, and wood chucks ran for their burrows, and any bird on or even close to the ground, was sent flying. Rover was gloriously happy. He ran about with his eyes bright, his tail wagging, and his beautiful golden hair blowing wildly in the breeze. At the brook he slurped the spring water eagerly, and when they came to Martel's he plunged inn for the sheer joy of it and swam happily around. Finally, he got out of the water, shook his shaggy coat vigorously, kicked up some leaves, lay down, and began watching the boys while they swam.

When other kids came, Rover wagged his tail when they talked to him, and politely let them pet him, but he let it be known that he was now on duty, and that Thos and Joe were his masters, at least for now.

With Rover gamboling around them or walking by their side, Thos and Joe were in a state of euphoria most of the day; but as they headed back home, reality began to set in.

"He's not really our dog, you know," said Joe.

"He likes us, Joe, and he loves the woods, I can tell; and I love him. Don't you Joe?"

"Of course I do, but he's not ours, Thos. Don't you get it? We're probably going to catch heck for taking him into the woods. Mrs. Parsons will probably be mad. Lizzie Horton said that she heard that Mrs. Parsons is an old battle-ax. Gee, Rover will probably get in trouble tool"

After they got out of the pasture, Rover seemed to sense that he might be in trouble too. His tail that he had been carrying like a battle flag, was now drooping -- not quite between his legs, but it was clear he was worried.

As they came within a block of Mrs. Parsons house, Joe said. "Maybe we ought to let Rover go home by himself, and we'll take the shortcut across the field to our house." Joe said.

"We can't let Rover take the rap all alone -- that's dirty!"

"Okay," said Joe, "but I've got a bad feeling about this."

Mrs. Parsons was waiting for them as they neared her house. Thos had never looked at her closely before. To him she was a crippled woman with her black hair done up in a tight bun on the back of her head. He had heard that her husband was dead and her son was away at college.

As they approached she ignored the boys and kept her eyes on Rover who now had his tail between his legs. When he got close to his lady, she crouched down, her leg with its ugly black shoe on it sticking awkwardly out.

"Where have you been, you naughty boy? I've been worried half to death."

Her voice was gentle and loving: not the least bit angry, and she put her arms around Rover and hugged him. the relieved Rover wagged his tail and whined softly.

Then she looked at the boys, and studied them. "You're Mrs. Robinson's boys, aren't you?" Again her voice was gentle. When most of the townspeople said those words, "You're Mrs. Robinson's boys," there was a hard tone to their voices, with some of them it was almost as though they were saying, "You're from the leper colony, aren't you?" That's an exaggeration -- it was more like -- "You're 'on the town,' aren't you?"

But in Mrs. Parsons' voice there was sweetness and kindness. She spoke to them the way that the teachers at Parting Ways School spoke.

Then she turned her attention back to Rover. "You poor thing! Now that George is away, you don't have anybody to run and play with." She looked at her leg, and looked back at the boys. "Did Rover go into the woods, with you?"

"Yes, Ma'am," said Joe.

She looked at Thos. "Little boy, don't you have a dog of your own?"

"No, Ma'am," said Thos.

"Have you any idea how precious Rover is to me?"

"Yes, Ma'am," Thos said.

She looked from Rover to the boys, and was lost in thought for a while. Then she said, "If I let you take Rover into the woods with you, would you promise to always bring him safely back to me, and always remember that he is my dog, and I love him very, very much?"

And that was it! From then on Rover became their best friend. This day might not have been at the very top of their all-time list of happiest days, but it was certainly very high up there.

CHAPTER 12

ON MOST DAYS, THOS and Joe, accompanied by Rover, were able to head for the woods. They became a familiar sight walking down the street that led to the pasture. Most neighbors ignored the two lads with their borrowed dog, but Mr. Lassiter, a disabled veteran of The Great War, would greet them warmly as they went by. When the weather was good he spent most of his time rocking on his front porch smoking his pipe.

"I know one of you is named Thos and the other is Joe, but I never can remember which one of you is which, so from now on I'm going to call you Joe-Thos and Thos-Joe. And that's what he did. They began to look forward to his cheery greeting: "Here comes Joe-Thos-Boy and Thos-Joe-Boy!"

Some of the Anneville kids, including Lizzie Horton, said Mr. Lassiter was a crazy old man and it was best not to go near him. Mother, though, told Thos and Joe that Mr. Lassiter was not old or crazy. She said that he was really only thirty four years old and the reason he looked so old was that he had been horribly disabled with mustard gas during the fighting in the Somme. He had been in a veteran's hospital for ten years after the war recovering from "gas shock." Now his sister Madeline, who never married, took care of him, and he was not expected to live long. Madeline sang in the choir, and this is how Mother had learned all this. Mother told the boys that this information was not to be discussed with other kids, and they were especially not to speak about the fact that Mr. Lassiter was dying of stomach cancer.

One day Mr. Lassiter stopped the boys and asked them where they went on their walks.

"We go to the woods, sir," Joe said.

"I thought so," Mr. Lassiter said, and for a few seconds, he seemed to be lost in thought. "I used to go there when I was a boy. Do you go swimming at Martel's where the log goes across the river?"

"Yes, sir," said Joe.

"You're a polite boy, Joe-Thos, but I wasn't an officer -- just a corporal. Instead of calling me 'Sir' you can just call me 'Harry,' okay? And, one of these days I'd like to ask you a few questions. But I want you to ask your Mother if it's okay to talk to me. For now, just go on into the woods with your dog and enjoy yourselves -go along now, Joe-Thos, and Thos-Joe." There was a grin on his face when he said this, but Thos noticed that there were tears in his eyes too.

That night Joe asked Mother about their talk with Mr. Lassiter, and if it was all right to call him 'Harry' and answer his questions. She said that she wanted the boys to do anything within reason to make Mr. Lassiter's last days as pleasant as possible.

When they told Harry that Mother said it was all right to talk to him and answer his questions, he was very pleased.

"Here's my first question ," he said. "When you go to Martel's, does the path cross over a little brook?"

"Yes," Joe said.

"Is the brook still clean? It doesn't have any junk or anything in it. Can you still drink from it?"

Thos did not wait for Joe to answer. "It's swell, Mr. Lassiter. We drink from it all the time."

"Good! And remember: please call me Harry. Would you boys like to play a little mystery game with me? The mystery has to deal with that brook. If you solve the mystery, I'll give each one of you a shiny new dime. Ask your Mother tonight if you can go ahead with this, and if you have her permission, I'll tell you more about it tomorrow."

This was exciting stuff. it was like a story -- like *Treasure Island* that Lorraine had read them last winter. This certainly sounded like an adventure, and the 'treasure' would be the shiny dimes. Neither one of the boys had had any spending money since Daddy had lost his job more than two years ago.

Mother readily gave her permission, and the boys had trouble getting to sleep that night for excitement.

When they told Harry that Mother had okayed the project, he smiled broadly, and picked up a pint Mason

jar he had placed near his rocker. "The first part of this game is to fill this jar with water from the brook." They were to wait until they had finished their day in the woods and were on their way back before they filled the jar. If Harry was not on the porch, they were to knock on the front door and give the water to Madeline. Thy would get further instructions the next day or the next time they went to the woods.

They took very good care of the Mason jar that day, and when they filled it on the way back, they made sure the water was as pure as spring water can be. Harry was not on the porch, but Madeline answered the door promptly, and she smiled as she took the water from the boys. "God bless you boys for helping Harry with this. He's sleeping now, but he said he will see you tomorrow if you come by."

When they received their instructions the next day, the mystery became more fascinating. Harry told them that the next step was to find the source of the brook. He said that when he had been a boy, he and his friend, Armand, had discovered the place where the spring bubbled out of the ground. When he said Armand's name, his voice broke, and he had to pause. He bit his lip, looked far into the distance; then he got his composure back. "Sorry, boys -- Armand and I used to go to the woods like you two." He paused and took a breath. "He bought it at the Somme. They say he was killed by the explosion of a gas shell. I was in the same trench, but I only got gassed--lucky me! Enough of this! That was over fifteen years ago."

He now seemed to get complete control of himself. "Armand and I were the ones responsible for that brook. We dug out the place where the spring was, made a little basin in the dirt and lined it with stones. Before we worked on it, there was just a swampy place in the leaves where you couldn't get a drink if your life depended on it. After we were through the brook flowed pure and sweet. But let me get back to your mission. You're to find the basin we made -- it's probably all covered with twigs and leaves; there are probably a million bugs there -- you two don't look like boys who are afraid of bugs -- you might even find a salamander or two. I used to love to see salamanders -- do you?" Joe nodded, but Thos had no idea of what he meant.

"Well, anyway," Harry continued, "On one of those stones that makes up the basin we put a little brass plaque -- Armand's dad made it for us: he was a machinist, He not only made us the plaque, but he engraved an inscription on it. Your mission is to find that plaque, write down the inscription, and then find out what it means. Then put the basin back the way it was -- leave the stone and the brass plate and everything the

secret way it was. When you show me the inscription and tell me what it means, you will have solved the mystery and I'll give you the dimes. You guys still game?"

The boys could hardly speak they were so excited. "Thank you, Harry," Joe said. "Thank you! Are we the only ones who know about this?"

"Yes," said Harry. "It's just us three -- and, Armand." Again, the mention of Armand's name was almost too much for him, but he got control quickly. He grinned and looked at Rover then. "What about Rover, there: Can you keep a secret, old boy?"

As they say in in the old mystery stories, "The game was now afoot!" Thos and Joe were about to have the best time of all the good times they had had that summer.

Harry had evidently planned his little game carefully. He reached in his pocket, and brought out a little notebook with a stubby pencil stuck in a loop attached to the cover.

He handed it to Joe. "This is what you will use to write down the inscription. Make sure you get it exactly right. Any little mistake you make, in any step of problem-solving, will prevent you from solving the problem. Armand's dad taught us that. Okay, boys! Off you go -- have fun!"

Joe and Thos wanted to run, but they had a long way to go, and settled for a brisk pace. The bird songs that morning seemed even happier and louder than usual, and when they reached the brook, it, too, seemed to flow with more energy.

Rover seemed slightly puzzled when the boys left the path and began walking up the slope through the underbrush. They made their way through briars and pushed aside creepers and vines. All kinds of flowers -- buttercups, daisies, violets, lady slippers, Jack-in-the-pulpits grew along the muddy banks, and Thos thought that this might be a good place to hunt for the 'first flowers of spring' when Parting Ways School next held its annual contest.

The basin that Harry and Armand had constructed was not big -- only about thirty inches in diameter -- and there was tall grass and some bushes growing around it, but the water made an agreeable sound as it splashed over the stones to form the beginning of the brook.

The boys broke off sticks from a nearby elderberry bush and began clearing the area so they could get at the stones. They were wild with excitement now, but Joe said they should work carefully so as not to disturb the basin anymore than they had to. "If we're lucky," he said, "we might be able to find the brass plaque without digging out any of the rocks."

They had no idea of exactly how large the brass plate would be or what it would look like. Harry had held up his fingers when he had mentioned the plaque to demonstrate that it was small -- maybe about an inch wide and three inches long. The rock could not be too large either, for Armand and Harry had taken it to Armand's dad to have him attach the plate.

As the boys worked, the romance of this situation became more and more intriguing. Though the time when this basin had been constructed could not have been more than twenty four years; yet to them it seemed as though they were discovering ancient ruins. James had told them that these woods had been used during the King Phillip's War by the Indians under the leadership of the sons of Massasoit circa 1675. To kids as young as Joe and Thos, the past is sometimes lumped into one mass known as "the olden days."

It wasn't long before Joe spotted the brass plate. Harry and Armand had placed the inscription stone at the place in the basin furthest away from where the brook began to flow. There was a patina over the brass that made the letters unreadable; but the discovery filled the boys with such excitement, they whooped with joy, and Rover ran over to see what was happening.

Thos wanted to start digging the stone out immediately, but Joe, always the patient one, said that they should think out their next step carefully; so they sat down on a nearby moss-covered rock to rest and discuss what strategy to use to make the brass plate readable.

They both agreed that it would be wrong to dig the stone from its place in the basin. Thos suggested that they find some dirt and use it to scour the patina off of the plate; but Joe pointed out that this would make the water muddy, making it difficult to see the stones and fouling their favorite brook.

"If we could get some sand," Thos said.

Joe agreed and they began to search the area. There was none to be found, but as they poked around in the leaves and twigs, they found, as Harry had predicted, many, many bugs. There may not have been a million, as Harry had said; but there were certainly many hundreds of them. There seemed to be a whole micro-wilderness under the decayed leaves and twigs: mites, ants beetles, spider lings, all kinds of worms-- Thos had never realized before how many different types of insects there were underneath the detritus on the floor of the woods. Remembering what Harry had said about "boys like you are not afraid of a few bugs," Thos tried not to be frightened, and did well until he saw a horrible little centipede slithering quickly away. After that he became very cautious.

Suddenly they saw a salamander, and Thos realized why Harry had mentioned the creature with such reverence. It was beautiful -- a smooth-skinned little lizard with eyes like tiny jewels. It looked like something created by Walt Disney, and it moved with such delightful grace, Thos wanted to capture it and keep it for a pet. Joe quickly explained that it would be wrong to take this little beauty away from this paradise, and it would quickly die in captivity.

"Besides," he said. "we didn't come here to look at bugs and stuff. Let's get back to work."

They tried scraping the plaque with a stick; then Joe took off his sock and vainly tried to rub the coating off the brass. All these efforts were useless.

The boys agreed that the only thing to so was to go to Martel's where there was not only plenty of sand, but there were also many smooth small stones that would work well as scouring pads.

They were soon back with plenty of sand and stones, and soon they were beginning to see the brass shine through the twenty four year old accumulation of grime and corrosion. Gradually the letters began to appear. Joe wrote them down carefully in his notebook: "is xii 3." That was all! What could it possibly mean? They sat down on the moss-covered rock and strained their brains until Thos started to get a headache . Even when Joe told Thos that the xii were probably Roman numerals that equaled twelve, the inscription still made no sense at all. Completely baffled, they tried to restore the area as best they could, and return home, disappointed, but by no means discouraged.

Harry was not on the porch when they came back, and they discussed whether or not they should tell Mother and the rest what had happened.

"We'll wait until we can ask Harry what we should do. Meanwhile it'll be okay if we just ask Mother and maybe James what the inscription means."

Mother was too busy when they came back to their house -- too busy to bother about the stuff they were working on. With the help of Patricia she had taken down the lace curtains and washed them. She immediately put Joe and Thos to work setting up the frames that had to be used to stretch the curtains on while they dried. These frames were hellish things to put up. They were stored in a closet as a set of fragile two by one inch slats that had to be assembled with nuts and thumbscrews to the exact dimensions of the curtains. The bad news was that these slats were studded everywhere with needle-sharp pins on which the curtains were to be anchored while they dried. Despite the fact that Mother gave them exact instructions on how to assemble this contraption, and gave them dire warnings to beware of the sharp pins, the boys' tender flesh was punctured again and again by the nasty little pins. Once the frames were assembled to Mother's satisfaction, she carefully stretched her precious curtains across the frames and left them to dry. The boys had to admit that there was a certain pleasure in seeing the whole assemblage when she was finished, and a wonderful aroma in the house as they dried. When the curtains were clean and dry, the boys had to carefully remove the delicate lace from the sharp little pins again and hand them to Mother to hang. This annual ritual was only one of many that left a lasting impression on the boys as to Mother's dedication to the axiom that "cleanliness was next to Godliness," or, as James would say, "Mother was sure a nut on keeping things clean!"

Thos and Joe had decided to wait until after supper to ask anybody about the inscription. They would say nothing about the brook or the basin or why they needed to know what the inscription meant. They would act as though it were simply a riddle. The only one who could make any sense at all about, 'is xii 3" was James: "I can't make head nor tail of it," he said. "it could be some kind of math formula -- like Roman numerals xii mean 12, and one plus two equals three. Thus xii is 3. But, if that's what means, it's a dumb riddle in my opinion."

The rest of the Robinsons soon gave up on trying to solve the riddle, so when the boys saw Harry the next morning, James's solution was all they had to offer.

Harry listened to what James had said; then he looked at the figures Joe had written. He shook his head. "Your brother is a smart fella'. This would be a dumb riddle if that's what it meant. But this is not really a riddle or a formula, it's just something that Armand and I thought might be right for where the spring comes out of the ground. We also thought that nobody would ever find it for a very long time -- like a hundred or even a thousand years. Then the people who found it would have fun trying to figure out what it meant. I'm not smart like Armand was, but I don't think the inscription is dumb. Now, you remember that I told you that when you are solving a problem, you must be sure that each step in the problem-solving is correct before you move on to the next. I'm sorry, but you boys have made a mistake in writing down these figures. Maybe I'm being too hard on you, but if I can teach you to be better at problem-solving, I'll be doing you a favor; so I'm going to insist that you don't get your dimes unless you get this thing right. Go back and check that brass plate again. If you study it carefully, you'll find your mistake. Do you want to try again, or do you think I'm cheating you by not giving you your dimes now for the good work you've already done?"

The boys looked at one another; then Joe said, "Gee, Harry, you aren't cheating us. Thos and I don't want any dimes until we get the job done right, do we Thos!"

Thos would have preferred to take his dime immediately, but he nodded affirmatively and kept his mouth shut.

Harry's old eyes almost sparkled. "You're good lads," he said, "both of you. Now, I'm just going to give you one clue: whenever you read anything, always be careful of punctuation and capitalization. That's all. Today is Friday and I know you kids don't go to the woods on

Saturday or Sunday, so I'll see you on Monday. Get along with you, good luck."

When the boys got back to the spring, it did not take them long to discover their error. They had failed to see that the first letter was the capital letter "I" and there was a period after the "s." and "3." The inscription really was: "Is. xii 3." They checked and double checked it before they wrote it down, but it still made no sense to them.

Even though they were pretty sure they had gotten it right this time, they still did not restore the area around the little pool to as natural a condition as they felt they should, but they determined to do so when they were positive that they had gotten the correct answer this time.

All the way home they puzzled over the strange figures, but they could not come up with anything that made any sense.

They showed the corrected inscription to Mother, James, and Patricia, but none of them could come up with a solution. Mother said that they should show it to Lorraine, who would be coming home from Hyannis for the weekend, but Lorraine was puzzled too. "I've seen something like that somewhere, but it's too far back in my brain for me to remember. What's it all about anyway?"

"It's a secret that Thos and Joe won't share with us, so we won't strain our brain anymore for them," James said good-naturedly.

Lorraine smiled at Thos and Joe. "A secret's not a secret if you share it. I like people who can keep a secret."

On Friday nights that summer, Lorraine, James, and Patricia were allowed to stay up late after the younger ones went to bed. Lorraine's friend, Trevor, who had forgiven her for the practical joke involving the plumber's helper, had been coming over on Friday nights to play cards. He had shown them how to play bridge, which was too complicated a game for any of the younger kids to understand.

On that Friday night Trevor had brought over some oatmeal cookies, and Lorraine had made tea. They took a break from the game, and while they were having the refreshments, the subject of the inscription came up. "Let me see it,said Trevor. When he read it, he began to laugh. "You mean none of you knows what this means?" Then he laughed again.

"Okay, wise guy," James said. "When are you going to tell us what's so funny?"

"This is too rich," said Trevor. "I've a mind not to tell you after that dirty trick you played on me about the posser."

"Okay, dear Trevor, I told you how sorry I was about that. Please let us in on your joke."

"It's just that none of you Catholics could figure it out. We Methodists all know our Bible better than you mackerel snappers. any good Protestant would know that thing is from the Bible: Isaiah, Chapter twelve, verse three. Oh boy, I love this!"

"All right," James said, "score one for the Methodists. We'll get back at you when Notre Dame plays Southern Methodist. Now what does that thing mean?"

"Well, even we Methodists don't know the entire Bible by heart. I don't suppose you Catholics have a Bible in the house? I can look it up in a hurry."

Lorraine quickly found the Bible and brought it in. Trevor shuffled through the pages. "Here it is: Isaiah, Chapter 12, verse 3." He glanced over it, and became very serious. In a very respectful voice, he read: 'Out of Me both little and great, rich and poor, as out of a living fountain, draw living water.'"

There was silence.

Finally Lorraine said, "Thank you, Trevor," then they went back to playing cards.

The boys told Harry on Monday and said that they would restore the fountain to the way it was when they found it. They also told him that they would not tell anybody about the brass plate. "We understand what it means. Armand and you did a very nice thing there," Joe said."

Harry, who looked tired, but very happy, ceremoniously presented the shiny dimes to Thos and Joe. "You're both very fine lads," He said. "I won't be able to be out on the porch anymore. I want to say goodbye to you here, and I want you to think about me whenever you go by this porch. The doctor says I'll be seeing Armand very soon. I'll tell Armand what good kids you are and how happy you made me these last days."

He shook both their hands; then he called for Madeline and she helped him go back in the house.

Harry Lassiter died two weeks before Labor Day. He was only thirty-four years old. He now belonged to the ranks of the other 116,000 American boys who sacrificed their lives in "the war to end all wars."

The Sit. Francis Xavier Church choir, with Madeline leading the altos and Mother leading the sopranos, sang the funeral mass. He was buried in the Anneville Cemetery, not very far away from the woods he loved. Men of the American Legion carried his flag-draped coffin to the grave site, and he was given full military honors, including the playing of Taps, and the traditional firing of rifles over his final resting place. One of the American Legionnaires said a few words over the grave. He ended with:

"To you with failing hands we throw
The torch, be yours to hold it high.
If ye break faith with we who die
We shall not sleep, though poppies grow
In Flanders fields."

Thos and Joe were hit hard by Harry's death. They talked this over with Mother, and they felt a little better when Mother told them that Maddie said that the boys had made Harry's last days very pleasant. she also told Mother about the boys bringing Harry the water from the brook. Madeline said that when Father Reynold had come to administer the sacrament of Extreme Unction, Harry had asked that Father Reynold use some of the water from the brook as part of the last rites.

The boys were especially troubled with what they should do with the dimes Harry had given them. Mother suggested that Joe, who had already made his first confession, should ask Father Reynold in the confessional what to do with the dimes. Father Reynold told Joe that he thought that Harry would want the boys to spend the money on themselves, and that they should make sure they enjoyed whatever they spent the money on.

Both the boys were greatly relieved by this advice, and set about planning what they would do with that much money. They talked this matter over with James, and he came up with an exciting idea: why not go to the movies? Mother had given him a quarter to spend on himself out of the money he had earned working on the Standish farm. The three of them would have enough money, not only to pay for the movie, but to buy a hot dog and a soda. there was one movie theater in New Bradford that would let two kids accompanied by an adult in for one dime. (This was called the Bailey theater: it had been named in honor of an American World War 1 flying ace named Frank Bailey.) James would be charged one whole dime for admission, so that would give them twenty-five cents to spend on hot dogs and sodas. There were two problems with this plan, though. They still needed another nickel to pay for the refreshments, and James would be paying a nickel out of his own money for Thos and Joe. Mother surprised them all when she agreed to supply the extra nickel. James assured the boys that he didn't mind at all kicking in one of his own nickels for such a magnificent expedition. He had been to the movies several times in the old days, and Joe had been once, but Thos had never seen a movie before in his life.

The Bailey Theater was approximately two and a half miles from the Robinsons" home. The boys would be taking Main Street down the hill, past the Russell Memorial Library, past the cemetery, the Ivy-covered old Methodist Church, and across the King Phillip's Bridge into New Bradford. From the bridge they would walk up hill to Anneville Avenue, the main commercial thoroughfare in the city, to Bailey Square, where the theater was.

As they hiked along, James gave them a short history lesson. This was the route the British took during the Revolutionary War after they landed on the west bank of the Anneville River near its mouth. The redcoats had marched north along what was now Anneville Avenue, burning businesses and warehouses as they marched. At the King Phillips Bridge the patriots of Anneville made a valiant but futile effort to stop the British regulars. The British could find nothing in Anneville worth stealing or destroying, and marched back to their ships in New Bradford and departed.

James told the boys that when school started again next week Lorraine would be walking this road on her way to Melville Junior High School. Instead of turning south at Anneville Avenue, though, she would continue up the hill another third of a mile to the school. This way eventually led across the border into Rhode Island, and legend had it that this route had been taken by George Washington on his way from Boston to Providence. The corner where the boys turned onto Anneville Avenue was called Lunds Corner, and it was here that the trolley line began that ran the length of New Bradford. A trolley car was stopped there and the conductor was busy moving his controls from one end of the car to the other. "What a modern marvel!" thought Thos! "Instead of having to turn the car around when they reach the end of the line, they simply reversed the controls and the trolley pole!"

James said they couldn't afford the fifteen cents it would cost for the three of them to ride car, but when Lorraine went to the tenth grade at New Bradford High School, she would be able to ride free every school day. Thos remembered the toy trolley car he had been given on this third birthday, but this sight of the real thing was thrilling.

The theater was not yet open when they arrived, but there was a line already waiting to get in. While they waited in line, Thos's excitement began to grow. The posters for the movie of the day, which was "Hell's Angels," had brightly colored posters that were almost worth a nickel just to look at -- biplanes, engulfed in smoke and flames heading for the ground, German and Allied aviators in leather helmets and goggles flying the plane while blasting away at each other with machine guns, and several wonderful pictures of Jean Harlowe looking like something that any red-blooded guy would be more than willing to die for.

When they finally got seated inside, the place was buzzing with anticipation. Thos was amazed at the size of the screen and curious about the projection booth in the back with its rectangular holes cut into it. The place had once served as a vaudeville theater and was decorated in garish art-deco style.

Then the lights dimmed, the crowd became silent, the screen lit up, and the sound track broke the silence. Thos was instantly transported into the land of enchantment.

A Pathe newsreel burst onto the screen. A cultured British voice charged with drama spoke the narration over stirring background music. There was a series of quick-moving news clips -- Nazi storm troopers arresting Jewish business men in Berlin, Mussolini, posturing absurdly, meeting with Chancellor Dollfuss of Austria, newly commissioned American warships plowing through heavy seas, and Mahatma Gandhi, weighing only ninety pounds after being on a hunger strike to non-violently trying to free his country from Britain. The whole thing was less than five minutes long, and Thos wished it had been longer. But as Thos was recovering from the excitement of the newsreel, the "Previews of Coming Attractions" started to roll, and Thos was soon holding on to James's arm with both hands. Max Steiner's music was so ominous and loud, it alone would have scared the bejabbers out of Thos, but what he saw on the screen would become a common figure in his nightmares in the weeks to come. "King Kong," the largest and most horrifying monster he had ever seen stood towering above him. If he hadn't been holding onto James's arm he would have exited that theater as fast as his skinny little legs would have taken him. Luckily this was only a short preview, and the other previews were mild enough to slow down his pounding heart. "It's just a movie," James whispered.

Then the introduction for the main feature began, and in Thos's opinion took forever. When the action finally started, it was worth waiting for. The posters outside had promised excitement, and they had not exaggerated. All three of the boys were mesmerized by the flying sequences Howard Hughes had worked so hard and spent so much money to produce.

All three of the boys were sorry when it was over, and reluctant to leave their seats when the lights were turned on. they were silent with awe as they followed the crowd out of the theater. What could be said about such a spectacle?

Finally, James said, "Who else is hungry besides me?"

The power and glory of the movie had made them forget about food, but now they realized how famished they were. The small diner James took them to was not far away. There were some tables, but the boys sat at the counter just in front of the grill where the man cooked the hot dogs and hamburgers which were the only things on the menu. A hamburger cost ten cents, a hot dog, a nickel. They ordered hot dogs and Nesbitt orange sodas.

"Everything on the hot dogs?" the counter man asked.

"You bet," said James, and the other two nodded eagerly in agreement.

The man knew his business. He did everything with a flourish, but with absolute economy of movement -- slapping the hot dogs on the grill, placing the buns on the edge of the grill so they would be warm, flipping the bottle caps off, slipping the straws in, and placing the frosted bottles in front of each boy without spilling a drop.

The boys savored each drop of the soda and each bite of the hot dog. They could have easily devoured several more of the delicious hot dogs, but they were used to not being able to eat their fill, and they were extremely pleased with the small feast they had.

On the way home, Thos said, "This was swell, wasn't it? This must be what it's like all the time when you're rich."

James slowed down his brisk pace and looked at Thos. "You don't have to be rich to be able to afford a movie, a hot dog and a soda; Lots of people do this practically every week. When Daddy was working, Lorraine, Patricia and I did this a lot -- you guys were too young."

"I hate being poor," Joe said.

They walked along silently for a while, then James said: "You know what? Mrs. Sylvia read something to us once from Shakespeare: 'That which is without remedy should be without regard.' That means, if you can't do anything about it, forget about it. All I hear around our house is, Poor us! Okay, we're poor; but the worst thing you can do in this world is to feel sorry for yourselves. We're supposed to be Anneville tough guys. Tough guys don't ever feel sorry for themselves. Just enjoy the fun we had today, and I don't want to hear either one of you ever again whining about being poor!"

CHAPTER 13

THE SUMMER WAS OVER, and though it had been a happy time for Thos and Joe, for Mother the miseries of The Depression were not over.

Some of Roosevelt's policies, though, were bringing hope to millions. By September he had cut through some of the red tape and made it possible to allocate federal money for relief without having to secure matching funds from state and local governments. He ordered that 700 million be allocated to provide food and clothing to the needy during the coming winter. But for now there were still bread lines and soup kitchens in many cities, and evicted families huddled in makeshift tents, and the ranks of the jobless continued to swell. All of the nation was affected by The Depression—both "little and great, rich and poor—"but some more than others. The mill towns in the industrial regions of America had been especially devastated, and Anneville was hit as hard as any of them.

The community made some effort to alleviate the misery of individual families, but in the end each family was on its own.

Mother did have faith in Roosevelt, and hoped that some federal food would reach her hungry kids soon. So far she had managed to keep her little brood from starving, but she was dreading the coming winter. The money that Lorraine and James had earned would help some: she would be able to buy much needed shoes for James and a warm new coat for Lorraine who would soon be taking a daily three mile walk to and from Melville Junior High School. Buying the shoes for James was no problem: there was a shoe store in Anneville and James was not fussy as long as the shoes were sturdy and they fit well. Buying the coat for Lorraine was more complicated. They would have to travel by trolley to a store in the center of New Bradford; and picking out something that would be both warm and attractive, and still be within their budget would be a tough job.

A woman in the choir told Mother about a thrift store that sold clean second-hand clothes a t reasonable prices.

Before they entered the store Mother instructed Lorraine in some of the basics in haggling over prices. "Above all, never let them know that you really like a particular piece of merchandise -- no matter how much you want something, be willing to walk out as though you weren't the least bit interested."

The minute they walked into the store Lorraine's eyes fell on a beautiful red coat with a black velvet collar. The coat had obviously been owned by someone with money. It was a full length woolen coat with a black satin lining, and it looked as though it were brand new. Mother spotted it too, but her eyes told Lorraine to pay no attention to it. Then the haggling began. Mother feigned shock when the price was mentioned, and began to walk out while Lorraine tried hard not to become teary-eyed with disappointment. The shop owner was a superb haggler too, but he was no match for Mother. They finally walked out of the place with not only the coat, but also with a nice wooden coat hanger which the shop owner had to reluctantly throw in to cinch the deal.

When the family saw the coat, they all agreed that the coat had been designed with Lorraine in mind: the color, the style, the fit -- all brought out the best of Lorraine's beauty. They were all now looking forward to cold weather, so they could see Lorraine sashaying along in that gorgeous coat.

The success of the buying of the coat incident had one more lasting benefit. The shop owner, Mr. Samuels, who had been so impressed with Mother and her story about her seven fatherless children (Mother often told this tale to anyone who seemed sympathetic), had sent a letter to Mother. From his conversation with Mother he had realized she was Roman Catholic (any conversation with Mother in those days would have told anyone that) and had contacted the Anneville parish to see if they would forward a letter to her. The letter contained a few dollars and explained that Mr. Samuels had discussed Mother's case with his wife, Leah. They had both agreed that whenever they had a good month with the store, which didn't happen very often, they would send a few dollars to the Robinson family. Thus, Mr. and Mrs. Samuels' names were added to the list of people the Robinson family prayed for each evening

There was a much more serious problem faced by the Robinsons. The bank, which had not received any rent payments for over a year, had finally sent an eviction notice to Mother.

Mother's powers of persuasion were useless against the bank,; so she added to the Robinsons' prayer list the following plea: "Please God, help us to find a decent place to live."

The Selectmen of Anneville offered Mother a hovel out in the farm area that had an outside privy and no running water. There were other families on the town who were reduced to these extremities, but Mother stoutly resisted such offers, and the pleas to Heaven now became a novena: a nine day prayer bombardment of heaven for a "decent place to live."

The nine days passed without any hope, and the bank had started legal action, when finally they received what all the Robinsons considered an answer to their prayers. Two Wesley coeds, Cynthia and Virginia, whose home was in New Bradford, heard about the Robinsons' plight and took the case on as a class project. They were sisters, very pretty and charming, and they had important connections in the area. On weekends and whenever they could get time from their studies, they drove down to Anneville and went to work. They soon found a place that was owned by a friend of theirs that met Mother's minimum standards. In addition, the coeds found a truck and driver to help with the moving. The Robinsons would have to do all the packing of their belongings, and the loading and unloading of the truck; but all the Robinsons were very much aware that these lovely young ladies had saved the family from a miserable fate.

The project of moving was not easy, but it was carried out by happy and excited Robinson children. The heavy work was done by James and some of this athletic pals.

Cynthia and Virginia visited the Robinsons when they could get away from Wesley and find time from their studies. They weren't exactly thought of as fairy godmothers--more like angels. In fact, Rosebud, after hearing Mother referring to them as "those angels," actually expected to see their wings.

All the children, prompted by Mother, gave their personal thanks to the coeds, who responded with wonderful smiles and the playful comment: "Now is there anything else you would like us to do for you children?"

Thos disgraced himself and the family when he took them up on their offer. "It sure would be nice," he said, " if maybe you could get us a piano?"

The neighborhood they now lived in was not as pleasant as the one they'd been evicted from. It was on a dirt street, and there was an undeveloped area not far away where some people dumped trash; but it was closer to Rover's house, and closer to the woods, which made Thos and Joe very happy. The school, the church, and the grocery store were all still within easy walking distance.

Mother was able to get the kerosene stove moved and set up by some men who knew how to do this safely, so she had a stove for cooking and keeping at least one room in the house warm. Mother knew, however, that the stove could not keep the rest of the house warm, and she remembered how much they had suffered last winter from the cold. This new place did have a hot air furnace in the cellar that could keep the rest of the house warm; but it would require fuel -- either wood or coal, and that would cost money she didn't have. This was a problem she would have to solve before the grim New England winter set in.

Getting used to a different home and a new school year kept the Robinson children very busy and excited. Thos was disappointed when he realized that not only would he not have Miss Moore for a teacher, (he had been prepared for that), but his dream-girl had gotten married over the summer and he would probably never see her again. His second grade teacher, Miss Kostello, was not as beautiful as Miss Moore, but she was every bit as kind and loving. She had survived polio as a child, and walked with a pronounced limp. Thos found this very engaging, and he soon was in love with her almost as much as he had been with Miss Moore. Miss Kostello informed Thos that she "had orders from Miss Moore" to see that Thos got his little bottle of milk during recess. She did this with such sweetness and diplomacy, it warmed his heart instead of embarrassing him as it might have done if Miss Kostello wasn't such a sweetheart.

The schoolyard was no longer as threatening to Thos now that he was in with the regular kids and he got to see Joe and James often. He quickly realized that Joe and James had their own pals, and Thos was not to hang around them unless he was in trouble. On one occasion he was able to rescue Leveret from a few kids who had given Leveret a small stick and asked him to show them how to direct a band. The rats told Thos to "scram" until he reminded them that Leveret was also under the protection of James and Joe Robinson.

That September was mild and the twilight made the days long enough that there was plenty of time after school to explore their new neighborhood. There was only one house next to them, and that was where the Pattersons lived. They seemed to be nice enough, but not very friendly. They ran a small business selling various kinds of perfumes, soaps, shampoos, and other sundries. They had only one child of their own, Melvin. They also had three teen-aged boys who were their foster children. These three were tutored at home and were not allowed to have anything to do with any of the kids in the neighborhood. Melvin, who was in his early twenties, was retarded and had the intelligence of only a four-year-old child. All this seemed very strange to the Robinson children, but mother told them to "pay no attention to them and leave them alone." It was pretty hard not to pay attention to Melvin, however. He was large --over six feet tall, and he must have weighed close to two hundred pounds. He was gentle as a lamb, and he was quick to smile. He would sit on his front porch for hours bouncing a ball and humming to himself. He would wave happily at anybody that walked by, and smile if anyone spoke to him. Mother reminded her children that Melvin was one of those the Lord referred to as the "least of our brethren," and "What you do to unto them, I will do unto you."

The friends of the Robinson children who came to the new house soon learned, after their initial shock, to ignore Melvin -- all but Lizzie Horton. She was totally fascinated and could not refrain from staring at him. she discovered that he would mimic any actions you would make towards him: wave and he would wave, thumb your nose and he would thumb his nose, place your thumbs on the side of your head and waggle your fingers -- he would do the same. Mother quickly forbade any such actions on the part of her children, but Lizzie would not stop this mockery until Mother threatened her with a thrashing if she did not.

Mr. Patterson was very handy with tools. He would make Melvin many fine toys that Melvin was never able to use. he made him a scooter to no avail, then made him a kite which he couldn't fly, and finally a beautifully made wooden automobile with wheels and upholstered seats.

The Robinson kids would often see Mr. Patterson vainly trying to teach Melvin how to use these toys. Eventually Mr. Patterson would give up, and the toy would disappear into one of his sheds or it would be disassembled. Never would Mr. Patterson let his foster boys touch any of the toys, and Thos would think to himself, "Why doesn't he let me or Joe or James have a crack at them?"

The Robinsons got used to these neighbors, though, and soon paid no attention to them. There were times when Thos and Regis would actually play with Melvin. One Sunday afternoon on a beautiful Indian summer day, Melvin was sitting on a blanket on their front lawn playing with an empty cardboard box.

Mrs. Patterson and Mother were sitting on the porch discussing the radio speeches of Father Coughlin, who at that time was a firm supporter of Roosevelt. "It's either Roosevelt or ruin," the radio priest had said.

Melvin, Thos, and Regis were taking turns putting the cardboard box over their heads and slapping the box with their hands. All three of them would laugh happily at the noise this made. The rules of "taking turns" had been firmly embedded in Thos and Regis by Mother and their older siblings; but Melvin did not quite understand the concept, and grew impatient when Thos or Regis had the box. The boys had grown so accustomed to seeing him they seemed unaware of the enormous size difference among them. Perhaps Mother and Mrs. Patterson had forgotten too.

When it came time for Regis to have his turn, the little guy (he was only three years and seven months of age at the time and scrawny as a baby bird) was indignant at the violation of the rules of fair play. With an angry, "It's my turn!," he tried to snatch the box away from his gigantic playmate. Melvin would have none of this and swatted Regis, catching him right in the pit of his stomach and knocking him breathless. All hell broke loose -- Regis crumpled over, gasping pitifully for air, Mrs. Patterson screamed, and Mother cried, "Oh! Dear God!" Poor Melvin looked totally bewildered.

The women were at the scene in an instant: Mother checking out Regis, Mrs. Patterson hugging her huge son who was now thoroughly frightened, Thos trying to explain what happened. "Melvin didn't want to wait his turn -- it was Regis' turn!"

Mother quickly calmed down when she realized that Regis was going to be all right, but both Mrs. Patterson and her husband (who had quickly arrived on the scene) were badly shaken.

"Hiram will take the boy to the doctor right away," said Mrs. Patterson. We're so sorry! It was my fault, Hiram. Melvin didn't mean to harm him --they were just"-

"It's okay, Hazel! Regis is all right. He just had the wind knocked out of him. My boys are all very tough. He'll be fine -- no need for a doctor." she turned to Melvin. "I know you didn't mean any harm dear. It's all right."

"I think I should drive the boy to the doctor," Mr. Patterson said.

"No thanks," said Mother, "He'll be fine, but I'll keep a close eye on him, and if need be, I'll let you know, and we can take him in."

That was the end of the matter. Regis was perfectly okay, except he kept insisting that, "It was my turn!" until Mother said firmly, "Shut up, Regis!"

Poor Melvin! From then on he was not allowed to play with any children and was usually kept out of sight when the Robinson children were outdoors.

There was one positive outcome of the affair. Hiram Patterson came over to the Robinsons' house several days later. "I couldn't help noticing you're using oil lamps for lighting," Mrs. Robinson. I assume you have no electricity."

"It's the least of my worries, Mr. Patterson, but I do miss it sometimes."

"I can fix that easily if you let me. The company will never miss it, believe me."

"I don't think I want to do that -- I got caught last time I tried it, and it's not right to steal. Thanks, but no thanks."

"I can fix it so you won't get caught. I heard about last time -- someone squealed on you. I'm your only neighbor this time, and I don't squeal on nobody. Talk about what's right. Is it right that those big companies can use our streets to put up their poles and wires, and then refuse to supply power to decent folks who happen to be down on their luck?"

The Robinsons had power the next day. There were so many advantages to this: Mother could now use the electric flatiron that had remained idle for so long, there would be no more smelly, dull kerosene lamps to take care of, and, best of all, they would be able to use once more the beautiful Spartan radio Daddy had bought shortly before he lost his job. The radio provided something for everyone: children's programs on Saturday, music for Mother, the Red sox broadcasts, the evening radio shows, news, weather, all the marvels of modern communication were now available. But this glorious time did not last. One night while the family was gathered around listening to "The Shadow," James noticed the smell of burning wire, then the radio burped a couple of times and died. No amount of twisting dials or banging on the beautiful walnut cabinet could bring the thing back to life, and the Robinsons were left once more without a connection with the modern marvel of radio.

James had a friend named Stanley Selwicki, a blonde, blue-eyed, round-faced boy of James's age. He was highly intelligent and could have earned the same high grades in school that James did if he had cared to compete. He played baseball with the easy grace of a natural athlete, and it was a pleasure to watch him scoop up a grounder and fire it to first base. He was always completely at ease with himself and everyone around him, and everybody liked him. Stanley could have been successful at anything he was interested in, but the only thing he wanted to do, the only thing he seemed to be interested in was electronics. He was an only child, his dad had a steady job, and Stanley was able to indulge his passion for electronics to his heart's content.

Lizzie called him a "radio nut." But most people called him a genius.

When Stanley heard about the breakdown of the Robinsons' Spartan, he was eager to see what he could do.

He appeared at the Robinsons' home on Saturday and checked out the radio. He moved the handsome walnut cabinet carefully out from the wall and sniffed the air around it.

"Was there much smoke just before it conked out?" he asked.

"Enough," said James.

"I'll have to take the chassis beck to my place to work on it. Is it okay if I use your red wagon to cart it back?"

Mother quickly gave him permission, and he went to work.

Since Stanley would be working in the parlor, and the children were not allowed to go in there except on Sundays or other special days, they could only watch Stanley work from the doorway. None of them had ever seen the inside of a radio cabinet; so when Stanley had removed all the control knobs, and taken off the back, they were astounded at the array of shiny metal and glass paraphernalia. How could all of this make it possible for humans to send voices and music all across the country and into their parlor? It was this first sight of the innards of a radio that ignited in Thos a life-long fascination for all things electronic.

Stanley finally got all the bolts unscrewed, and the wires disconnected, and with the help of James he carried the huge chassis out to the red wagon and set off for his house pulling the red wagon by its black handle. Sitting in the bed of that wagon as it rumbled through the Anneville streets was the working heart of one of the great marvels of the twentieth century, and the hopes of the Robinson family.

On the following Saturday Stanley returned with the precious Spartan, and without a word began reinstalling the chassis into the cabinet. he not only was an electronics wizard (they no longer considered him a nut), he also understood the basics of drama. As the Robinson kids watched silently in the doorway of the parlor, and Mother busied herself preparing the lemonade and cookies she planned to give Stanley whether he had successfully repaired the radio or not, Stanley, poker-faced and totally focused, prepared for the great moment. He carefully attached the antenna, stretched out the power cord, plugged it in, turned on the switch. The yellow dial light came on immediately, and after a moment of silence, the magnificent Spartan burst forth in a glorious rendition of one of the "oldies but goodies" of the day: "Wish I Had a Talking Picture of You."

There was spontaneous applause and cheers from the children, and Mother rushed in and led her brood in a stirring chorus of "For He's a Jolly Good Fellow."

Stanley carefully moved the Spartan to its rightful place in the parlor. Mother suggested that they turn it off for now and go to the dining room where they celebrated with lemonade and cookies. Stanley explained that the radio had broken down because a condenser had short-circuited and caused a resister to burn out. He was the only one there that had the vaguest notion of what he was talking about. The only thing they understood was that their family entertainment center was finally back in business.

All the family enjoyed the radio, but no one more than Mother. It stimulated her life-long love of singing. She would not only sing along with any music on the radio, but she frequently sang at full voice when the radio was off and she was busy doing her housework. The neighbors often remarked about how good her voice was, and Keats Gidney told Joe that half the time he couldn't figure out whether the singing was coming from Mother or the radio. When Joe told Mother this, she was quite insulted. Like most good singers she was convinced that other singers weren't half as good as she was.

One of Mother's favorite programs was the Texaco Company's weekly broadcasts of the Metropolitan Opera, and she listened to them faithfully. Once Bobby Ellison told Thos and Joe, "Your Mom sure likes to listen to weird songs. Last Saturday I was going to the store, and when I passed your house some lady was singing this song at the top of her lungs in some crazy language. I went all the way to store, bought some stuff for my ma, and -- you won't believe this – but I'm telling you, it's the truth! That same lady still hadn't finished singing that same old crazy song!"

CHAPTER 14

THE RADIO BROUGHT MOSTLY joy into the Robinson home, but it brought some gloom too in the form of the domestic and worldwide news broadcasts.

The fascists and the Japanese militarists continued their vicious aggressive rampages.

On the domestic front too there were ominous signs: the economy was not improving, joblessness was increasing, and strident voices were demanding changes in the very foundations of the American society. The communists were becoming more powerful and brazen, and so were the Nazis. The Ku Klux Klan was spreading from the Deep South into most of the industrial regions of the country. Mother, who had been born and raised in Maryland, was shocked to learn that a mob of 2,000 had lynched a Negro who had been falsely accused of raping a white woman.

Klansmen were spewing their hatred now, not only against their traditional victims, the blacks, but were including Jews and Catholics in their campaign of hate.

Roosevelt had to use all of his considerable political skills to steer the ship of state through all of these rocks and shoals. He was attacked viciously from all of the extremist groups, and opposed often by moderates of both the Republican and Democratic parties. Somehow, however, he was able to maintain his popularity with the vast majority of the American people, including the Robinson family.

Mother and James were the only ones in the family who paid any attention to the news, whether it were delivered by radio or the printed page. The other Robinsons considered news broadcasts second only to commercials as boring interruptions of what they really were interested in.

Their new neighborhood contained some unusual young people: the most interesting being Keats Gidney, a lean, hatchet-faced lad with hawk-like eyes and nose, and a shock of black hair that was almost always covered by a Red Sox baseball cap. Keats was two years older than James, but he had never been to school. He had severe asthma and his mother had tutored him at home. She was a well educated woman and there was nothing lacking in Keats's education or intelligence, but he was undeveloped physically. On rainy or very cold days he was not allowed outdoors, and when he was allowed out, he loved to play baseball with James, Joe, or Thos. He had developed a form of the sport which James contemptuously referred to as "sissy baseball," but which Thos and Joe found very relaxing and a great deal of fun. It was played with a tennis ball and a stout stick. The rules of the game were pretty standard, and the distance between the bases could be negotiated by the players. The main advantages of this game were that it required no equipment but a tennis ball (one could easily make a "bat" out of a tree branch or a rake handle), and Keats could obtain old tennis balls from a relative of his who was rich enough to own a tennis racket and played tennis on the public courts of New Bradford. Of course, no glove or protective gear of any kind was needed.

There was an unused pasture surrounded by stone walls across the street from the Robinson home and not far away from Keats's house, which became the playground for the neighborhood kids. At the time no one knew who the owner of this pasture was, and no one seemed to care who used it as a playground. Later it was found that the pasture belonged to an old Yankee family, and the present owner, Mr. Taber, had said that as long as young people wanted to play in that pasture he would not sell it or develop it.

The games played in that pasture may have been a mockery of the real game of baseball, but they provided as much fun and excitement as any game played in the entire United States.

Pitching was an especially fun-filled part of the game. Keats was the Cy Young of that Anneville pasture. He could make a tennis ball do almost anything: curves, sliders, "drops," and a specialty he called an "up-shoot" mowed opposing batters down like wheat. His best strike-out pitch, though, was the "cigar ball' which was nothing more than a change-up which bounced a few inches in front of home plate.

Joe was almost as wily a pitcher as Keats, and he learned somehow to throw a tennis ball at a very high speed. James was a power hitter, and the ball usually left his bat as a flattened piece of fuzz. Thos was only useful as a player when they occasionally were able to find an umpire. At such times Thos was so small the pitcher had trouble hitting the strike zone, so Thos often got on base with a walk. He was a fast base runner, so he frequently scored.

One Saturday morning Keats, James, Joe, Thos, Bobby Ellison, and Gerry Durant had gathered at Taber's field for a baseball game when it suddenly began to rain heavily. James suggested they all go to the Robinsons' cellar where they could wait until the rain stopped. As they ran towards the house they had to go over one of those old New England stone walls. Going over a wet stone wall is a little trickier than crossing a dry one, and Bobby slipped off a boulder and banged up his leg. "You've got to learn how to cross these rocks in any kind of weather, Bobby," Keats told him. And, showing no sympathy at all for Bobby's painful leg, Keats added, "Always show a lot of respect for these ancient stones; there was plenty of care and hard work put into building these old walls."

When they got to the house, James lifted up the large cellar doors. Keats stared at the rough cement stairs that led down into the dark basement. "This looks like the entrance to an old tomb," he said in a sepulchral voice. They all walked into the dimly lit cellar and arranged themselves on the crude wooden stairs that led up into the house. Keats continued to talk about the old stones of New England. "I've been reading about them," he said. "You see these big old field stones that the foundation's made of? They're hundreds of millions of years old . . ."

Gerry Durant interrupted. "Come on, Keats, This is Saturday. We don't want no history lesson. Tell us a ghost story or something."

"Don't pay any attention to Gerry," James told Keats, "tell us more about the rocks."

"Well, Keats said, "during the last ice age, the glaciers moved down from the north and covered this whole area. They were over a mile thick at one time -- probably right here where we sit. As they moved along they ground up the bed-rock into boulders of all sizes. When the glaciers melted, about twelve thousand years ago, they left the boulders scattered all over the place. The sun began to warm the earth, and grass and trees started to grow. Then the animals moved up from the south -- mammoths, saber-tooth tigers, giant bears -- all kinds of ancient beasts. That's when the ancestors of the Indians came -- Paleo-Indians, we call 'em. You think you're tough? Those guys were really tough. They started running around killing all those huge monsters with nothing but bows and arrows, spears, and stones. Think of what feasts they could have on those big suckers! Then they would celebrate by dancing, chanting, and beating on drums and stuff. Boy! I sure wish I'd been alive then!"

"Me too!" said Thos.

"Well, you know the Indians believe in leaving Nature the way they find it; so those stones lay undisturbed for at least ten thousand years. Then, about three hundred years ago ," Keats continued, "when the pilgrims came, they had to clear the land for farming, so they used all the boulders to make stone walls. Ever since then the farmers of New England busted their butts to build these walls. There is a government report put out in 1872 that claims there were 240,000 miles of stone walls in New England." He paused to enjoy the look of wonder on some of the boys' faces. Then he said with a smile, "Now Bobby here is trying to bust all these beautiful stones with his crummy leg."

"Very funny," Bobby said, "Maybe I ought to kick your skinny butt with this crummy leg of mine, Keats!"

"Come on guys," James said, let's settle down. "How'd you learn so much about the rocks, Keats?"

"Oh, I read a lot. During the winter Ma doesn't let me go out much, so that's what I do: I read."

He looked around for a moment, then he said, "I know I talk too much. I was only kidding about the leg, Bobby. I really hope it's going to be okay."

The rain stopped, but the field was too wet to play ball, so they decided to go exploring the saw mill dump, which was only a mile away. The dump was used not only by the saw mill, but a lot of other businesses too, so they never knew what they would find.

This time somebody had dumped a load of empty five-gallon cans. These had been drained and flushed, but when James removed one of the caps, he could still smell alcohol. Keats figured that these shiny, like-new cans had probably been dumped by bootleggers who had been put out of business by the repeal of prohibition -- whatever -- now here were all of these interesting cans available to him and the boys. 'Finders, keepers' was the universal rule that applied to anything found in the dumps of Anneville.

He took one of the cans and tapped on it with his hand; it made a wonderful sound. He began drumming on it with both hands: a rhythmic, primitive drumming. Other boys picked up cans and began drumming along with Keats. the beat was irresistible and soon the air was filled with the pounding of the boys' impression of jungle drums. Finally Keats led a procession of the six boys away from the dump and through the woods back to Taber's field. No one spoke, they just moved along beating on their "drum" and following Keats. Keats was in his element now. His imagination evidently knew no bounds. When they got to one of the darker parts of the woods, he stopped drumming and held up his hands for silence. "Watch me," he said.

He set down his drum, took out his jackknife, found a suitable bush, and cut himself a stick. He trimmed it into what looked something like a spear, but he didn't sharpen it. Then he held the knife out. "Anybody else want to make a spear?" he asked.

Bobby and Gerry both made spears; and Thos wanted to make one too, but he noticed that James didn't make one, so he decided he better not make one either.

"What are we going to do with the spears?" Bobby asked.

Keats got one of those great dramatic looks on his face. "From now on, until we get out of the woods -- no more drumming. Keep your spears ready, and watch out for mammoths or saber-toothed tigers. When we get to Taber's field, we'll assemble and figure out what to do next."

By the time they got back to the field the sun had dried the stones in the wall enough to where the boys could sit on them. They stuck their spears in the ground and began pounding their drums again -- just drumming away in that same primitive, now almost hypnotic beat.

Soon other neighborhood kids started to show up. When they found out where Keats and his "tribe" had found the containers they headed for the saw mill and returned with "drums" of their own. Before long there were two dozen boys beating drums and parading around

Taber's field. Other kids simply went to the woods and cut themselves spears and returned to join the ever growing crowd of boys. The noise was deafening, and the sight of all these kids waving spears, chanting, and dancing so wildly around was something that made some of the adults very uneasy.

Usually the grown-ups never came to see what their kids were up to, but this time the commotion was so great, and the scene so disturbing, several mothers appeared and tried to talk to one another over the infernal din. Somebody called the Anneville police and they all responded -- both of them. Chief Mueller and his assistant discussed the matter and finally decided that this was a clear-cut case of "disturbing the peace."

Chief Mueller stood on top of the stone wall and began giving loud blasts on his whistle. The blasts could hardly be heard above the pounding of the drums; but gradually, one by one, the little savages began to stop whacking on their shiny new drums, and the spear wielders stopped waving their spears.

Chief Mueller, once he had their attention, announced that he was declaring this an illegal assembly that was disturbing the peace, and he was ordering them to disperse forthwith and return to their homes as soon as they returned "those damned tin cans to the dump where they belong."

The adults gave him a round of applause, and the boys reluctantly went about carrying out his orders.

Then Keats began waving his spear, hopping up and down in a savage dance and chanting in angry gibberish. The other boys joined in the chant, and the drums began to beat faster and faster. Wilder and wilder became the dance. It was like a bunch of Hollywood cannibals about to descend on some of Tarzan's friends. There's no telling what would have happened if some of the kids hadn't started laughing. The laughter was even more contagious than the dancing, and soon everybody, including Chief Mueller and his deputy were roaring with laughter.

When the police and some of the adults discussed this incident later, they agreed that Keats was a bit of a trouble-maker; but with the kids of Anneville he had now established himself as "a real fun guy."

Near Keats's home there was an abandoned house and garage. The door of the garage had long since been removed, and the place had become a popular shelter for the neighborhood kids during rainy weather. On such occasions the kids would ask Keats to show off some of his dramatic skills. He could do hilarious impressions of Dracula and King Kong, but his best act was a bit he called the "trance." He would bow his head, cover his face with both hands, then slowly withdraw his hands, revealing a zombie-like visage that would unnerve all but the most unimaginative of his audience.

He had a dog named Hecuba, a Pomeranian, that was almost as unusual as he was He always mouthed his dog's name, "Hek-you-bah," with a Shakespearean flourish. He said that Hecuba was named after the queen of Troy, that she hated Greeks, and that she considered anyone not in her immediate family as Greek. Because of this she had bitten the mail man, the paper boy, and several door-to-door salesmen. The chief of police said that if she bit anybody else, she would have to be destroyed.

Keats fancied himself the "leader of the pack," but was not universally recognized as so except on a few occasions. At the back of his property was a small stream that had eroded his yard in several spots. Keats conned the neighborhood kids into forming a construction gang. those who had a red wagon at their disposal were invited to join. (This included the Robinson kids, of course). The idea was to pull their wagons to a near-by hill which at one time was used as a sand pit, fill up their wagons, drag them over to Keats's yard, dump them into the eroded spots, and return for more sand. Most of the kids realized they were being conned "a la 'Tom Sawyer," but they had such fun carrying out the project, that Keats managed to finish the job before the kids became bored with it all.

Keats's most successful bid for leadership came one rainy day while the kids were congregated in the abandoned garage. In this garage was an old flat-bed truck that had been stripped of everything except its wooden-spoked wheels and a battered steering wheel. The truck was so old it had wooden-spoked wheels and solid rubber tires, very hard riding, but they would never go flat. The brakes were non-existent, but the steering mechanism still worked. Kids would often sit on the wooden seat, grab the steering wheel, and with very poor imitations of the sound of the motor, pretend to be truck drivers.

One day, Keats stood with his jaw in his right hand, silently eying this old truck. Suddenly he took his hand from his jaw, made it into a fist, held it high, and exclaimed, "Sisyphus! Yes, by Zeus!! Sisyphus!" And Thos could sense that Keats was pleased with all the sensuous sibilance of his pronouncement .

Most of the kids thought Keats had finally flipped his lid. Only James had the slightest clue as to who or what "Sisyphus" was.

"You mean the Greek guy that was condemned by the gods to spend eternity pushing a large boulder up the hill, and then, after it rolled down he had to push it up again?" James asked.

"Right," Keats said. "Homer said he was the wisest and most prudent of mortals."

"Swell!" said Gerry Durant. "Now, tell us what the hell you guys are talking about."

Keats ignored the sarcasm.

"Don't you see?" he continued, "That truck is like the rock Sisyphus kept pushing up the hill. We can all be Sisyphus. We push the truck up the hill, all pile on, and have one wild ride down the hill. I'm not saying it will make us wise and prudent, but we can have one heck of a time!"

Most of the kids didn't have the foggiest notion of what the Sisyphus business was all about, but the idea of riding that truck downhill sounded very exciting.

James was the only one who objected to the plan on the grounds that it was too dangerous: how would you ever stop the truck? Even without its motor and parts the truck was heavy enough to kill any kid that fell in front of it. Also, at the bottom of the hill was the dirt road. What if a car happened by as the truck loaded with kids came hurtling down the hill?

Keats brushed all these objections aside. Only a very young or stupid kid would get in the way of their truck (he had already begun to call it "their truck"); and they would carefully time their descent so there wouldn't be any cars coming. And if a car did show up when they were coming down the hill, those cars have brakes don't they?

So, with Keats at the wheel, Joe, Thos, Bobby Ellison, and Gerry Durant pushed the truck over to the hill next to the sand pit. James would have nothing to do with the whole thing. Before leaving he warned Thos and Joe. "Whatever you do, don't push from the back of the truck. If any of the other kids lose their grip the truck will roll right back over you, and you'll be flattened like flounders.

Pushing the truck over to the sand pit was arduous enough, but getting it up the hill with only four scrawny kids pushing was impossible. Joe finally enlisted the aid of his old pal Vasco who was probably strong enough to push the truck up by himself. Joe warned Keats not to say anything about Sisyphus. "If you start talking like that, this guy will beat you up just on general principles."

Vasco liked the idea, but would participate only if he were allowed to steer the truck down the hill. Keats reluctantly agreed to the arrangement, and they all set to work pushing the old wreck up the steep slope. At the top of the hill was a flat spot where they could maneuver the truck around for the ride down. When the truck was pointed in the downhill direction, Keats gave up the driver's seat to Vasco, and they all pushed the truck to the edge of the down slope. As soon as the truck began to roll, they all piled on; and yelling with sheer joy, they headed down the hill. The momentum of the truck carried it completely across the dirt road and within a few feet of the back of a neighbor's garage. That ride down the hill, though, was so exciting, they repeated the whole operation until they were so exhausted they barely had strength to push the truck back to its garage.

As they rested there in the garage, bone weary but happy; Keats looked around and said, "Did anybody notice that we spent a lot more time pushing the thing up the hill than we did riding it down?"

Vasco looked at him with disgust. "Like we didn't notice," he said.

Ignoring the sarcasm, Keats went on; "Well, I read an article by this guy who said that this is the way life is--you spend most of your life working and being miserable, then, once in a while, you get some fun--you enjoy yourself. And the really smart guys are the ones who learn to get some fun out of pushing the thing uphill."

There was silence for a short while; then Vasco turned to Joe and said, "You know? Sometimes this sonovabitch makes sense."

That was the only time they were allowed to carry out this wonderful game, though. One of the neighbors, perhaps the one whose garage was endangered, called the police. The chief himself took charge of the case. He visited the boys while they were assembled in the infamous garage, and solemnly informed them that all of them were in violation of a number of laws: operating a vehicle without a license, operating an unregistered vehicle, endangering people and property. "And that's just for starters," he added.

He would refrain from arresting and jailing them only on a "cross my heart" promise that they would never take the truck out of the garage again. He also promised not to inform their parents if they promised to consult him before they carried out any more of these "damned hare-brained' ideas."

The pasture across the street was mostly the domain of the boys, but occasionally a few girls would come to watch the guys play baseball, football, soccer, or whatever game that happened to be in season at the time. Also, the type of game chosen might depend on the number of kids available. Usually, when they played in the pasture, if the weather was not too chilly, Thos did not wear his overalls, but instead he wore a pair of old kaki shorts he had inherited from Joe, who had inherited them from James. They were faded and baggy, and looked like heck with his skinny legs sticking out, but they were comfortable.

One Saturday afternoon there were only a few kids available, and they decided to play "King of the Mountain." Near the northwest corner of the pasture there was a grassy knoll that served very well as the "mountain." The rules of the game were simple and universal: whoever could get on top, and throw the others off his ground was king of the mountain for that moment.

That day Patricia, Lizzie, and Beatrice Langervine had come by to watch. Thos, Joe, James, Bobby Elision, and Roland Bouchard were all participating. James was most often the king, but by ganging up on him the other guys were able to dethrone him. It was a rough and tumble affair, but the knoll was surrounded by thick grass; and when the smaller kids, like Thos, were thrown down, they were usually not hurt. One time, though, Roland Bouchard flung Thos down the hill into some tall grass. Thos's bare knee landed on a broken milk bottle and a jagged piece tore an ugly gash in his tender flesh. He yelled with pain and everyone ran to him. So deep was the cut, a piece of white tendon could be seen in the bloody mess.

Lizzie, who was the first one to reach him, let out a horrified squeal, "Oh, yuk! There's a big white worm in the cut!" And before anybody could stop her, she began to tug on the tendon. At this Joe fainted dead away, and James grabbed Lizzie, and threw her roughly aside. "It's not a worm, you idiot, it's part of his body! We've got to get him to a doctor."

Patricia attended to Joe, who quickly came to and was perfectly okay in a few moments. Beatrice wrapped her handkerchief around Thos's bloody knee, and they carried him home.

Mother sent Lorraine to get Mr. Patterson to see if he could drive Thos to the Anneville hospital, but Mr. Patterson was not home. She made a solution of warm water and Lysol (her cure-all for all wounds), and washed Thos's knee thoroughly. Then she tore up an old, but very clean pillow case, and made bandages of it. She sent Joe out to clean up the red wagon. "After you get it cleaned up, Patricia will put that blanket in it. Thos can sit in it while James and Lorraine take him to the hospital. Thos, you hold tightly on to the sides of the wagon. James, go quickly, but don't bounce Thos out of the wagon, whatever you do."

All this time Thos was trying hard not to cry or complain and was rewarded with encouraging remarks about how "tough" he was.

When they got to the hospital, Dr. Cavanaugh cleaned the wound, swabbed it with iodine, and wired the two sides of the cut together. During the ordeal Thos had trouble remembering that he was supposed to be "an Anneville tough guy," but he bore it all stoically, and Dr. Simpson's nurse, Loretta Ducette, said that he was a "brave little man."

The doctor said he would send Loretta by in a few days to check and re-bandage the wound.

As they were leaving, Thos noticed that Loretta, who served as the doctor's secretary as well as nurse, looked at the Robinson kids and asked, "Pro bono?"

"Pro bono," the doctor wearily replied.

Luckily there was no infection and the wound healed very well. Loretta came by and removed the wire suture, and all that remained was a prominent scar which looked exactly like a pirate's dagger, and was the envy of every guy that saw it.

The whole episode was a favorite topic of conversation for a while, and Thos heard Lizzie talking about it to Patricia.

"James actually grabbed me and spoke to me," she said.

"He practically broke your arm and he called you an idiot," Patricia said.

"OOh! I know! I know!" she gushed. "Isn't he wonderful!"

From then on she had a hopeless crush on James; and he, terrified at the very thought, did everything he could to stay out of her way from then on.

CHAPTER 15

THE DEPRESSION CONTINUED TO cause unhappiness throughout America. It was like a dreadful disease that resisted all attempts to cure it, and it continued to ravage the economic health of the nation. The Dow Jones average, which was at 381 in 1929 was now at 41. People who still had hope in the entrepreneurial spirit were now standing on street corners trying to sell apples or pencils and getting their meals from soup kitchens; and the hopeless were struggling desperately to obtain food, clothing, and shelter by any means they could.

One day in Anneville posters began to appear proclaiming a promotional campaign for a new brand of apple butter that was about to hit the stores. large pictures of the red-labeled jars containing this "deliciously nutritious" product were plastered everywhere. The exciting news was that on Saturday, November 14, at 10:00 A. M., there would be free samples of this stuff spread over fresh slices of --- bread available to "one and all" in front of the town hall.

Mother said that any of her boys that wanted to go had her permission, but Lorraine, Patricia, and Rosebud would have to stay home.

A huge crowd gathered well before the allotted time. Men and women of all ages milled around in an expectant, but almost embarrassed, manner. When the truck appeared, a man stepped out of the passenger's side and asked the crowd to make way so that he could position the van in a way that would provide the best service to everyone "who had been kind enough to come and witness this demonstration of the best thing that's happened to bread since we learned how to slice it. Have no fear, ladies and gentlemen, boys and girls, there is plenty for everyone. We ask however that each of you only take what you can consume on these premises, thank you."

Then he lowered the tailgate on the van and revealed three men in clean white smocks who began the process of slapping the apple butter on the slices of bread and handing them out to the hungry crowd. People lined up and there was little pushing and shoving. Thos, like most people, was able to get a slice in each hand, and he ate them quickly. By the time he finished the two slices, though, the line was so long, he and his brothers decided they would not wait for "seconds." It wasn't that they weren't still hungry, and that the bread and apple butter weren't delicious; it was just that there was something unsettling about the whole spectacle. Later, Thos found out that one of his pals, who was almost as poor as he was, couldn't come to the feast because his mother said there was something about this event that was too much like begging.

Food was not the only problem, though. With the winter rapidly approaching, Mother had not yet been able to get any coal for the furnace. Their house was poorly insulated, and she knew that the kerosene stove would not be able to keep her kids warm when the temperature dropped below freezing. Her weekly stipend of seven dollars a week was not enough to buy food, so she would have to battle the selectmen to get fuel, but she was making little progress in that quarter. Their advice was to put the younger children in the Catholic orphanage, and have Lorraine, James, and Patricia wear their warmest clothing indoors during the cold days.

She firmly refused to cease her demands that her family be given coal for the winter.

When Thanksgiving came, Mother was given a small break. Mrs. Shields, who sang in the choir with Mother and shared her love of music and good books, invited the Robinson family for Thanksgiving dinner. The Shields were not rich, but Mr. Shields still had a job with the phone company, and their home was one of the nicer ones in Anneville.

Several baskets containing the groceries for a Thanksgiving dinner were delivered to the Robinson home, so Mother stored these to be used for family meals in the days following Thanksgiving.

The dinner at the Shieldses' home was a memorable event. The Robinson kids were scrubbed and arrayed in their best Sunday clothes.

The Shieldses had four children of their own who were well known to the Robinson children, and the Robinsons were treated as honored guests rather than like a family "on the town," which is the way most well-to-do people treated them.

The table was set with the finest silver and China Thos had ever seen. The adults had wine to drink and the children were given cranberry juice served in the same kind of goblets the adults were using. It was a feast fit for royalty, and when Mother used this phrase in thanking Mr. and Mr. Shields, the host grandly announced that it was only fitting, for everyone knows that all the Irish are descendants of kings.

The Shields family moved to a town in Maine a few months later, but that Thanksgiving dinner, and the kind people who shared it with their less fortunate neighbors, remained in the memory of all of the Robinson family, and would be mentioned many times in the years to come as a wonderful example of how nice some people can really be. When the Shields's eldest son, Merrill, was killed in action in Europe ten years later, Mother asked all of her children to offer up their Sunday mass for Merrill and his family.

At Parting Ways School, Thos was now in the second grade, Joe was in the fourth grade, Patricia was in the sixth, and James was in the eighth. The superintendent, Mr. Ford, the principal, Mrs. Phillips, and all the teachers did their utmost to make the school an outpost of civilization and hope in a wilderness of uncertainty and despair. At every grade level, in addition to drilling their students in reading, writing, and arithmetic, they emphasized the importance of the humanities: history, literature, music, and art. They hammered away at the importance of brotherly love and tolerance for ethnic groups other than themselves. This latter point was especially difficult because Anneville was a heterogeneous mixture of many nationalities, races, and religions. Instead of being a "melting pot," Anneville was a stew pot full of separate hunks of humanity: French-Canadians, Portuguese, Polish, Old Yankees, many of whom traced their lineage back to Colonial days, and a sprinkling of African-Americans, Irish, Italians, and Germans.

Largely due to the valiant efforts of the schools, these disparate groups managed to live in relative peace. The larger groups tended to cluster into neighborhoods, and there were unpleasant slang names for each group, but they rarely hurled racial epithets at one another, and their children usually played and associated with one another.

There were only two African-American families in the town of Anneville, and while they were generally treated with respect and never persecuted, the "colored people" (in the Thirties this was considered almost a polite appellation) were treated with condescension. It was almost as though the "whites" in Anneville felt proud of themselves because they didn't mistreat their black brothers and sisters as did the whites in some other parts of the country, and therefore were trying hard to treat them like fellow members of the human race. This resulted in some strange contradictions. On the rare occasion that a black boy was in a class at Parting Ways School, he would invariably be elected class president (a powerless but honorable position); and, of course, if he happened to be an athlete, he was eagerly accepted on the team, but it was rare that strong friendships would develop between a white and a black.

Thos found this particular contradiction puzzling. In his class was an African-American girl named Heather Kingston. Heather's family was much better off than the Robinsons, she was a better student than Thos, she was always immaculately groomed, and her clothes were much nicer than Thos's. She sat in front of him, and sometimes Miss Kostello would ask her to help him -- usually with his art projects. Thos was hopelessly bad at art, and he appreciated Heather's expert help. He noticed, though, that when he smiled at her and sincerely thanked her, there was a look in her large brown eyes of pathetic gratitude. Why should she be grateful to someone she was helping so much? Then he began to notice that he was the only kid who ever talked to her. They didn't call her names, or persecute her, they simply ignored her. What kind of a world was this in which a human being as nice as Heather could be so lonely?

In the schoolyard one of the boys in his class razzed him about being in love with a "jigaboo." Thos challenged the little rat to a fight, but the kid quickly backed off. "Jeez, Thos, I didn't mean nuttin.'. What you so sore about?"

None of the other kids ever said anything like that again in his presence.

A few days later, on December 15, 1933, a Tennessee mob lynched a Negro who had just been freed by a court.

Ten days later most of America celebrated the birthday of the Prince of Peace who tried to teach people to love one another, and is reported to have said: "What you do to the least of my brethren, you do unto Me."

* * *

Not all people, though, think of Christmas as a religious holy day. They think of December 25 as another excuse to try to have a good time -- have a "Merry Christmas." For these folks there was something that was going to make Christmas a little merrier this year. The 18th amendment had been repealed on December 5 of that year. And Prohibition, which had been in effect since 1920, was finally over.

Mother didn't need booze to have a good time. She had provided her kids with a merry Christmas last year despite everything, and she would try to do the same this year. With the help of Lorraine, James, Patricia, the American Legion, the Salvation Army, plus many other kind souls, she produced a Christmas celebration that was every bit as good as last year's.

Mother, Lorraine, James, and Patricia worked tirelessly to provide the younger kids with a celebration that was again the high point of the whole year. For Thos the humiliation of having to tell Miss Kostello that he couldn't afford to pay the ten cents to buy the gift for the class Christmas party was much easier to bear when he discovered that he wasn't the only kid who had to do this. He also found out that the teachers in these cases had to pay for this out of their own pockets. Many teachers, including Miss Kostello, bought little boxes of hard candy for every student in their classes. There was no money for this in the school budget, so the teachers paid for this out of their own meager salaries. When Thos heard about things like this, it reinforced his opinion that teachers, at least at his school, were some of the nicest people in world.

In 1934, New Year's Day came on a Monday; so the day was made a little less happy with the realization that the kids would have to go back to school the next day. They did have a great feast, though, as Mother cooked up the last food that had come with the Christmas baskets. After

119

the meal the boys listened to the Rose Bowl game in which Columbia beat Stanford 17 - 0. James was quite happy with the outcome because he had been predicting this to his pals. When the game was over, he sat back in his chair and sighed contentedly. "Sometimes I almost feel lucky being poor. I'll bet the rich kids didn't enjoy the last two weeks as much as we did. When we had money, I never realized how wonderful it could be not to be hungry for two whole weeks."

After New Year's Day winter came on quickly. The Robinsons' bedrooms grew so cold at night the kids had to not only use every blanket available, but they had to pile their coats on top of the blankets as well. Getting up in the morning was a terrible ordeal. They had to stay huddled under the covers until Mother announced that the bathroom was clear, and then they grabbed their clothes, and raced downstairs, clad in their skimpy pajamas so they could dress in the bathroom that was warmed slightly by the heat from the kerosene stove.

Mother knew that if she didn't get fuel for the furnace soon, she would lose her battle to keep her family together. She heard on the radio that Roosevelt had persuaded the Congress to authorize funds to pay for emergency relief for heating fuel for states that were being hit by the cold weather. She went over the heads of the selectmen and walked to the trolley which took her to the State offices in New Bradford. In order to dramatize her plight she took along Thos who had developed a very croupy cough. Her strategy worked and the officials agreed to expedite the paper work and get her help as soon as possible.

Two weeks later when Thos came home from school he saw a mountain of firewood dumped in front of their house.

Mother said that they couldn't get coal, but that this wood had been cut to function in a furnace. The truck driver said he couldn't help them stack the wood in the cellar, but he wished her luck.

A snow storm was on its way, and the temperature was rapidly dropping, so there was no time to lose. James, Joe, and Thos would have to get to work as soon as they could change to their work clothes. James took charge of the operation. He opened the large cellar doors and several of the small cellar windows. They world throw all the wood into the cellar -- first filling the coal bin, and stacking the remaining wood along the cellar walls.

It was the hardest and most miserable work Thos had ever done. The weather was bitterly cold; and the logs were heavy and covered with dust, dirt and bugs. They worked like slaves of old -- not actually under the lash, but urged on by the realization that if they didn't get that wood into the cellar before the snow covered it, it could be weeks before they could get it to where it could become dry enough to use.

By nightfall they still hadn't got all the wood thrown into the cellar. Mother told them that they did not have to stack the wood that night, and once they got the wood out of the weather they could have their supper. When the last log was thrown into the cellar, the cold, hungry, and exhausted trio dusted off their clothes, washed up, and ate their supper like hungry hounds.

The next morning the snow covered everything with a beautiful blanket, but it wasn't heavy enough to close the schools. Mother told the exhausted boys that they did not have to go to school, but James insisted on going. He said he couldn't miss any class work if he wanted a chance to become valedictorian that year. Mother made him some oatmeal and hot chocolate, he devoured this quickly, put on his warmest clothes and his tasseled stocking cap and trudged wearily off to school. Thos and Joe wrapped themselves in their blankets and went back to sleep. Later in the morning they went down into the cellar, and under the supervision of Mother, they began stacking the wood along the cellar walls. they hated this kind of work, but they both understood that with the weather getting colder, they had better be prepared for it.

Everyone in Anneville took the cold weather for granted, the way some people take gravity. Just as anyone who went around complaining about gravity, so anyone who complained about the cold would be considered a nut by any natives of Anneville. Bobby Ellison had an aunt, his mother's sister, who lived in Florida and who had come up accompanied by her husband, to visit the Ellisons in the middle of January for a week.

Bobby said to Thos one day: "My uncle was born in Florida and I think those people are nuts. All he does is sit by the stove drinking whiskey and cussing out the Anneville weather and anybody crazy enough to live here."

Lorraine was happy with the cold weather because it gave her a chance to wear her "new" coat. Even the long walk down to the river and up to Melville Junior High School did not bother her because she knew she looked great walking along in that cherry-red coat and the navy-blue beret that went so well with it. She liked the school too and was getting "A's" in all of her classes. There was little time to make new friends, though, because during the noon break she worked in the cafeteria to earn a nourishing free lunch. she couldn't linger after school to socialize because of the long walk ahead of her, and Mother grew worried if she wasn't home on time. There was one short block in Anneville where some of the local boys used to congregate in the afternoon. These louts were harmless, and would never molest any girls, but they considered it very funny to make a few remarks if a pretty girl happened to pass by. One of these louts was Bud LePierre. He was the strongest boy in town, and a good athlete, but he was also the most insensitive and loutish of the town louts. Thos hated and feared him because whenever he saw Thos, he thought it was funny to grab Thos by the seat of his pants and hold him aloft like an Indian displaying it like a newly taken scalp. Thos always bore this without complaint, but the crotch of his pants dug deeply into his little family jewels, and he was relieved when Bud would finally set him back on the ground.

One day in late January when the Robinsons' food supply was unusually low, and Melville Junior High had a lot of corn chowder left over from lunch, Lorraine asked the cafeteria supervisor if she could take some of the left-over corn chowder home to her family. The supervisor told Lorraine to come by after school and she would have the chowder ready for her in a container.

The best container she could come up with was an enameled steel pitcher. She put a brown paper bag over the pitcher and fastened it with some rubber bands. "If you walk carefully, Dear, I don't think it will spill, " she said to Lorraine.

Lorraine, not wanting to spill any of the chowder on her precious coat, walked carefully downhill to the bridge, across the bridge, and then uphill to Anneville.

Waiting at the usual corner were Bud LePierre and his fellow louts. Flagpole -- said with a friendly enough tone: "What 'cha got there, Lorraine -- a pitcher of beer?"

The boys laughed, but Lorraine ignored them and walked bravely by. Bud, though, who never knew when to let well enough alone, walked after Lorraine and tried to pull the pitcher away from her. As she struggled, to hold on to it, the paper bag popped off and the chowder slurped all over her coat. Totally humiliated now she hurried away, spilling more chowder on her coat.

"I'm sorry, kid," she heard Bud blurt out as she hurried home.

When she opened the door of the house, she just stood there where the Robinson kids would stand if they had to remove their dirty or snow covered shoes . Mother took one look at Lorraine's face, turned pale, and with a wave of her hand ordered her kids to be silent. "Go upstairs, all of you. I'll call you down later."

Lorraine's beautiful coat was now smeared from top to bottom with corn chowder, and her face was now distorted by her attempts to keep from screaming with rage and frustration.

Mother gently took the pitcher away from her and set it down. Then she went to her and put her arms around her. "For God's sake, Lorraine. Are you Okay?"

"My coat!" she moaned.

"Never mind the coat, Dear, for now. Are you hurt? Who did this?"

"I'm okay, Mother -- I'm just so--. Here, take the coat. I'll tell you all about it, but first I have to --" Then she handed the coat to Mother and ran into the bathroom, shut the door, and they heard her sobbing uncontrollably .

When Mother finally got Lorraine calmed down and found out what happened, she told Lorraine that she would get the coat cleaned, and said that it would be just "as good as new." Then she said grimly, "I'll fix that son of a bitch Bud LePierre, too; you see if I don't." Lorraine nor any of the other kids had ever heard Mother use such language before and it frightened them.

"No, Mother, it's not just him -- it's the whole thing -- being poor, the Depression, the squalor! I'm so sick and tired of the whole thing!"

Mother's rage at Bud LePierre could not be assuaged; she never could forgive Bud. When James heard the story, he stormed out of the house in search of Bud, despite Lorraine's pleas not to get in a fight over "this."

When Bud saw James striding towards him, he held up both hands, open palms facing James. "Look, James, I don't blame you for being teed off. I'm sorry -- really sorry -- tell your sister, I'm very sorry. Tell her I'll pay to have the coat cleaned -- buy her a new one – whatever. I'm not going to fight you, James, I'm not afraid of you, you know that, but I'm not fighting you. You want to punch me out, go ahead! It might make me feel better if you did."

The other guys tried to calm James down. "Come on, Professor, take it easy." Flag-pole tried to be funny. "Come on, James. If you really want to beat up Bud, we'll help you. Settle down. We've all been friends too long to let this break us up. He said he was sorry -- give him a break, for Pete's sake, James!"

James's shoulders sagged, and he unclenched his fists; then he just turned, and walked back home.

When he told Lorraine what happened, she gave her brother a hug. "I'm so glad you didn't get in a fight over this. I'm all right now. Let's forget the whole thing."

Mother, though, was not so easily mollified. "If that -- that rat -- ever comes around this house, I'll take a rolling pin and give him a wooden shampoo he'll never forget!"

Thos also was still furious. He imagined himself suddenly becoming the size of King Kong, and lifting Bud LePierre up by the seat of his pants until the crotch dug into his family jewels and he yelled with pain. Then he would dunk the bugger into a large vat of corn chowder until he was half drowned.

Mother cleaned the coat so that it was almost as nice as it was before, but Lorraine would never wear it to school again. She would wear it to church once in a while, but the kids never knew whether she did that for penitential reasons--to humble herself; or she did it out of defiance to the "pitchfork of poverty."

CHAPTER 16

As FRANKLIN DELANO ROOSEVELT neared the end of his first year in office, the vast majority of Americans were pleased with his performance. He had "stemmed the hemorrhaging, stopped the downward spiral, and saved us from going over the brink."

Whatever metaphor that was used, most people believed that his imaginative innovations had replaced chaos with order, and despair with hope.

He still had many critics; those whose ox was being gored -- the high and mighty, the wealthy and powerful who saw their positions being threatened; and the fascists and communists who saw chaos and despair as allies in their attempts to take over America -- all of these used every nasty epithet in the dictionary to describe FDR. There were people of intelligence, wisdom, and education, including his wife, Eleanor, who felt that he was neglecting one of the most oppressed segments of our society, the African Americans, in his quest to bring a better life to the downtrodden of America.

The Great Depression had hit the black people even harder than it had the rest of the nation. Roosevelt seemed to totally ignore their plight. He argued, often with Eleanor, that if he tried to bring justice to the "Negroes," he would lose all of his southern support in Congress, and would be unable to get through any of his legislation at all. Whether or not he was justified in this matter is something for History to judge, but there is no doubt that his failure to include all citizens in his reforms is a blemish on his otherwise great record of achievements. It seems only fair, though, to remember that the same blemish is on the record of all white people in America who pledged allegiance to "one nation under

God with liberty and justice for all," and yet ignored the plight of so many Americans to whom "liberty and justice" was only a sick joke.

The Robinson family, though, like most of the white people in the country, idolized FDR, and his picture had an honored place in their homes, and his "fireside chat" radio broadcasts were the most popular show on radio.

Most of the victims of The Depression had little time for hero worship or politics. Their concern had to be how to keep body and soul together for themselves and their families. The cold was just one more enemy to defeat in their grim battle for survival. In the case of the Robinsons, the furnace, fueled by the wood, kept them from perishing from hypothermia, but it was not easy to keep going. James had learned how to split kindling to get it going in the morning, but it was tough on him. In the cold dawn, while the rest of the kids were still wrapped in their blankets, he would have to rise, pull on his warmest clothes in the freezing cold, and go down into the cellar to fire up the furnace before the rest of the house got up. He was only a boy of 13 and wouldn't be 14 until April; but his siblings all considered him already a man, and few could disagree with that assessment.

This was the time of the year when Mother faced her toughest challenges -- the time that the Indians called "the hunger moon." Her immediate problem was to get shoes for her brood. She had been able to buy shoes for James and Lorraine last fall, but the snow and mud had been hard on the worn-out shoes of her other five children. Rosebud and Regis could get by because they didn't have to walk to school, but the shoes of Patricia, Joe, and Thos were worn out. She had been using cardboard to patch the holes in the leather soles, but this did not work well in the snow, and now even the uppers of Thos's and Joe's shoes were falling apart.

Many other kids in the town were in similar straits; some, like Vasco and his brothers, even walked to school barefoot in the snow.

When Mother heard about this, she gritted her teeth. "No child of mine is going barefoot in the winter!" and she once more went to war against the selectmen. She had found out that Roosevelt had pushed some bills through Congress that would provide federal funds for emergency relief to the states. She demanded that the selectmen obtain some of that money to pay for shoes for the destitute of Anneville. They resisted, claiming that it wasn't their responsibility, and that the people themselves would have to petition the state for this money.

For Mother and the rest of the poor in Anneville it was almost impossible to get to the state offices in the middle of winter -- they had no transportation, no telephones, and some of them didn't even have shoes. She decided to take a bold step to force the selectmen to act -- she told Patricia, Joe, and Thos that they were not to attend school until they got new shoes. Lorraine and James could continue to go, but the rest of them would stay home.

The selectmen reacted by sending Chief of Police, Mueller, who also acted as truant officer, to remind Mother that she was breaking the law, and threaten her with arrest. Mueller tried to reason with her, but Mother stood her ground. "Go ahead and arrest me!" she said firmly. I already have a press release written out for The *New Bradford Times* relating how you arrested me for refusing to send my little children to school barefoot in the middle of winter. I've entitled it, ' Anneville or Valley Forge?'"

Mueller went back to the selectmen. "If you want me to arrest that woman, you'll have to put the order in writing, and I want the order signed and dated by every member of this board!"

One of the selectman, Warren Brewster, came personally to visit Mother, presenting her with vouchers that would allow her to buy shoes at the local shoe store   for all five of her kids who attended school. He was a kindly man, and told Mother that all of the other selectmen were furious at her, but they all admired her guts.

The next day, as soon as James had returned from school, Mother told him to watch Regis and Rosebud while she took Patricia, Joe, and Thos to the local shoe store. The owner, Mr. Petain, was genuinely glad to see the Robinson quartette. He had heard from the selectmen about the vouchers, and the prospect of selling three pairs of shoes in one day was very good news to him.

He lived in the back of the store with his wife, Clara, who was, like most of the good wives of Anneville, "pleasantly plump."

Petain served as shoe salesman and cobbler. The cobbler shop was in the rear of the store and could be entered either directly from the street or from the shoe store itself. Each door had a bell that jingled loudly when either door was opened. He did not have much business these days so he took pride in keeping it very neat and attractive. The hardwood plank floor, though not stained or varnished, was kept polished with a heavy brush. The display shoes were arranged in geometric patterns and were dusted several times a day. The place had a marvelous smell of polished leather and the aromatic pipe tobacco Petain liked to smoke when there were no customers in his store.

The store sold only one brand of shoes -- Triangle Brand--which boasted on every shoe box that "Guaranteed genuine leather: $50.00 reward if any paper is ever found in any Triangle Brand shoe!"

Thos was excited about this. He thought it was a promotional thing -- that somewhere, maybe in one shoe out of a thousand, a piece of paper was hidden, and the finder would be entitled to the treasure of $50.00. Until James explained how dumb his idea was, Thos was sure that the precious piece of paper was hidden in one of his shoes, and he would find it and make his family rich.

"It's so nice to see you, Mrs. Robinson," he beamed. "And how are you, Patricia, Joe, and Thos? I've heard very good things about you children."

Then there was just the briefest of uncomfortable pauses before he said to Mother, "You understand, of course, about the vouchers. They entitle you to one pair of shoes for each of your three children. You may choose any of the shoes I have on display today. Of course these here are only display samples. I have all sizes available on my shelves. First I have to measure the feet of the children to see what size will fit them. Where shall we start?"

"You'll be first, Patricia, then Joe, then Thos." Mother said.

Thos watched fascinated while Petain, using an elaborate instrument, measured Patricia's pretty foot while Mother examined the shoes on display. Petain measured all three of the children and wrote down their sizes on a small pad he kept in his pocket.

Mother picked out a pair of sturdy brown oxfords for Patricia. "Do you have these in her size, Mr. Petain?" she asked.

Patricia knew better than to express her disappointment that the shoes were not more feminine, and, besides, she was very thrilled at the idea of getting any shoes at all.

Petain was a model of patience while Mother carefully selected shoes for Joe and Thos. He encouraged her to be sure that the shoes fit perfectly, and personally pinched and squeezed the leather around the children's toes, instep, and heel to be sure that the shoes were comfortable.

This was the first time Thos could remember getting new shoes, and he was so excited about the whole process he would have gladly clomped out of the shop with any shoes that would stay on his feet without falling off.

The kids had to do some big time pleading before Mother agreed to let them walk home in their new shoes. All three of them could not help strutting a little, and they spent much time glancing down at their new footgear just to be sure that they really had such beautiful and comfortable covering on their feet.

When they got home, they all thanked Mother; and Patricia said, "That Mr. Petain is such a nice man, isn't he Mother."

Mother remained grimly silent. She knew that Petain always gave the children of cash-paying customers a toffee caramel whenever they bought new shoes. She was thinking: "What would it have cost that weasel to give my children just one little piece of candy?"

Back at the shoe store Petain's wife was asking him that same question.

"You women! You do not understand such things. Roosevelt is ruining this country with his "New Deal." He gives away our tax money to people who don't work for it. He is teaching people to be lazy. Why should people work if they can get things like shoes free from the government? Those children are old enough to earn money. Roosevelt! He even got laws passed that prevent honest business men from hiring children. I'm not going to encourage such things by teaching children to think that they can get shoes without working for them."

"But, Francois, would you have them go barefoot to school in the winter?"

"Hush, Yvonne! You women think with your hearts and not your heads. That is why God put men in charge of the world. I love you, but you are beginning to sound like that ugly bitch, Eleanor Roosevelt! You women do not understand politics. You take care of your housework, we men will take care of running this country."

The Robinson kids were allowed to wear the new shoes only to go to church and to school. The rest of the time they would have to wear whatever other miserable, worn-out shoes they could get on their feet.

In late January a blizzard hit New England--a nor'easter. They closed the school and sent the kids home early, but the storm was already so furious, and the temperature was dropping so fast, Thos was afraid he'd never reach home alive. he had no gloves or mittens, so he had to jam his hands deep into his pockets to keep them from freezing. Luckily he had a woolen stocking cap which he pulled down over his ears and as much of his face as he could.

Visibility was almost zero, and the wind was driving the sleet directly into his face, so Thos could barely make out the edges of the dirt road that was rapidly being covered with the snow. He was frightened, and the sleet cut his face, but there was a certain glory in fighting against the storm. At least this blizzard played no favorites. It blasted both rich and poor alike, and it didn't give a hoot whether or not he was on the town or what.

Finally he reached home, and as Mother helped him out of his snow covered clothes, and as he carefully wiped off the ice and mud from his precious shoes, he felt like an arctic explorer who had just successfully reached the North Pole. His fingers were so numb he had to run them under tap water to bring life back into them. As he warmed himself by the heat from the furnace transom, he felt proud that he had worked so hard to stack the wood in the cellar earlier in the winter.

All of the children except Lorraine had reached home safely. Mother was worried about Lorraine making that long walk up from Melville Junior High, and she finally ordered James to go out into the storm to check on his sister. On his way James passed the corner where Bud LePierre and his pals usually gathered. There they were: Bud, Flagpole, Ziggy Janowski, and Pee-pee Bouvias. Evidently they were there just trying to show off how tough they were.

When they found out what James's mission was, they insisted on joining him. They found Lorraine just after she had crossed the bridge and was bravely making her way up the hill. James took her hand, Ziggy got to carry her books, Flagpole and Pee-pee brought up the rear, and Bud was the point man, guiding the group and doing his best to protect Lorraine from the stinging blasts.

At first Lorraine was embarrassed, but she was relieved too; and the more she thought about it, the more she enjoyed the whole situation. Here she was, escorted by some of the huskiest guys in Anneville, and being treated as though she were the Snow Queen herself.

When they got home, Mother invited them all in for hot chocolate, but the storm was getting meaner every minute, and they were smart enough to realize they better get to their houses as soon as possible.

After they got Lorraine and James thawed out, they all had a great time telling about their adventures in the great storm.

When James told Mother about how the boys had helped him, she seemed to have almost forgiven Bud, and was grateful to the other lads. She had never heard of Pee-pee Bouvais, though, and she tried to correct James on the pronunciation of his name.

"It's not Pee-pee, dear, it's Pepe'. The French pronounce it, Peh-pay."

"No, Mother," James protested, "it's Pee-pee. He got the name as a kid when he used to wet the bed."

Mother managed to keep a straight face, but Patricia and Lorraine burst into a major giggling jag.

As soon as they finished their supper of dried lima beans, boiled beets, and hot cocoa, Mother led them in a short prayer: "Thank you, Dear Lord for the food, and especially for getting all of us home safely from the blizzard. Please get us safely through this night. And please, Lord, have mercy on any poor souls who have no shelter from this terrible storm."

Then, like a sea captain battening down the hatches for a coming gale, she began barking orders: "Joe, You'll have to bundle up and take the kerosene bottle out to fill it. We can't be running out of oil tonight. After you get it back on its stand, you and Thos clean up the dishes. Lorraine and Patricia, get the lamps filled and ready; we may lose electricity before long. James, whatever you do, don't let the furnace go out. Set the alarm clock so you can check on it every two hours. The radio said the temperature might go below zero tonight. If the furnace goes out, the pipes will freeze and burst, and then we're in real trouble. The bedrooms are going to get very cold, so all of you can go to bed with your clothes on, and be sure to pile all your coats on top of the covers. Rosebud and Regis, if you still get too cold, come in and crawl in with me. In the morning, listen for the bells from the school. I'm sure there will be no classes tomorrow, So you can all sleep in. Now get moving! That wind's getting louder every minute!"

Thos knew that he should be feeling sorry for anyone out in the storm, and that he should be concerned for the safety of his family, and sorry for poor James who would be down in the cold cellar, stoking the furnace while the rest of them were snuggled warm in their beds; but instead he was wildly excited about the whole adventure. He loved the howling of the wind, the rattling of the sleet against the windows, and the thought of no school in the morning. Again he got satisfaction out of knowing that this blizzard played no favorites: it hit the "little and great, rich and poor'" with equal fury.

That night the wind rose to gusts of over 45 miles an hour, the electric wires were downed, and most of New England lost power; but Mother's little crew weathered the storm unscathed.

In the morning all the kids heard the bells announcing the joyous news that school would have to be temporarily closed. They all slept in except James, who had to throw more logs into the furnace to warm the house enough for the rest of the family to get up for breakfast.

The storm was over, and the sun began to shine on a landscape of pristine beauty. The wind had sculpted the snow into unearthly patterns. In some places the drifts were more than fifteen feet deep, and every tree and bush was flocked with a virginal white veil. All of the Robinsons were overcome by the wonder of it all. "I wish all our lives could be transformed into such beauty overnight!" Lorraine said.

"If wishes were fishes, no one would die of starvation," said Mother, remembering a quote she had heard from her Irish grandfather who had survived the Potato Famine.

Chapter 17

MOTHER HAD HOPED THAT before the end of the winter of "33-'34, Roosevelt's relief programs would be in full swing, and she would be receiving the food provided for in the Agricultural Surplus Commodities Act. One of the provisions of this act was that the government would help the farmers by buying their surplus commodities, and then use those commodities to send food to jobless families. It was an excellent plan, but like most bureaucratic schemes, it took time to get going. By February, 1934, Anneville still did not have a distribution system in action.

Mother's food supply was dangerously low. Gabrosski's grocery store had reluctantly refused her any more credit, and she had been buying food at another store, farther away. This store was owned by Caleb Thornhill. Caleb had agreed to give her credit only if she would sign over her seven dollar a week stipend to him. She had no choice but to agree, and by Ground Hog day, she had overdrawn her account to where Caleb told Patricia that he would not let her buy any more food on credit. Mother sent James back to the store to ask Caleb if he could at least let him buy three loaves of bread and add it on her account. Caleb angrily refused and sent James back with an insulting reply. Mother told him that she would return personally with James to demand the bread from the grocer. James begged Mother not to force him to go with her.

"I'm telling you, if that bastard (it was the first time in his life that James had ever used foul language in front of any family member) gives you a bad time, I'll punch his stinking lights out, and I don't like to hurt people, Mother."

Mother looked at James, and bit her lip. "That's all right, son, you stay home, I'll take Thos with me. I'll get the bread, you just wait and see!"

She threw on her coat and hat, and with Thos hurrying on behind her, she headed for the Thornhill store. Thos was as frightened as he'd ever been in his life, but he was not about to let anybody know that.

When she got to the store, she said firmly to the surprised Caleb, "I'd like three loaves of --- bread, please, and you can put it on my account."

Caleb stood his ground. "I told your son that I will not give you any more groceries until you pay up for what you already owe me."

Without another word Mother scooped up three loaves of bread and began to leave the store. Furious, Caleb made a move towards her. She fixed him with her blazing Irish eyes. "You lay one of your filthy fingers on me, you old fool, and I'll have you in jail for battery!" Then, cradling the bread in her arms, and with the wide-eyed Thos close behind her, she headed home.

As soon as she left, Caleb closed the store, placed a "be back soon" sign on the door, and called Chief Mueller. "Meet me at the Robinson home right away," he said.

"What's this all about?" Mueller asked.

"I'll tell you when you get there," Caleb said huffily.

Mueller could tell that the man was really upset. "Okay, okay! But it'll take me about ten minutes to get there."

Caleb sat waiting in his Whippet sedan about a block away from the Robinsons' house until he saw Mueller's Chevrolet pulling up in front of their house; then he pulled up behind the chief's car. As the grocer got out of his car, Mueller hurried up to him. "What the hell's going on?" he demanded.

"Look, Herman, we pay you a good salary in this town to uphold the law, and you have little enough to do. Now it's time to earn your money. That uppity Robinson bitch in there is a thief, and it's your job to go in there and arrest her."

"Is this some kind of a joke? What did she steal?"

"Three loaves of bread. I saw her just take them into her house."

"Right! Three loaves of bread, and you expect me to arrest her:"

"You are sworn to uphold the law! I don't have to tell you I have some clout with the selectmen, and you could be fired tomorrow. Jobs don't grow on trees these days, you know. Get in there and do your job, you Kraut.' At the word, 'kraut," Mueller bristled: he squared his broad shoulders, and the muscles on his thick arms tightened; for he had fought against the Germans at Belleau Wood, and one of his ancestors had been with Washington at Valley Forge; but he took a deep breath and remained calm.

Then he turned on his heel and headed up to the Robinsons' door. By now some curious neighbors had gathered near the cars. When the chief knocked on the door, Mother opened it, and stood pale, but with her head held high. James stood resolutely next to her, and the rest of her children were clustered around her like frightened sheep.

Mueller could see the three loaves of bread setting on the kitchen table. He stood silently for a minute, then he said respectfully, "Please excuse me for a few minutes, Mrs. Robinson." Then he walked quickly back to Caleb. "Get in the back of my car, Thornhill, I want to talk to you where these people can't hear us."

When Caleb was in the car, Mueller rolled up the windows. Speaking in a low, firm voice he said, "Mr. Thornhill, you're right. I have a sworn duty to uphold the law. I take that duty seriously; so if you insist, I'll go in there, arrest that poor woman, write her a citation for petty theft, and release her on her own recognizance. Then because you reminded me that I must uphold the law, I'm going to go back to the station and pick up the book on the health and safety code for grocery stores in the Commonwealth of Massachusetts. Then I'm going over to your store and check to see if you've violated any of those regulations. Now, if you insist that I do my duty in there, you'd better get back to that rat-trap store of yours and get ready for the kind of inspection that only a good Kraut like me knows how to conduct. How do you like them apples, Mr. grocery man?"

Caleb was silent for a moment, then he said, "I get the picture, Herman. Okay, I'm sorry I called you a kraut. Now I've got to get back to the store, but you tell her I'm going to put that bread on her account. You can also tell her that if she ever tries to steal anything from me again, I'm calling the state troopers: they know how to act like real policemen."

Mueller went back into the Robinson house. "It's all just a big misunderstanding, Mrs. Robinson. Mr. Thornhill didn't realize you wanted to put the bread on your account. But if you want my advice I wouldn't do business with that old skinflint anymore." Then Mueller turned to James. "How are you doing, James? Has Anneville got a pretty good team this year?"

James relaxed for the first time in several hours. "We're going to do our best, Chief Mueller."

"That's the spirit, son!" he said heartily. Then he looked at the rest of the children. "You can be very proud of your mother, kids," he said as he walked away.

But Mother was not proud of herself. She knew she had set a very bad example for her kids. Stealing was not only against the law of man, it was also against the law of God. Sure, it was stealing for her to use electricity without paying for it, but she had been able to make excuses for herself because of the big corporation idea and all that. But this last act was shameful. The Depression had turned her into a beggar and a thief, and now it had crushed and broken her the way it had crushed and broken her husband and so many millions of others. For the first time in her struggle, she was afraid. The three loaves of bread would not last long, and then what? She was finally at the end of her rope.

She went into her bedroom and shut the door for a few minutes; then she opened it and called Lorraine in. "Shut the door, Lorraine, I don't want the kids to hear this."

Mother's bedroom was off-limits to the children. She always kept it tidy and immaculately clean. The two windows had lace curtains on them, and there was a brass bed which she had brought with her from Pennsylvania. She had told Lorraine that all of her children except Regis had been born in that bed. It was now covered by a white chenille bedspread with matching pillow shams. On her bureau were framed photos of her Father and Mother on their wedding day, and a picture of her only sibling: her brother Timothy. Scrawled on the bottom of the photo was the inscription: Here's looking at you, your brother, Timothy.

Although he shared the same mother and father as Mother, they did not resemble each other. Timothy's was a lean face with prominent nose and ears. He had an intelligent look in his eyes, and a mouth that looked like it was used to smiling. His hair was dark, and it looked as though it was already growing thin even though he was younger than Mother—probably about thirty-three years old when the picture had been taken. His most striking feature was a "widow's peak" which had evidently been carefully combed and brushed for the occasion.

On the wall opposite the bed was a group picture of all of her children standing on a snow-covered porch. It had been taken in better times, and all the kids looked well-fed, well-dressed, and happy. In the corner of the room was a small table and chair that served as her desk. Everything on the table was arranged neatly: There was a box of stationery, some pens and pen points, a bottle of blue-black ink, and a blotter. Her correspondence was stacked carefully at the back of the table.

After Lorraine had closed the door, Mother said, "I'm awfully blue, Dear. Don't tell them -- just say I'm sick."

The way Mother said this and the way she looked, worried Lorraine. She had heard of other Anneville women who had had "nervous breakdowns." It usually happened to women with many children, and whose husbands were out of work. It had happened to Mrs. Menard, Beverly's mother; and now Mrs. Menard was in the state hospital at Taunton, which most Anneville people called, "the nut house."

Mother was sitting on the bed. She pointed to a wicker rocking chair which was also a remnant of the good old days. "Sit down, I've got to talk you."

Lorraine was really getting worried now.

"You're going to have to be in charge for a few days. I'll take care of Regis and Rosebud while you're at school, but I'm staying in bed for the rest of the time. You know things are very bad. We have very little food in the house, and we can't get any credit at Gabrowski's or Thornhill's." She pointed to a small decorative teapot on the top of her bureau. The only money we have in the world is in that pot, probably about five dollars in coins. I was saving it to buy a suit for James's graduation. You take the money in that teapot: Gabrowski will sell you food if you pay cash. Have James buy the stuff for soup -- potatoes, carrots, onions, cabbage, and a soup bone. Tomorrow while you're all at school, I'll make some soup. Better get about five pounds of flour too, I'll make biscuits.

The soup and the biscuits and the little we have left in the cupboard will have to do you until Monday. That's four days. I think we have enough canned milk, oatmeal, sugar, and cocoa; but that's not much. If I can't come up with something by that time, I really don't know what we can do." She began to cry, and between sobs she continued. "I'm very, very sorry to put this on you, darling. Sometime tonight I'll get up and write a few letters. In the morning come in and get them. I want you to mail them on your way to school. God bless you, my dear Lorraine, and please pray for me."

The next day Lorraine mailed three letters: one was to the selectman, Mr. Brewster, asking him to see that Mr. Thornhill could no longer have control over her weekly check. Another one was to her brother, Timothy, and the other was to office of Federal Relief in Boston.

Somehow Lorraine, James, and Patricia kept things going, but the soup was all gone by Thursday night. They would have to get by now on oatmeal, stale biscuits, and cocoa. Mother would not get out of bed except when the older kids were at school when she had to get up to take care of Regis and Rosebud.

On Friday as Lorraine trudged up the hill from the river, she wondered what would happen to the family if Mother didn't get well soon?

When they lived in Pennsylvania and Daddy was working, she had attended Catholic school, and one of her favorite nuns had told the kids that when things were really bad, they should ask St. Jude, patron of things despaired of, to ask God to help them. She prayed to St. Jude for the rest of the way home.

Her prayers were not answered until the next day when the mail came. There was only one letter. she took it into Mother, and when Mother saw it, she held it up to the light. "Lorraine, Dear! Wait a minute! My hands are shaking too much, You open it for me!"

With fumbling hands Lorraine opened the letter and gasped. A five dollar bill fell onto the chenille bedspread. "Read me the note, please, Dear." Mother said with tears in her eyes.

"Dear Mrs. Robinson," Lorraine read,

"Sorry we haven't sent you anything for so long. Business has not been good this winter, but Leah and I could not help thinking about you during this terrible weather. We wish we could send you more, but we hope this will be useful to you.

Shalom,

Leah and Jacob Samuels

Mother hugged Lorraine. "Isn't God good?' she said.

"Mr. and Mrs. Samuels are good too," said Lorraine happily.

When Lorraine went to confession that afternoon, she told Father Reynold how St. Jude had helped her. "I have a strange question to ask you, Father, "Why do you think God answered my prayer by using those nice Jewish people? Some of my dumb friends say that the Jews are Christ-killers.""

"Your friends, dear child, are indeed very dumb; for don't they know that Jesus and St. Jude were Jews; and that all of us who sin against God or our fellow man are the real Christ-killers of this world?"

Naturally, five bucks alone could not solve Mother's problems. But that act of kindness which the five dollars represented was powerful enough to, as Mother used to say, "Knock the 'blue gunkies out of me and give me a new lease on life."

She got out of bed, and on Sunday she went to church and sang in the choir -- something that always lifted her spirits.

On Monday, when Thos got home from school, a cheap cardboard suitcase was at the bottom of the stairs, and a man was sitting in the parlor drinking tea with Mother.

"This is your Uncle Timothy, Thos," he's going to stay with us for a while."

"Thos, I hope you call me Uncle Tim from now on." He smiled and stuck out his hand, and Thos was a little uncomfortable to notice that the last three fingers of Uncle Tim's right hand were badly mutilated

Uncle Tim saw Thos trying to avoid looking at the fingers. "That's all right, Thos, you're the first one of the kids to see these. I'm going to explain to you what happened, and you can tell the rest of the kids so I won't have to keep explaining it to the others. They got munched up by a lathe I was working on in a machine shop. They look like hell. Sorry, Mary, I'll have to start watching my language around the house, but no matter how bad they look, they don't bother me at all. If I can get used to them, so can you kids. Okay, Pal?"

Thos wanted to be polite and say, "Yes, Uncle Tim," but he was so startled by the whole thing and by the feel of the fingers, that he just nodded affirmatively.

The other kids came in and Mother introduced each one of them, even though she knew that Uncle Tim remembered Lorraine, James, Patricia, and Joe quite well. Each time Uncle Tim shook hands with them he would tell them Thos would explain what had happened to his fingers. "It happened after you all left Pennsylvania, and it's no big deal, so we won't talk about it any more. Now, I've got to find out what you all have been doing."

Mother quickly broke in. "Uncle Tim is tired. He hitch-hiked all the way from Maryland today. James, you move your things into Joe and Thos's room for now. Uncle Tim will sleep in your room until we get the storage room ready for him. Don't worry, Timothy, we have plenty of room for everybody."

Uncle Tim had come in response to Mother's plea for help. He was a bachelor who had been a merchant seaman for sometime, but he was now out of work because the business slump had hit the merchant marine as hard as it had hit the rest of the world's commerce. He had saved enough money to hold him over for quite a while; so the plan was that he would pay Mother for board and room, and at the same time help her with the upbringing of the children.

At first Uncle Tim was almost as popular with the kids as Santa Claus. He had saved Mother from her "blues," and he was exceedingly entertaining. He had somehow managed to bring a ukulele with him in his suitcase. He accompanied himself on the 'uke" when he sang in his fine baritone. When he and Mother sang together, they made the "welkin ring with their song," as Mother loved to say.

Uncle Tim and Mother reminisced about their childhood -- about crabbing in the Chesapeake, and about the delicious crab cakes, about the music in their family when their mother was alive, and about the sorrow when she died, and about how things got so unbearable when their father remarried. They both agreed that this woman was not half the woman their mother was, and how Mother had moved away to her aunt's house as soon as she was old enough to work, and how Uncle Tim had left as soon as he was old enough to go to sea.

They talked of how the Ku Klux Klan had burned down the flagpole at their church school, and then spread rumors that the Catholics were planning an armed revolution. One of their best childhood friends had begged them not to kill him when the revolution came.

"What makes you think we're planning an armed revolution?" Uncle Tim asked.

"My Dad saw them unloading rifles in the church school basement," their friend replied.

Mother and Uncle Tim both laughed. They had to explain to their friend that what was being unloaded at the church were crates containing some new folding chairs for the school.

Then Uncle Tim reminded Mother that the Ku Klux Klan treated the Catholics a lot better than they treated the Negroes.

Mother reflected then said, "Let's not talk about that in front of the children, Timothy. It's too horrible."

Uncle Tim's sea stories were eagerly listened to by the kids. Their favorite story was about a particularly mean first mate they served under. The man's name was Gatsby: a powerfully built sadist who was especially cruel to men who were much smaller than he, which included Uncle Tim.

Things got so bad, the crew decided to kill Gatsby in the dark of night and throw his body overboard. They drew straws and swore to each other that the man who got the shortest straw would pound on the mate's cabin door at one o'clock in the morning, and when he opened the door, they would plunge a knife into his heart and throw him over the side.

Of course, Uncle Tim drew the short straw. They provided him with a suitable knife, and that night Uncle Tim, shaking with trepidation, approached the door and knocked. When the door opened, Uncle Tim completely froze. Gatsby, with one quick move, wrested the knife from his clutch, and pulled Uncle Tim into his cabin.

"Moran, you dumb shit! So this time it's you!! You look like you could use a drink." Gatsby laid the knife on a small desk, opened a cabinet, took out a bottle of brandy, and poured them both a drink.

"Sit down Moran!" he ordered. "Have a drink while we talk about this." Uncle Tim's hand was shaking as he tried to drink the brandy. He was sure the drink would be his last.

Gatsby took a healthy swig of his drink and said calmly "Relax, Moran. Hell, you think this is the first time this has happened? Every damned time I get on a new ship the crew tries something like this. Sometimes the short straw goes to guys a helluva lot bigger'n you, but always it's the same thing--I have the knife or the club or whatever-- before they know what hit them. Now I want you to give those weak sisters down there a message: 'After this voyage, if any of them wants to meet with me anywhere, I'll take 'em on, and they can use any weapon they want, I'll go at it with 'em. But also tell them that I say, 'a tough ship' is a good ship, and I don't intend to be mate on nothing but a good ship. Tell them that sneaking around in the middle of the night is something that bilge rats do. I won't hold this against you personally, Moran, and you ought'a thank God that I don't. Now, finish your drink and let me get back to sleep."

Uncle Tim paused at the end of the tale, then he said, "You know, I thanked God a lot after that -- not that I didn't get killed -- but I thank him for not letting me kill Gatsby. I can't imagine trying to go through life with such a thing on my soul. Remember, kids,that before you do anything that is so clearly against the law of God, always take time to think carefully. If you do, you will always be, not only good enough, but smart enough not to do it."

Thos and Joe were especially fascinated with the way Uncle Tim rolled and lit up a cigarette. That such a complicated operation could be performed with such style and dexterity was a wonder to them. The paper, the little bag , and the tobacco all had to be fashioned with easy precision into a perfect little cylinder; then the match had to be struck, and the cylinder lit -- all of this done without the least indication that any of it was difficult at all. The actual smoking of the cigarette was an art unto itself, and it seemed in those days that most adults took great pride and satisfaction in the grace with which they smoked a cigarette. No one ever seemed to be concerned about the question of why, with money so scarce and difficult to obtain, people, no matter how poor, would waste time and money on the habit of smoking. Nor was the question ever really considered as to why cigarettes were frequently referred to by doctors and health workers as "coffin nails," and coaches of sport teams would forbid their athletes to smoke because they claimed it would shorten their wind and stunt their growth.

Uncle Tim's pleasant personality, good looks, and sense of humor quickly endeared him to all of Mother's friends and children. He was a welcome addition to the church choir, both for his excellent voice and musical talent, but also because several of the curvaceous French girls were single and found him very exciting. Such was the character of Uncle Tim that everyone quickly disregarded the fact that his right hand happened to be different than other people's.

For a while the brother and sister team of Mother and Uncle Tim worked to the advantage of all concerned. Uncle Tim took over most of Mother's household chores -- cooking, laundry, cleaning, and, to some extent the management of the children. It was in the latter category that friction began to develop. Uncle Tim could not help thinking that a household was a ship, that the children were the crew,that Mother was the captain, and he was the first mate. He had adopted Gatsby's doctrine that "a tough ship is a good ship."

He told Mother that there was too much turmoil and confusion in her house, and he would show her "how to bring order out of chaos, and make things shipshape around here."

He set up a strict schedule for weekday mornings. He rose with James, and as James got the furnace going, Uncle Tim prepared breakfast. Then, he called the family down in groups -- Lorraine and Patricia first, Joe and Thos second, James and himself third, and finally Mother, Rosebud, and Regis last. This system worked well, as long as the crew followed orders, and Uncle Tim made sure they did. The kids generally appreciated the procedure, for it helped alleviate the problem of trying to make one bathroom serve nine people.

He got along very well with Lorraine, James, and Patricia because he had known them very well in Pennsylvania. Thos and Joe could handle Uncle Tim's toughness for they had adapted to the streets of Anneville, and they probably would agree that "a tough town is a good town," but Regis did not respond well to the Gatsby way of dealing with discipline. Rosebud, with her shy beauty and charm quickly won Uncle Tim over, and she could do no wrong in his eyes. Regis though, soon began to fear and dislike his uncle. The ex-seaman's answer to any failure on Regis's part to learn quickly or carry out his orders with speed and accuracy was a slap or even a stroke or two from the razor strop. Mother, so far, had not interfered because she believed, as did most of the parents of that day, in the doctrine of "spare the rod and spoil the child."

Regis, who had just reached his fourth birthday, had not yet mastered the art of tying his shoes. Uncle Tim decided that it was high time for the little boy to learn.

"Come here, Regis, and bring those shoes with you," he ordered. "I want you to pay close attention to how I tie these shoes. See, it's very simple." Then he slowly and carefully went through the motions of tying Regis' small, hand-me-down shoes.

Then he handed the shoes to Regis and helped him put them on. "Now, you do exactly what I did."

Regis tried, but became confused and crossed the laces incorrectly. "Whack!" Uncle Tim slapped him hard, and took the shoes back. "Now, I'm going to show you again, and this time, pay attention!"

By now Regis was terrified and incapable of concentrating. after the third failure and slap, he began to wail, and Uncle Tim lost his temper. "I'll give you something to cry about, you little brat!" Then as he took another whack at poor Regis, the kid managed to duck the blow and take off like a little red headed elf. He scrambled into the bathroom with Uncle Tim close behind him, and tried to squeeze his skinny body behind the claw-footed bathtub. In his panic he wedged himself between the wall an the edge of the cast iron tub. By now Uncle Tim's wrath was beginning to wane and he realized the situation had gotten out of hand. "Get out of there! Come on, Regis, I'm not going to hit you, get out of there!"

It was too late. Regis was painfully stuck. Any amount of struggling on his part just wedged him in further, any tugging on his little body caused him to scream hysterically.

Mother rushed into the bathroom, and sprung into action. "Everybody clear out of here except Lorraine -- that includes you, Timothy! James, you heat some water in a saucepan. As soon as it becomes lukewarm, bring it in here -- get moving!"

She climbed into the tub so she could get near her youngest child and put her arms around him. "It's all right now, dear, I'll get you out of here in a minute. Try to stay still. Let me see."

By the time James came back with the warm water, she had Regis calmed down and he was only sniffling. She took a washcloth, soaked it in the water and began making some suds with a bar of Palmolive soap. "Stay here and help us, James. Keep everybody else out."

After she had washed Regis's legs thoroughly around the stuck area, she told James, "I want you to try to move the tub away from Regis when I give you the signal. Go easy, you don't want to break off any of the pipes -- just move it enough to get his legs out of there."

James got into position to where he could use all of his strength, then when Mother said she was ready, he moved the heavy tub a fraction of an inch, and Mother was able to lift Regis out of his trap and smother him in her arms."

The crisis was over, but so was Uncle Tim's career as the first mate of that ship.

The kids never knew whether he left because Mother ordered him to, whether it was a mutual agreement, or whether he departed in anger and frustration. He did not say goodbye, and Mother did not say anything about him until several years later, when she told the family that Uncle Tim had married a schoolteacher from Baltimore, and that he had gotten a job with the government.

Uncle Tim had left near the beginning of March while the weather was still very cold. Mother's "blue gunkies" returned, but they were not as severe as before. Two events helped to cheer Mother up: one was that signs of spring were definitely in the air. The snow melted, Parting Ways School had posted the chart for "the first flowers of spring" contest, and Joe reported seeing the first robin. But the event that cheered Mother the most was that finally the surplus food from Roosevelt's Agricultural program began arriving in Anneville.

First to be delivered to the Robinson home was a large sack of raisins; then a few days later several quart jars of peanut butter, and a twenty-five pound bag of flour. The raisins caused some distress in the lower gastrointestinal tracts of the kids who consumed too many of them, but the food was sorely needed and put to good use, and Mother gave thanks that she and her brood had survived another "hunger moon."

CHAPTER 18

ONCE MORE SPRING WITH its beauty and promise began to lift up the spirits of the whole Robinson family. Joe was excited about the return of the birds, Thos was excited about the idea that there would be more food available -- wild berries and fruits and nuts, and more farm produce. James was excited about the return of baseball -- his school team, and the Red Sox; and everyone was thrilled about the return of warmth, greenery, and flowers to the earth.

Spring fever gripped Parting Ways School. The teachers enriched their lessons with more poetry, more history and art. Preparations began for the Decoration Day ceremonies, and the class leaders began to whisper about how the girls should start preparing the May Basket for the teacher: This was a carefully decorated basket full of little treats to be presented to the teacher on the first of May. Of all human beings in their lives, with the possible exception of their mothers, the poor children of Anneville loved their teachers; and why not? These angelic women, all of them unmarried (at that time the law did not dictate that all female teachers be unmarried, but custom still demanded that they be "maidens"), these women devoted all of their lives, their love and nurturing instincts towards their students. They maintained iron discipline in their classrooms because their charges dreaded the possibility that one of their beloved teachers would look with disfavor on them. The quality of the teachers was very high, partly because teaching jobs were scarce and the school boards could select only the best of the applicants.

Also in spring an epidemic of "puppy" love affairs sprung up everywhere on campus. Joe was enamored of a pretty Italian, Doris Albergetti, James was smitten by Madeline Morrison, Patricia was besieged by so many swains she couldn't settle on any particular one. Thos was still in love with Miss Kostello, but he still couldn't take his eyes off the sweetheart of the school, fourteen year old Violet Harrington. Thos secretly told Lorraine, "Violet's eyes are so pretty, it hurts to look into them."

"I'll bet you don't even know what color her eyes are, Thos," Lorraine teased.

"I do too! They're Vi . . ." He stopped when he realized he was being "had."

James, with his sturdy physique and personality, caused many a maidenly heart to flutter, but Joe, with his wavy blond hair and dimpled cheeks, was the dream-boy of the lower grades. Thos got tired of having girls tell him that "Your brother, Joe, is So cute with those dimples!" Thos had not yet adjusted to the fact that his was the lot of the majority of males in the human race who just did not quickly activate the sex sensors in the systems of the females of our species.

Joe's crush on Doris Albergetti led to a bitter rivalry with Gerry Durant, who also had his eye on Doris. This rivalry led to some bad words between Gerry and Joe, who normally got along well, and finally it led to bad blood. A challenge was issued (no one knew who issued it), and it was accepted. The fight would take place after school on a Thursday at the sand pit. Word of the affair quickly spread. Joe and Gerry both had reputations for being good fighters. Money would have been bet on the battle, if any of the kids had any money, but, of course, they were all penniless, so they would just settle for bragging rights: "I knew (either Gerry of Joe) could whip him."

Thos felt sorry for Joe. Gerry was bigger and stronger than him, and even if Joe won, he would have to take a lot of hard punches. Thos also remembered what it was like in those hours before an impending fight. You wished there were some way of getting out honorably, but you knew that there was no way out but to punch or be punched.

A crowd had gathered, and the older boys took charge of the officiating. James would be Joe's "second," and Bud LePierre would be Gerry's. This time, instead of using the "chip on the shoulder" method of starting, they would use the "line in the sand" system. A line was drawn on the ground between the two combatants, and the battle would begin when either boy crossed the line.

Joe crossed over first and the fists began to fly. From the first blow it was obvious that this would be an epic struggle. They traded blow for blow, each fighter knew how to counter-punch effectively; so soon there was a great deal of bobbing and weaving. The crowd was made up of boys of all ages and from both Parting Ways School and St. Francis Xavier School. There were no girls present: it was not seemly for girls to be present at such affairs, and there were no adults, but it was well-known that both girls and adults were very interested in the outcome of this match.

The fight quickly moved into the street and down the hill; and as the battle moved past, people viewed it from the windows, and some even opened their doors to get a better view. Both Joe and Gerry landed some very good punches, but neither drew any blood except on their knuckles.

Nobody kept a record of exactly how long the fight lasted, though most agreed later that it was one of the longest fights in the history of Anneville, and that the fight was definitely the best street fight anyone had ever seen, and that the two gladiators were both very worthy of being called "Anneville tough guys."

Mercifully, the older boys decided that the exhausted warriors could not go on any longer, and the fight was declared a draw, and there were cheers and applause when Joe and Gerry shook hands. Whether Doris ever found out why Joe and Gerry fought so valiantly is not known. Also, no one could ever determine which one of the two lads she favored: she bestowed her smiles and charms on each one of them equally from then on. Thos wondered if this was because the fight was a draw, and would she have chosen Joe exclusively if he had won? Or was Doris hoping for a re-match? For the rest of his life he continued to be mystified by the ways of women.

Watching nine-year-old boys slugging it out in a street fight was not the only sporting interest of the good people of Anneville. As April approached, the standard New England greeting of, "Cold enough for you? (pronounced, "Coldnuff faw yaw"), was replaced with, "How the Sox gonna do this yee-ah."

Then there would be the perennial answer, "This is their year; they're going to take it all this time."

"I think you're right. You see where they're finally getting a good manager -- Joe Cronin -- he can hit too."

"They got Lefty Grove too. Wait'll those damn Yankees get a load of his fast ball ."

And so it went. Thos, Joe, and James were all Red Sox fans; but nobody was a bigger fan than James. Fenway Park was sixty miles away, so James had never seen a Red Sox game. He never missed one on radio if he could help it, and during the season you could walk through the streets of Anneville and hear the game on the radio from every house you passed.

An incident happened that spring which was very unimportant in the big scheme of things, but which stuck in James's craw for a long time.

A Massachusetts canned milk company had a promotional campaign with the local stores that encouraged them to stock their "Pilgrim" brand milk in a prominent place in the store. Customers who bought the cans of milk were told to keep the labels, and the first boy to turn in one hundred labels would win two free tickets to a Red Sox game and free transportation to and from Fenway Park. The campaign was voluntary on the part of the grocer, and the company did not have the money to advertise publicly.

Gabrowski's store did not participate, but a small variety store, "Bonard's," did. Mother often bought her canned milk at Bonard's, and over the months this amounted to a considerable number of cans of milk. Eddie Bonard, the proprietor, never told the Robinson kids about the promotion, and James never knew about it until Lester White, the son of one of the Anneville selectmen, was announced the winner.

James confronted Eddie. "Why didn't you tell us about the contest, Mr. Bonard? We buy a lot of Pilgrim milk from you."

"Yes, son, but you buy it with the taxpayer's money. I don't believe that kids "on the town" should expect to get free trips to Fenway Park."

James tried to talk Mother into not buying anything from Bonard's from then on, but she wouldn't go along with him on that. "I know you're disappointed, Dear." Then she added one of her more brutal axioms: "Remember, those who expect nothing will never be disappointed."

One of the reasons why Mother was so unsympathetic about James's situation was that she had just learned some very bad news: she was being evicted from her home again. The news was a cruel shock to her; She had been feeling pretty optimistic about things: they had survived another winter, food from federal relief was beginning to trickle in (she had just received a small crate of grapefruit), there was a good chance that James would be chosen valedictorian, and her home and neighborhood, though not anything to brag about, was still adequate. Now the specter of having to move into squalor haunted her. Once again the family prayer sessions included a plea for "a decent home to live in." Once again her prayers were answered. this time the home was not as "decent" as she would have hoped for. It had been built for speculation in the late twenties, just before the crash. It was a large barn-like structure, but it had plenty of room, and it had a furnace. To paraphrase the realtor's cliché, there were only three things wrong with it: location, location, location.   To the back of it was a small swamp, which the neighbors used as a dump. There were empty lots on both sides of the house, and a rutted dirt road running downhill in front of the house. This street was called "Hill Street." The good news about it was that it was closer to the school and the church; and it was not far from Rover's house and Taber Field.

The house was owned by the Standish family, and Mother suspected that Beth Standish had been instrumental in getting the house for them. When she thanked Beth, the gracious lady said, "Oh, don't be silly, Mary, we are very grateful that you're moving in. We couldn't get anybody to rent it, and we know you'll take good care of it.

Mother decided that they would move during the Easter vacation, which was the week before Easter Sunday; what Catholics called Passion Week, and she stated that they would offer up the miseries of moving in memory of the Passion of Christ.

All eight of the Robinsons were involved in preparations for the move -- even Regis and Rosebud. Not only did everything have to be made ready to be loaded on the truck, but the old house, as well as the new one, had to be cleaned from stem to stern. It was during the cleaning of the new house that Joe found ominous signs of rats. Mother contacted the health department, and the best they could do was to provide her with rat traps, a brochure on pest control, some chicken wire, and some stucco ready-mix. The idea of the latter items was that you mixed the chicken wire and the stucco mix, and used the mess to plug any holes the rats were using to enter the building.

Joe, the family's resident naturalist, was put in charge of getting rid of the rats, and Thos was to be his helper. According to the brochure, the first step was to find the places where the rats were getting in.

Both Joe and Thos hated and feared rats, so they asked James to help them make some clubs to defend themselves with. James shouldered his ax, and Joe and Thos followed him into the woods. He located a suitable oak sapling.

He studied it carefully, and said to the boys, "Your Irish grandfather showed me how to do this."

He trimmed it, cut it down, and the boys carried it home. Then James took their buck saw and cut the sapling's trunk into two lengths of about eighteen inches long, making sure that there was a knot at the end of the two clubs. He handed a club to each one of the boys. "The meanest rat in the world will not come near you if you're carrying one of these," he said.

When Mother saw the clubs, she immediately asked, "Where did you ever get those little shillelaghs?"

Armed with their vicious little cudgels, Joe and Thos inspected the new house carefully. Joe quickly discovered places where the mortar in the foundation had fallen out, and plugged these with the concoction of stucco and chicken wire. In the attic Joe could see daylight in several places at the edge of the roof where the ugly pests were getting in. The brochure said that rats can easily run vertically up the side of a clapboard house.

When they were sure that all the entrance places were plugged up, Joe and Thos set the traps and baited them with some of the peanut butter they had received from the government relief agency.

There were two types of traps: the spring loaded type which almost instantly killed the rodents, and the cage type, which captured them alive. Joe decided that he preferred the quick death method because he could put dead rats in a bag, and dump them at the edge of the woods where they could quickly be recycled by crows and other scavengers.

The live captives were much more of a problem. The recommended disposal method was to drown them by immersing the traps in any convenient body of water. Neither Joe nor Thos could stomach this method, so Joe asked Vasco for help.

"No problem," said Vasco eagerly. "Just hand one of those clubs to me and open the cage. The little bastards will be dead before they take three steps."

Thos would have nothing to do with Vasco's plan. He insisted that they carry the cages into the woods, open them and let the rats take their chances with weasels, blacksnakes, hawks, and owls. They both agreed that they would no longer use the cage traps in their campaign of extermination.

They soon had the Hill Street house free of rats. Mother was very pleased. Eyeing their shillelaghs she said, "I don't want to hear how you did it." Then she got a faraway look in her eyes. "My father told me that in ancient days the Irish used to rid their cottages of rats by reciting poetry."

Whether she was serious about that story or not, the kids could never tell.

James, Joe, and Thos worked hard at scrubbing, disinfecting, and deodorizing the Hill Street house. When Mother inspected the premises she could find only a few smears on the windows that needed to be wiped clean. She also noticed that the bedroom windows had no screens on them, and in the summer they would not be able to get fresh air unless they wanted to be eaten alive by mosquitoes. She prevailed upon Mrs. Standish, and she got her grumbling husband to have screens installed on all the windows.

The actual moving took place on the Monday before Easter. James got some of his buddies to help him with the heavy stuff, but most of the loading and unloading was done by Mother and the kids. The truck and driver was provided by the selectmen, but the driver would do no loading or unloading. At he end of the day, everyone was thoroughly exhausted, but the beds had been re-assembled, the food put away, and the house was ready to be lived in. The next day the whole family went back to the old house and made sure it was clean and neat enough to keep Mother's reputation as a "woman with a respectable family" intact.

By Easter Sunday the Robinsons were already becoming accustomed to the Hill Street House. There were many disadvantages to their new dwelling. The most apparent problem was that they no longer had electricity. Mother never did feel comfortable about stealing electric power, and she felt that the legal and ethical risks involved in this practice were no longer worth taking. All of the Robinson family hated to go back to using kerosene lamps, and they were all very sorry that they would no longer have the radio. Mother said that if Lorraine and James were able to make any money this summer, she would use any money earned to pay for electricity during the winter, and that with any luck they might have lights on their tree next Christmas.

The new neighbors they now had were an interesting bunch. For one thing they now lived closer to Lizzie Horton, and she was over to their house much more frequently than she had been for a while. She was still smitten with James, but he managed to keep out of her sight as much as he could. Lizzie was still the same old Lizzie -- forever doing or saying dumb things. That would be bad enough, but she had the strange power of convincing other dumb people that what she said was Gospel truth.

When a rainbow appeared one day after a rainstorm she had some of the neighborhood kids, including Thos, running down the street trying to find the pot of gold said to be at the end of the beautiful arch in the sky.

One of her most memorable con jobs (no one ever figured out whether she personally believed all of this silly stuff herself) was perpetrated on Joe and Thos one day when they were looking at a picture in the Saturday Evening Post, of a scale model of a Yankee clipper ship enclosed in a large bottle.

"How did they ever get that thing in there?" Thos asked.

Lizzie was quick with the answer. "My uncle Ethan, who lives in Vermont, has a friend who does that kind of stuff -- builds the ships and puts them in the bottle. He says getting it in the bottle is no problem at all. All of those big bottles have a secret way of unscrewing their bottoms. My Uncle told me to keep that a secret: otherwise the guys will not be able to charge such big prices for the ships in the bottles."

Soon every kid in the neighborhood, but especially Joe and Thos, were working away trying to figure out how to unscrew the bottoms of large glass bottles. Sadly, the kids who were most victimized by this what Lorraine called, "Lizzie-isms" were those who tended to refuse to admit defeat in anything they wanted to accomplish. Thos, who was wont to give up too easily, quickly abandoned the project. Joe, the opposite of Thos in this quality, tried every way he could to figure out the secret of the "ship in the bottle." He even got Vasco to help him. Vasco, whose answer to all problems was to use brute force, quickly tired of the attempt, and smashed the bottle against a nearby rock.

The land in back of the Hill Street house was about two acres of "common land." That meant it could be used for agriculture by whoever wished to use it, and that usage would be respected by the law and by the neighboring citizens. This made for some strange arrangements. Part of the land was swampy, and many people used it for a dump. Another part of the property was used as grazing land, and when grass was growing, some small farmers would tether their cows there during the day. When milking time came they would return them to the barn.

There was one plot that was used by a farmer for growing potatoes. There was a long-standing tradition that everyone, including the most disrespectful of children, would not interfere with anyone using this property for legitimate purposes. Thos never once witnessed any discord caused by this tradition.

The kids generally watched the agricultural activities with fascination and awe. A cow grazing, chewing its cud, or relieving itself of waste, was a wonder to behold. A farmer preparing a plot of land with only the aid of a horse was also a pleasure to watch. Perhaps these positive feelings towards agricultural activities was some genetic response to the fact that over the millennia mankind had survived by planting, growing, and keeping domestic animals.

The fact that part of the common property was used as a dump by nearby residents was not simply a matter of ignorance or slovenliness on their part. It was a matter of necessity. The town could not afford any organized trash disposal system. People had to work out their own method of getting rid of refuse. Most people, including the Robinsons, had incinerators fashioned out of fifty gallon oil drums. They burned all combustible waste, then dumped the ashes and the charred tin cans in the nearest dump. Some people didn't even bother burning their trash before they dumped it.

Organic garbage, though, was not allowed to be dumped anywhere. There was a large pig farm on the outskirts of town owned by the

Mesisio family. They would made regular rounds of the town in their trucks. Anyone who wanted to get rid of their garbage (swill) could leave it in front of their house in a covered container, and the Mesisios would pick it up. The Mesisios would then feed it to their hogs. It seemed like a good plan, but the town did enforce the rule that the containers be tightly covered, and the Mesisio family would not pick the containers up if they were not kept reasonably clean; thus occasionally there would be some rotten garbage illegally thrown into the town dumps.

The Mesisio kids, who attended Parting Ways School, would often smell of swill because they had to help the family with the garbage pick-ups. A sick joke of the day, which some people thought was hilarious, ran like this: "If you need a job, you can get one working on the Mesisio garbage trucks: they pay ten cents an hour and all you can eat. Ha, ha."

The major dumps of Anneville were located at the edge of the woods. They were ugly and unpleasant places, but a treasure trove for kids to find useful junk. The Robinson boys, despite Mother's pleas for them to "stay away from those filthy places," would occasionally go on junk-picking expeditions to some of the larger dumps. The saw mill dump where the kids had found the infamous five gallon cans used in the drums and spears fiasco was one of the best dumps around.

A part of the dump was covered by water, especially when the river that fed the pond was swollen with spring rains. Most of the trash was from businesses in Anneville or New Bradford -- the usual stuff -- bottles, cans, pieces of old cars, discarded batteries, tires, and inner tubes. There was also refuse from construction sites: hunks of lathe and plaster, electrical wire, barbed wire, and pieces of broken cement.

Sometimes, when Thos would look at all this ugliness, he would think of what Miss Kostello had told the class about what this country was like before the white men had come. The stone age Native Americans believed that the things of the natural world belonged to the Great Spirit and were to be used by humans for their good, but could not be owned by them, and in no case should they ever be destroyed. She told them that before the white men arrived, the country from the Atlantic Ocean to the Mississippi River was one great virginal forest -- a continuous expanse of trees so vast that a squirrel might travel by tree top to tree top for over a thousand miles without ever having to touch the ground.

Now, all that was left of that magnificent wilderness were a few isolated patches of woods such as the one where he and Joe and Rover had wandered in so happily last summer. This dump was on the southern edge of their woods, and it seemed clear to Thos that this ugliness was beginning to encroach slowly but surely into their beautiful refuge.

It made Thos sad to think such thoughts, so he quickly switched to thinking about what he might find in this place-- maybe a soda pop bottle that he could turn in for a few pennies, or an old aluminum pot or a piece of copper. The junkman paid two cents a pound for copper and four cents a pound for aluminum. Mother would let them keep half of any cash they made this way.

One day just before Patriot's Day, Thos, Joe, Bobby Ellison, and Citron Moulette were poking around in the sawmill dump when Joe dug up a piece of shiny metal. "Looks like it's nickel- plated," he said.

He began digging up more nickel-plated objects, until he finally realized these were parts of a revolver. someone had gone to the trouble of taking the gun completely apart. He could not find any of the screws that once held it together, and he couldn't find the firing pin; but he was sure he had all the other parts of this gun. the other three began digging furiously in the same area. Soon they too began to find gun parts. Before long they had dug up parts of five guns: a nickel-plated revolver, a blue steel 32, two anodized steel 38's, and a few pieces of an automatic of undetermined caliber. All of these had been completely disassembled, and their bolts and screws were missing.

Joe claimed ownership of the nickel-plated pistol, and the other three boys agreed as to how the other three revolvers would be divided. Their was a short discussion as to whether they should report this to the police, but it was quickly decided that the 'finders keepers' rule over-ruled other considerations, and so the guns, if they ever could get them put together, belonged to them.

They went to Bobby Ellison's garage to work on assembling their new-found treasures. No one ever knew where Bobby's father was, and his mother was too busy with Bobby's three younger brothers to ever pay any attention to what Bobby was doing.

There were no screws available, so Bobby found an old pair of electrician's pliers and a can of miscellaneous nails. They found that by putting the nails into the screw holes, bending them over, and clipping off the excess part of the nail, they could assemble the guns into a reasonable facsimile of the originals, but any close look would quickly reveal the absurdity of the way they had been put together.

Word quickly spread that the boys had found the guns, and it wasn't long before Chief Mueller decided to investigate. He found the three boys in Taber Field playing cops and robbers with some of the other kids. Several of the boys scattered at the approach of the police chief, but Thos, Joe, and Bobby realized the futility of flight, and stood there with their guns in their hands.

Mueller could quickly see that the guns were nothing but junk, but, being the big ham he was he decided to play his hand. Making sure his police special was near to his dangling right hand, Wyatt Earp style, he walked slowly up to the guilty looking trio. "All right, boys! Let's have no trouble! Just lay your weapons on the ground and step back two giant steps!"

The boys quickly complied, and Mueller picked up and examined the three guns. "Where did you get these?" He demanded.

"We dug 'em up at the sawmill dump. They don't have any firing pins or anything," Joe said defensively.

"What do you intend to with them?"

"Nothing," Joe said.

"What if I confiscate them?"

"We found them," Bobby said. "Finders keepers."

Mueller examined all three of the guns closely. It would have taken a first class gunsmith to get them in firing condition, and even then they would be more dangerous to the person doing the shooting than the person being shot at.

"If you promise to ask your parents' permission if you can keep these, I have no problem with that. The serial numbers have been burnished off; they probably belonged to bootleggers in the old days. Keep out of trouble, lads." Mueller said, leaving the guns on the ground, and striding briskly away.

The kids who had run away came quickly back. "What happened?" they asked.

"I told him, 'finders keepers," Bobby bragged.

"Are you going to get to keep them?" Citron Moulette asked incredulously .

All the boys were envious of Joe, Thos, and Bobby. Guns were the "in" thing at that time. Some of the kids had seen the Howard Hughes film classic, *Scar Face,* which came out in 1932, but was still playing in some theaters in the spring of '34. Those who had not seen the film had heard it childishly but enthusiastically re-enacted by those who had parents rich enough to take them to the movies. This was also the era of Baby Face Nelson, Bonnie and Clyde, and above all -- John Dillinger. The papers had been filled with the sensational exploits of this trigger-happy bank robber and his gang of killers. Despite the efforts of teachers and parents to explain to their children that there is nothing glamorous about robbing and killing, the kids on the streets of Anneville generally thought of gangsters as folk heroes, if not role models. The gun, therefore, was popular with the street urchins of Anneville because it was the symbol of the gangster era -- all that was exciting and glamorous about the time of the gangsters could be compressed into that little hand-held killing machine -- the gun. "A gun makes a guy really feel like a man!" Bobby Ellison used to say.

Toy guns were great, and there was even a certain thrill in simulating a gun by holding the fingers and the thumb in a certain way and trying to imitate the sound of a pistol shot, but to have a real gun in your hand, even one held together with bent nails -- that was a thrill! At least many of the Anneville tough guys thought so.

Some kids hurried to the sawmill dump and dug everywhere, but they could find no other guns. Evidently Joe, Thos, and Bobby had found the only ones available. As a result the other kids began offering them some pretty good trade Items.

Thos finally decided that he would trade his gun, but could not make up his mind whether he would accept a white rat, a jackknife, or a Model T Ford magneto and spark coil. It was an agonizing decision, because he wanted all three of the items, but he finally settled on the Model T magneto and spark coil because electrical gadgets had always been irresistibly attractive to him.

Joe received some equally tempting offers -- a harmonica, a Red Sox baseball cap, or an old Benjamin air rifle. He chose the latter, even though it was the old model in which the compressed air was pumped in by aid of a long rod which resembled the ramrod of an old musket. This rod was kept clipped beneath the   barrel, and when more compressed air was needed, the rod was unfolded and used as a pump rod. The gun used BB's, and was single shot, but it was well designed, and packed a pretty good wallop if it were pumped up enough.

Both of the trades were well made: Thos was to have much fun with his magneto, and what is more important, he learned much about electricity from playing with it. Joe was to put his air rifle to good use in the coming battle against the rats.

CHAPTER 19

SPRING CONTINUED TO WORK its magic upon the fields and woods of Anneville, and, indeed upon the streets of the little town. Everywhere could be heard the songs of returning bobolinks, robins, bluebirds and meadowlarks. The air was filled with the scent of lilacs, apple blossoms, and wild roses, and the earth once more felt soft under the feet of children. Poor people responded to the thrill and promise of spring almost as much, or perhaps, even more than the rich people; for with spring there would be more food available and less struggle to keep warm; and natural beauty meant as much to poor souls as it did to others. The Robinson family in their new Hill Street home were able to look out from the back of their place and see the common land with the cows grazing, the buttercups and daisies blossoming, and the newly planted potato patch turning greener with each new day. Unfortunately though, they could also see the swampy dump, and occasionally they would get a glimpse of a rat scrounging for food in the trash.

Joe, with his sharp eye and newly acquired BB gun, was able to pick off a few of the disgusting pests, but there was no way to exterminate them this way. Traps and poisons were too dangerous to children, birds, and squirrels to be an effective way of getting rid of rats.

For a while there was a stalemate in the rat battle, but then something happened that alarmed the whole Robinson family. In the middle of the night, when Thos got up for a bathroom visit, he saw by lamplight, a large rat running down the hall. The next morning James and Joe found some rat droppings in another part of the house, and the battle was on!

Mother rushed to the Health Department and demanded they send a man out to investigate.

A man finally showed up. He was middle-aged, with a fringe of grey hair making a half circle around his pale, bald pate. He was short and pot-bellied, and he smelled of pipe tobacco; but he seemed to be competent and sympathetic.

After a quick survey of the situation, he said to Mother, "Look, lady, I don't know what to tell you. They told me we do not have the funds to conduct any rat control. All I'm allowed to do is give you some advice. These are Norwegian rats: They're determined and resourceful. No matter how you try to stop them they'll get into your house if they want to. Cats aren't worth much against them, and they'll soon get wise to traps and poison. A rat terrier can kill them, and it's fun to watch them do it, but for every one they get there will be two more show up. As long as that dump is there, you'll have rats getting into your place. I'll be willing to bet, they're getting into other homes around here too."

"Won't the health department help us get rid of the dump?"

"I'm sorry, lady, we can't do that; you'll have to get a private businessman to take care of that."

"That's ridiculous! Mother said, raising her voice. "The people around here don't have enough money to feed their. . ."

"Don't raise your voice to me lady. It's not my fault. I'm just doing what they tell me to do, and I'll tell you the truth: I don't like this job, but I'm darned glad I got it."

Then he made some notes on a yellow note pad and walked away.

Mother ordered Joe and Thos to get out their shillelaghs and do what they did before to "get those filthy little buggers out of my house!"

Then she appealed to the board of selectmen for help; but sometimes bureaucrats are more difficult to deal with than Norwegian rats, and this was one of those times. They wrung their hands and professed sympathy, and swore they knew how Mother felt, but also swore that they were powerless to help her.

Mother bit her tongue. She wanted to tell them that they were not powerless, but spineless, and that in her opinion the rats on the board of selectmen were as bad as the rats in the dump. "No!" she told herself. "I've got to focus on the problem."

Then she smiled sweetly. "Oh, I know you gentlemen are doing the best you can. But is it possible that you could provide us with a dump truck to haul the trash away if we clean it up and load it into the truck for you?"

Mr. Brewster made a move that the board meet later in executive session and discuss this proposal. A few days later Mother received a letter saying that the board had agreed to provide a dump truck for one day. If Mrs. Robinson could get the dump cleaned up and get the truck loaded in one day, they would see that the trash was hauled away and dumped at a site away from any residences. Mother had won the opening skirmish in the battle against the rats.

Now Mother went door to door in the neighborhood and pleaded for help. Her pleas were at first met with astonishment, and then cold indifference. The men were openly opposed to her.

Her strongest opposition came from Mr. Laval, father of five children, and a man who had lost his farm in the crash. He worked part time as a day laborer on a farm on the outskirts of Anneville. He was a bitter, irascible man -- red-faced, and quick tempered. Mother had already had a run-in with him.

The Laval's house was on the corner of the common land next to the area where the cows were sometimes tethered. The Robinson home was only an empty lot from Laval's, and one day when Mother was hanging out the wash, she heard a child screaming. she looked out to see little Gilbert, Laval's two year old son sitting on the back porch steps with his wet under-pants draped over his head, wailing uncontrollably. Mother rushed over; and as she drew near she could smell the urine from the poor child's pants. Angrily, she pounded on the Laval's door.

When the door opened, Laval appeared. "Sir," Mother said, "Do you know that there's a baby sitting out there with wet underpants draped over his head?"

"Sure, that's the best way I know of house-breaking the little bugger."

"Mr. Laval, that is a cruel and unsanitary thing to do to a child. I must protest."

Laval's re face became almost purple. "Just who in the hell do you think you are, telling me how to raise my kids? Get the hell out of here!"

Mother could get angry too. "What you're doing is against the Constitution of this country! I can't enforce the law, but there are people who can."

"Don't give me that fancy talk, woman! What you need is a man to keep you in your place. I've hear about what an uppity . . ."

His wife had now come out on the porch. Cecile Laval was compact and curvaceous, and despite the fact that she had given birth to several kids, she was still a pretty woman. Even without make-up, her cheeks were pink, and her lips red and full. Her hair and eyebrows were jet-black and her eyes as blue as a Canadian lake. She put her delicate hand on her husband's brawny arm. "Now, Hector," she said, "Calm down, dear. You know it's very bad for you to get so upset."

Laval shot her an angry look, but went back into the house. Mrs. Laval leaned confidentially close to Mother. "Poor Hector! He's never been the same since they took our farm from us. He will be very sorry about what he did to little Gilbert. I wish I could get him to apologize to you, but that would be impossible for him. I hope we can be friends even so, Mrs. Robinson."

Laval never apologized, nor did he ever speak to Mother again. When she began to ask for support in her campaign to get the dump cleaned up, she learned that Laval was saying that he would have nothing to do with anything "that that Robinson dame" was organizing."

When Laval was at work, though, his wife came to visit Mother. "I admire you for trying to get rid of the rats. I'll do what I can. Don't worry about Hector, Mary," she said. "I don't think he'll help you at all, but he won't give you any trouble." Then she smiled moved her body coquettishly, "There are ways to handle big mugs like him," she said.

Getting rid of the dump would be no easy task: the neighbors had been throwing their trash there for years, and bad habits are difficult to break. But hatred and fear are powerful motivational tools, and the women hated and feared rats. Mother soon convinced most of the women to join in her campaign. They agreed to let their older boys help in the clean-up and the loading of the truck. They also agreed to help to provide and serve refreshments for the project. The neighborhood men were not very enthusiastic. Not only were they not intimidated by rats, they were also so mired in their own economic misery they gave little thought to neighborhood improvement. The major burden of the war against rats, therefore, would have to be carried by the women and children.

Mother told the selectmen to have one of the Town's dump trucks parked and ready at the swampy dump on the Saturday before Memorial Day. she held a meeting for all volunteers in her backyard on the night before the "battle."

The neighborhood mothers and a motley collection of boys showed up. The boys ranged in age from seven to seventeen. Most of them were from the neighborhood, but the best of the lot were some of James's athletic pals and team-mates -- Bud LePierre, Ziggy Janowski, Flagpole, -- Pee--Pee LeFerriere, Moosey Oliviera. All in all, there were about eighteen boys. Mother was quite pleased.

"All right men," she said, good-naturedly taking on the tone of a commanding general,, "We will attack at first light! Your weapons will be shovels, rakes, and hoes. Your uniforms will be the worse clothes you can find: you will get wet and dirty. Wear old shoes, but be sure your feet are covered well. Beware of broken glass. There will be a large dump truck parked here in the morning. Our objective is to move all that ugly trash out of that dump and into that truck. By this time tomorrow we'll have this neighborhood looking a lot better, and their will be no room around here for any more dirty rats!" Then the commanding General became the cheerleader at a rally. "Whadda you say men? It's gonna be the dirty rats against the Anneville tough guys -- Who's gonna win?"

The boys got in the spirit of the moment and the chant went up: "Anneville! Anneville! Anneville!"

Everyone was laughing and the kids never saw Mother looking happier.

The Robinson boys were the only ones attacking the dump at first light, but soon others started to work. Mother thanked God for the beautiful May day.

"It'll be hot in the afternoon," she said," so we better get as much done as we can while it's cool."

The plan was to move all the trash to a big pile at the edge of the empty lot next door to the Robinsons. When the dump truck came, Mother would have it back up as close to the pile as possible. Then she would have two teams: one moving the trash to the pile, the other loading it into the truck. Only boys over seven would be allowed to do the shoveling and raking. The Robinson girls would take care of any Saturday household chores, then come out and help serve water or lemonade to the boys. Any volunteers from the neighborhood would fall into similar work details.

The dump truck arrived at about 8:25. The driver, Lou Plant, parked the truck exactly where Mother told him: then he explained that this was his day off, and he had to take care of some family business. He said he would come to drive the truck away at about 5:30. Before he left he once again explained that he was doing this on his day off and he wasn't getting paid for it. Mother, thinking of how much work her crew was going to have to do that day, thanked Lou politely, but murmured something uncomplimentary as he headed for his house four blocks away.

The work went well at first; James's team-mates wielded their shovels and rakes with gusto. Occasionally a rat would pop out of the trash and make a break for it. A cheer went up from the boys whenever one of the slower pests was dispatched with a shovel or rake. When the third carcass was thrown into the truck, Flagpole yelled, "Anneville Tough Guys--three, Dirty Rats--nothing!"

This received the best laugh of the day. Most of the girls and women did not join in the laughter. "The poor little things," Lorraine was heard to say.

For a while it looked as though they might easily have the job done before the truck driver returned; but the work was hard, and after three hours, even Bud LePierre was getting very tired.

"Let's take a break," Mother said.

Cecile Laval and some of the other women had brought cookies -- oatmeal, peanut butter, and one batch of Toll House cookies. The boys sat in the shade and ate every cookie in sight. Most of them drank water and some had lemonade. Lorraine and Patricia were not the only pretty girls there; there was Doris Albergetti, Madeline --, and, of course, Lizzie Horton. Lizzie avoided making any Lizzie-isms except for one time when she got Citron Moulette so mad he almost brained her with his shovel. Citron (pronounced, see-twonh") was only a nickname; his real name was Gascoigne. He was given the name Citron by his French-Canadian buddies because his head was shaped somewhat like a lemon. Such cruel appellations were given and received with good humor by the French-Canadians of Anneville, but they resented anyone using the term derisively. Poor Citron! He had worked with the best of them shoveling trash, and sat exhausted, taking a well-earned rest and some lemonade.

Lizzie, who had been staring at him, burst into giggles. "Now I know why they call you Citron," she giggled. "Your head is shaped just like a lemon!"

Citron, usually a good-natured lad, went after Lizzie in a blind fury. Bud and James grabbed him before he could get to Lizzie. "That bitch!" he shouted. "I oughta' kick her ass!"

Such language was used a lot in Anneville, but never in the presence of women. Mother quickly settled everybody down. "Lizzie! You're to go home this instant, and don't come back!"

After Lizzie, in tears, had hurried home, Mother comforted Citron. "Don't pay any attention to Lizzie, Dear," she said. "Lizzie sometimes says things to me that makes me want to kill her. She's going to hang herself with her own tongue one of these days. Citron, I watched you today. You worked as hard as any of these tough guys. Let's hear it for Citron!" and she began the chant, "Citron! Citron!" and everyone joined in, and Citron finally smiled.

After the break the boys renewed their work, but they had slowed down considerably, and Mother began to despair of finishing the project before the truck driver returned. The heat of the day was coming on, and the poor boys could not keep working that long.

At twelve o'clock she dismissed everyone for an hour lunch break and urged them all to come back for the afternoon session. She realized, though, that not all of them would have the grit to come back. Sadly she realized that if they didn't finish that day, it would be a while before she could get this operation started again. It was unthinkable to work on Sundays; the next weekend was a holiday. There was no alternative; she would have to do her best to get the job done that day.

At one o'clock things turned definitely for the better. Wes Harrington, the farmer whose potato patch was next to the swampy dump, had heard about the clean-up project from his daughter, Violet. He drove up in his Ford model A pick-up. In the back he had a hoe, a rake, and several shovels. He was dressed in bib overalls and wore a straw hat. He definitely had come to work. At first Mother thought he had come to work on his potato patch, but he strode up to Mother, and announced, "Sorry I couldn't be here earlier, Mrs. Robinson, I had some important stuff to do at my place, but I got here as soon as I could. Violet wants to help too, so put her to work."

For Mother, this was a double gift from Heaven. Not only would Wes's strong back be welcome, but Violet, by her very pretty presence, would generate new energy in the hearts of the young men.

"How pretty that child is!" Mother thought, "I remember. . . Enough of that," she told herself. "We've got a dump to get rid of."

Then a second bonus appeared. Hector Laval, in bib overalls and straw hat, carrying a shovel, came striding up to Wes Harrington. Evidently they were old pals. He spoke briefly to Wes; then Wes said to Mother. "We'd appreciate it if you'd keep the little guys out of the way. We're gonna see what we can do."

Both of the men spat on their hands, picked up their shovels and went to work. The rest of the crew could not believe their eyes. "They're like human steam shovels!" said James.

Wes pointed to James and his pals. "You guys pile the stuff in the truck, we'll put the stuff in the pile."

Their shovels never stopped moving. Even when a rat tried to dash for safety, they killed it with one deft movement of their shovels and continued moving the trash to the pile. Sweat poured from their faces and large areas of their shirts became soaked. No matter how hard James and his pals worked, they could not keep ahead of these two farmers glorying in their trade. The two of them, not used to an appreciative audience, were putting on a show -- competing with one another -- having the time of their lives.

The boys too were now glorying in their work. They began to really put their backs into their labors. Now they were showing all the pretty girls present what unleashed testosterone could really do. For Thos and Joe this was even better than watching a movie show.

By two-thirty the sun was beating down unmercifully on the sweating men. Mother told James and his buddies to take a break in the shade even though the pile of junk waiting to be shoveled into the truck was getting bigger despite the efforts of the strong young men.

The boys had been doing their best, but they were just schoolboys. Wes and Hector were farmers -- old fashioned farmers, muscle, sinew and sweat farmers --farmers who came from the old school where if you didn't put every shred of your energy, and every ounce of your sweat into your work, you and your family might well starve to death.

Mother, out of fear that the men might collapse from heat and exhaustion, begged them to take a break.

Wes, continuing to scrape and shovel, looked at Hector, who shook his head.

Thanks, Ma'am," Wes said, "but we're just getting our second wind. We'll take a break when the work's done."

At that Cecile Laval ran out, and taking her apron off, she wiped the sweat from her husband's face and eyes. Violet, taking a towel from Lorraine, ran out and wiped her father's face. This was such a spontaneous and beautiful move by the young beauties, everyone just gaped in wonder. Thos whispered to Joe, "That's almost as beautiful as Veronica wiping the face of Jesus!"

Mr. Brewster came by and was astonished at how well the project was going. "That's some swell thing you're doing, Mrs. Robinson."

Then Brewster looked at Cecile Laval, who was now sitting in the shade some distance away. "Who's that cutey?" Brewster, the most eligible bachelor in town, whispered to Mother."

"That's Cecile Laval," Mother said. "And that big guy with the shovel, there, is her husband."

"Okay, okay, I get the message," Brewster said with a big smile. He left shortly after that.

Before long it became clear that the project would be successful. The dump, which had for so long been an offensive reminder of man's defilement of Nature, was now just a pile of stinking rubble waiting to be carted away out of sight. Wes and Hector could now see the results of their labors. As they raked away the last pieces of sodden paper and broken glass, and threw the last rusty tin can on the junk pile, they could take pleasure in seeing that all that remained was natural -- earth, weeds, grass, roots and water. The place was still fetid and musty, but a few days of sunlight would bring it back to the way it was before the dump.

When the farmers had shoveled the last scrap of trash on the pile, they quickly raked the area until it looked trim and neat. Then they went to work on the pile, and soon it was all safely in the truck. Then they covered the mess with a tarpaulin, and tied it securely down.

It was 4:35 in the afternoon. They quickly cleaned off their tools and graciously received the thanks of Mother and the admiring looks of their audience. Wes climbed into his Model A, and he and Violet, grinning broadly, drove away. Hector and Cecile went home and so did everybody else; so that when the truck driver returned, all that was left were Mother and her very proud brood.

"Jumping Jehosaphat!" Lou said. "I've never seen anything like this! How'd you ever get it all done?"

Thos tried to be modest. "We didn't do it all by ourselves. Mr. Harrington and Mr. Laval were sure a big help," he said.

"It looks like you still got some work ahead of you, Mr. Plant. Will you need any help getting this unloaded," she asked, to the horror of the exhausted James, Joe, and Thos.

"Heck, no thanks, Ma'am. I just back old Betsy, here, up to the dump, hit a couple of levers, back will lift up and the whole mess will slide out." Then I'm through for the day." Then he pointed to where the dump used to be. "That's one hell of a job, Ma'am!" he said as he fired up his engine.

The clean-up of the swampy dump was quite a triumph for Mother. Her friends and people of good will all over Anneville talked about her achievement. The selectmen had signs posted on the site reading, "No Dumping At Any Time!" and the neighbors found other ways to get rid of their trash. They also waged a campaign to get rid of any stray rats remaining in the homes of the neighborhood, and everyone was happy to be free of their disgusting house guests. For a few days it could be said that Mother was the talk of the town.

There were other triumphs too. On Decoration Day, when Parting Ways School presented their annual tribute to the men and women who had given their "last full measure of devotion" to their country, the Robinson children were all asked to give solo performances: James delivered "The Gettysburg Address," Patricia recited, by heart, Whittier's entire "Barbara Frietche," Joe did Emerson's "Concord Hymn," and Thos presented Sir Walter Scott's "My Native Land."

As usual, veterans from the Civil War, the Spanish American War, and World War I were the guests of honor. The whole town turned out, and patriotic fervor was at a fever pitch. There was not a dry eye in the entire assemblage when the audience joined the students in the singing of "The Battle Hymn of the Republic."

Mother's greatest triumph that spring, though, was at the graduation ceremonies. James not only was the valedictorian, he also was awarded the American Legion Citizenship award. This was the first time anybody could remember that the two awards were given to the same student. When the citizenship award was handed to him, all the members of the American Legion, resplendent in their blue and gold overseas caps, rose as a man and gave James a standing ovation. The entire audience also rose to their feet and joined the applause. Mother, with tears streaming down her cheeks, was telling everyone around her that Irish people cry when they are happy and laugh when they are sad.

CHAPTER 20

ALTHOUGH, BY THE SUMMER of 1934, the Robinson family had won some grudging respect from many other good folks of Anneville, there were still people who resented and even hated them. These people never would let Mother and her brood forget that they were newcomers to Anneville, that they talked differently than the other townspeople, that they had never paid taxes to the town, and that they were "on the town."

People who felt like this were usually those who hated Roosevelt and his New Deal. The New Deal, they felt, was simply a "soak the rich" scheme. One anti-New Deal spokesman said that Roosevelt wanted to "take money from the thrifty and give it to the improvident." Whether or not the idea implicit in that statement is fair or accurate has been a subject of lively debate ever since.

But in the thirties, the large majority of the people favored the New Deal, and the popularity of Roosevelt, especially in places like Anneville, continued to increase.

When school vacation began, Mother made plans to get some money for the long winter to come. Lorraine and James would work on Cape Cod where they would get board and room and wages to help with the family budget. Patricia would take care of Regis and Rosebud, and most of the housework while Mother tried her hand at selling silk stockings door to door. With any luck she hoped to get enough money to pay for the winter fuel, to re-connect the electricity, and to buy some much needed clothes for James and Lorraine, who would both be attending school in New Bradford: James at Melville Junior high, and Lorraine at New Bradford High School.

Patricia at this time was only ten years old, and she would have quite a responsibility to take care of the smaller children and do the cooking and cleaning for the household in general.

Joe and Thos, although they would have many specific chores, would be mostly on their own and were looking forward to once again roaming the woods and fields. Joe's pal, Vasco, would be working as a farm hand and would have little time or energy for wandering the woods with Joe and Thos.

During the winter, Keats Gidney had moved to Arizona because of his asthma, so his fascinating personality would no longer liven up the street life of Anneville.

Joe and Thos heard from Citron Moulette that one of his relatives was hiring kids to pick strawberries on a farm in the outskirts of Anneville. The bad news was that they would have to walk over two and a half miles to the strawberry fields, and then, after a very hard day's work, trudge the two and a half miles back home. The good news was that they would be paid two cents a box for the picking, and that Mother said they could keep half of all the money they made. The other half of the money would have to go into the family kitty.

She said they must wear a straw hat in the sun, and they were not to take off their shirts, no matter how hot it got, for sunburn was a real danger to any Irishman.

Citron gave them directions to his uncle's farm, and said he would tell his Aunt Pauline that they were friends of his, and to be looking out for them.

He hesitated for a few seconds, then he said, "Aunt Pauline is my mom's sister. She's nice, but my Uncle Lester is a son-uva-bitch. That's one of the reasons I'm not going with you: the other's that the work's too hard."

Thos and Joe donned their summer uniform of bib overalls, and with their straw hats they felt like real farmers. When Thos thought of how hard real farmers like Mr. Laval and Mr. Harrington had to work, though, he felt a little uneasy about what lay ahead of them.

The road to Uncle Lester's farm led through one of the nicest parts of Anneville--an area of tree-lined streets, neatly trimmed box hedges, flower gardens, and green lawns. The kids who lived in this section of town had bicycles, sleds, and ice skates. Their parents owned cars, and their homes had hot and cold running water. Most of the homes were old but well cared for. A few of them dated back to the late eighteenth century, and quite a few of them had been owned by sea captains in the days of the whaling industry.

Walking along this road on that beautiful June morning, while the great elms arched overhead providing almost continual shade, and where they could look up and see the Baltimore orioles building their "pendant cradles" at the ends of the drooping branches, was extremely agreeable to the two boys. They tried not to be envious of the kids who lived there (Mother had told them that envy was one of the cardinal sins), but they could not help day-dreaming about how nice it would be to live in one of those houses.

When they arrived at the farm, they found Citron's aunt checking workers in. She took one look at Thos and Joe, and shook her head. "You boys don't look strong enough for this work, I'm sorry."

"We're a lot stronger than we look," Joe said.

"Well," Aunt Pauline said, "You walked all the way out here, I should give you a chance. You won't last long, though."

Then she entered their names on her list and gave them instructions.

The procedure was simple: pick up an empty basket at the check-in station, go to a certain area of the fields, fill the basket with ripe, undamaged fruit; and when the basket was full, return to the check in station where Citron's aunt made sure the basket was filled with attractive fruit and entered a number by their name. if the basket had any bruised or unripe fruit it was thrown into a bucket which would be fed to the hogs, and the picker was sent back to fill the basket properly. For Joe and Thos this was grueling work. they had to either bend way over to find the berries on the low-growing bushes, or work on their knees on the muddy ground. They had arrived at the picking fields about seven-thirty. By eleven they were totally exhausted, and Joe had been given credit for only twelve boxes and Thos for only ten. As they ate their lunch, which consisted of the raisin biscuits Mother had given them in the morning, some bruised strawberries they had rescued from the swill bucket, and fresh water provided them by the farmer's wife, Uncle Lester informed them they no longer needed them to pick strawberries. He said that they were really too small to work at this, and that their production was so slow they were only in the way. They were half glad and half very discouraged by this news. On one hand they were so tired, and their backs were so sore, they wondered how they could ever manage to finish the day, and on the other hand the idea of earning money for themselves and Mother had been very exciting.

As they walked wearily home in the hot afternoon sun, they cheered themselves up with the thought that Joe had earned twenty-four cents and Thos had earned twenty. They had been promised that the farmer would drive by the corner next to Eddie Bonard's store on Saturday, and he would pay them their wages. Tired and discouraged as they were, this was something really wonderful to look forward to.

When they got home, Patricia gave them a snack of biscuits and lemonade. She let them take an old blanket out in the shade, and they lay down to rest and dream of what they would do with the big money they had earned. Even after they had given Mother the family cut from their wages, they would each have enough to go to the movies -- wow!

Mother came home about an hour after. She was tired and discouraged too. "AT least you two guys made some money. I didn't make a cent. I did get a couple of promises, though. I'll go back at it tomorrow. You can't let yourself get discouraged when you're trying to sell stuff." Then she looked at the sad faces of her two sons. "Cheer up, you two. You made twenty-two cents for the family -- we can use every penny of it. When did you say you'll get your money?"

"Saturday. Citron's uncle is going to drive by Eddie Bonard's store sometime in the morning and he'll give it to us then," Joe said.

"What time in the morning?"

Thos and Joe looked at one another." We don't know. They just said it would be sometime Saturday morning."

Mother frowned. "How strange!" she said. "Did they give you a receipt -- a piece of paper that says what they owe you?"

Joe and Thos looked at each other again.

"They didn't give you anything that showed that they owed you money?"

"No."

Mother looked worried. "Oh, well," she finally said. "Most farmers are honest. We'll see."

The next day Joe decided he wanted to make a bird house. He had seen an article about building bird houses in an issue *of Popular Mechanics*. A friend of Mother's would sometimes give her old copies of magazines, and *Popular Mechanics* was one of the boy's favorites.

The article made it look as though anybody could easily build a very nice looking bird house. This was probably true if one had the proper tools. The Robinson family had very few tools -- an ax, a buck saw, a rake, Joe's jackknife, and a pair of old water pump pliers -- that was it. They had no lumber, no nails or screws -- no adult male to give them advice. Most kids would not have even thought of trying to build a bird house under those conditions, but Joe was not easily discouraged. He found a few boards in one of the Anneville dumps, and he began searching everywhere for old rusty nails. He also had a piece of rubber inner tube, from which he had cut a number of heavy rubber bands he used when he was making sling-shots.

He had found a few pieces of old board fence, Which he carried home and began tearing apart for material with which to construct his bird houses (By now he was determined to make at least two).

With the aid of the ax and the water pump pliers he was able to disassemble the pieces of the fence until he had several boards, and some rusty old bent nails.

He went to work on the cement steps of the back porch. He worked in the direct sun while Thos, Rosebud, and Regis sat in the shade watching him.

With the ax he chopped the boards into the correct lengths he needed for the walls of one of the houses. One of his most challenging problems was cutting an entrance hole in one of the boards, so the birds could get in and out. The conventional hole should be circular in shape. With the tools he had this was an impossibility, but he did the best he could. He traced a hole in the middle of the board he would use for the front of the house. Then with the aid of one of his larger nails, and using a stone for a hammer, he punched a series of holes in the circle he had traced in the board. With the small blade of his jackknife he cut the pieces of wood between the nail holes until he was able to knock out a ragged, but almost circular entrance hole for the birds.

Assembling the walls and roof of his rough-hewn structures was the most heart-breaking part of his project. Most of the nails he was using were bent and too big for the job. Trying to hammer them into the old, almost rotten wood, with only a stone for a hammer, resulted in the splitting of some of the boards he had worked so hard cutting into the proper shape. He managed to get the four walls put together, but it was impossible to nail the roof and the floors to the four walls. By this time he had been working well into the afternoon in the hot sun. Rosebud and Regis had long since gone back into the house because of boredom. Only Thos was still there in the shade offering what help he could, but actually doing very little for the project. Suddenly, Joe gave a little moan and slumped over. His face beet red, and his breathing labored and fitful. Thos hollered for Patricia, and ran to his brother. Patricia appeared quickly, and together they dragged the unconscious Joe into the shade. Patricia got some water, soaked her handkerchief in it, and bathed Joe's temples.

"Loosen his belt, and unbutton his shirt!" Patricia said.

Joe regained consciousness, but he was very groggy.

"Take it easy," Patricia said.

Patricia kept gently bathing his face with her damp handkerchief, and gradually Joe's face became less flushed, and they helped him into the house and up to his bed. "Thos," he asked, "could you get all of my stuff, the nails and everything, and put it in the cellar? I'll finish the bird house tomorrow."

"You stay in bed 'til Mother gets home," Patricia ordered.

Mother came home in the afternoon. When she heard what had happened to Joe,, she hurried upstairs and checked him carefully. "Dear God!" she said. "I think it was sun stroke. It could have killed him. Wasn't he wearing a hat?"

"No," Thos said.

"How many times have I told you kids to wear a hat out in the sun? Where were you, Patricia?" she asked angrily.

Patricia began to cry. "I was in the house keeping an eye on Regis and Rosebud. I . . ."

"That's okay, Dear. I know it wasn't your fault. I know you did your best." She felt his forehead and took his pulse. "He seems fine now, but we'll keep him in bed until we're sure he's all right."

Mother had made a few sales that day, so she became more cheerful once she was sure Joe would be okay.

Later she told Patricia that what had happened to Joe was very dangerous, and that what she should have done was send Thos up to Eddie Bonard's store and got him to telephone a doctor or a nurse to come and check him out. "I know this is a tremendous responsibility for you, Patricia, but you're a very smart girl, and I'm counting on you. It's just possible that I might be able to make a few dollars selling these stockings, and God knows we need every penny we can get."

Thos thought to himself, "Wait 'til Saturday comes! Then Joe and I will be able to donate some pennies to the family budget."

The next day, Wednesday, Mother went out again to sell silk stockings, and Joe went back to work on his bird house. The only way he was able to fasten the roof and the floor to the walls was with the aid of rubber bands cut from his old inner tube. This method served its purpose, and he was finally able to climb an apple tree in the empty lot next to their house and hang it on a branch in a place that would protect any tenants from cats or any other furry predators. From the backyard of his house he could watch to see if any of his feathered friends decided to nest in his strange box.

Joe was certain that the birds did not care whether their home was fancy or not. Lizzie Horton, though, irritated him when she sneered that his bird house looked like "a shanty from one of the Hoovervilles she had seen pictures of in *The Saturday Evening Post*."

By Thursday Thos saw a bird checking out the bird house. He ran to get Joe. "What does the bird look like?" Joe asked as he waited to see who his tenant might be.

"I don't know," Thos said. "Kind of a medium sized black thing."

"It better not be a starling," Joe said ominously.

"What's the difference?" Thos said. "A bird's a bird."

"No," Joe said, "starlings are pests. They're not native American birds. They keep the good birds like the bluebirds and the wrens, and tree swallows from nesting cavities. I've read that the blue birds are becoming very scarce around here. Oh, heck! Look! That's a starling sitting on the perch outside the hole. I didn't build that house for those flying rats!"

He went in the house, got his Benjamin air rifle, and began pumping it up. The starling had flown away now, but he loaded the gun with a BB and began sighting it in on the entrance to the little house.

"If that bugger comes back, I'll fix him," Joe said grimly.

Thos was kind of hoping the bird would stay away, or Joe would change his mind about murdering the poor thing. But the bird, his iridescent wings flashing in the sun, circled in and landed on the perch. Thos heard the snap of the air exploding the gun, and the bird fell like a stone. Joe and Thos ran over to where it lay motionless on the ground.

"Don't touch it," Joe said, "Birds can carry disease."

Joe got a piece of newspaper, wrapped the bird in it and threw it in the incinerator. It would be burned when they burned the trash after supper.

The whole incident was very troubling to Thos. It was one thing to see a dead rat. There was something ugly and disgusting about a rat. He hated them -- they came into people's homes, fouled food, bit babies, caused serious disease -- he had no problem killing them, or seeing their dead carcasses. But a bird! Such a marvelous beautiful thing! One minute it was sparkling in the sun; then a few minutes later, it was a dead thing being thrown into the trash. He tried to see Joe's point about the good and bad birds, but he could only think of how sad it was to see that starling toppling from that apple tree.

They got up very early Saturday and went up to Eddie Bonard's corner. The store was not open yet, but Joe figured that Citron's Uncle Lester was a farmer and would be up early too. A few cars and trucks were going by on Main Street heading north toward the farm country or perhaps to Cape Cod. This route was not the shortest to Cape Cod, but it was a very scenic way, and some people preferred to go this way.

"When do you think he'll come," Thos said.

"I hope you're not going to be asking that anymore," Joe said. "I don't know when he's going to come, we just have to wait and see. If he comes early enough, maybe we can go to the movies. Bobby said there's a Buck Jones picture at Bailey's Square."

"That's swell," Thos said. "Is Bobby going to be here to wait with us?"

"Yep, and Citron too. He knows what his Uncle's truck looks like."

"At 7:30 Eddie Bonard opened his store and began to roll down his awning. He looked at the boys. "You kids gonna buy anything?" he asked.

"No," Joe said. "We're just waiting for somebody." He said guardedly.

"Well," don't wait right in front of my store, please. You can wait over there," he said, pointing across the highway to where a low retaining wall, made of small field stones, held back a plot of grassy ground which in colonial days had been the yard of the old Quaker meeting house. Beyond the meeting house was the old Anneville cemetery where Joe and Thos sometimes walked to read the dates on the old gravestones, many dating back to the 1700's, and a few even to the 1600's.

The wall was a pleasant, shady spot, and a good place to sit and watch the cars roll by.

Then Bobby Ellison joined them.

"How much is Citron's uncle owe you?" Thos asked.

"Sixteen cents," Bobby said. "I picked eight boxes, then he fired me. He's kind of a mean old guy, I think."

"Be careful," Joe said. "Here comes Citron."

Citron had promised to wait with them so he could identify his uncle's truck which he said was an old flat-bed Dodge.

"Did your Uncle say what time he's coming by?" Bobby asked.

"I haven't talked to my uncle."

"Did your ma talk to your uncle?" Bobby asked.

"Nope," said Citron.

"While we're waiting why don't we count cars. I get Plymouths." Said Joe.

"I get Chevrolets," Citron said.

"I get Fords," said Thos.

"I get Buicks ," Bobby said, and they all nodded in agreement.

There were only a trickle of cars going by; most of them coming from the south. Whenever any truck came from the north, they all craned their necks eagerly.

By nine o'clock none of the boys had seen more than ten of their cars come by.

Joe, who wasn't talking much, finally asked Bobby if the farmer had given him any idea of when he would be coming by.

"No," said Bobby. "I asked him twice, and all he said was that he would be coming by 'in the morning.' He got kinda mad when I asked him the second time."

They all looked at Citron.

"Don't blame me, guys," Citron said defensively. "I told you he was a sonuvabitch. Heck, my mom was mad at me for telling you guys about the strawberry picking."

"Don't worry," said Joe, "we'll get our dough. But whatever happens, it's not your fault, Citron. We oughta thank you for trying to help us out."

The morning dragged by. The only good thing that happened was that Violet Harrington rode by on her bicycle to get some groceries from the store. she flashed a bright smile at the boys as she sailed by, and left four young hearts beating faster in her wake.

The boys could hardly wait until she made her return trip.

"Wow!" thought Thos. "What is it about that one girl that makes the whole world around her look so exciting?"

"The car game is over when the first guy gets to eleven. Okay guys?" Bobby said.

At about ten-thirty, the eleventh Ford, an old Model A, came by, and Thos was declared the winner; but he got no satisfaction from his victory.

For a while they talked about the news. The Dionne quintuplets had been born on May 28, and that was still a major news story. The boys could not quite understand why this was such a big deal, but they still all knew the names of Annette, Cecile, Yvonne, Marie, and Emilie. They also knew all about the exploits of Dr. Defoe, who kept the five little dark haired cuties alive by keeping them warm in the oven of a farmhouse kitchen.

A more recent front page story, and one that interested the boys much more, was that Primo Canera, the heavyweight champion of the world, was knocked out by the colorful Max Baer who was now the new heavyweight champion. Max Baer was famous for having punched two of his former opponents to death in the ring.

Joe reminded the boys that the Irish-American James J. Braddock had surprised everyone by kayoing his opponent in one of the preliminary matches at Madison Square Garden.

All four of the boys were considering the same horrible possibility -- "What if Uncle Lester did not show up?"

"The morning ends at twelve o'clock," said Joe. "If he's not here by then, I'm giving up for today."

"I'm leaving now," said Citron. You can't miss his truck -- an old dodge with slats on the side of the bed."

As he walked off, Thos's heart began to sink. "If I don't get the money today . . ." He didn't know how to finish the thought.

When twelve o'clock came, they waited another half hour and then walked away looking over their shoulders to see if just maybe they might see a Dodge truck stop at the corner.

Uncle Lester never did pay the kids a penny. Citron's mother was told that Lester would "come by" Eddie Bonard's store the next Saturday, but he never showed up. When Citron's mother tried to pursue the matter, Uncle Lester lied and said the kids were more bother than they were worth, and they ruined or destroyed so many strawberries the kids should owe him money.

The whole heartbreaking incident was never forgotten by the boys; and several years later, when Uncle Lester was publicly denounced by the SPCA for cruelty to his horses for letting them stand in their own muck until their hooves rotted, the boys got a grim satisfaction out of realizing that now everybody else knew what a son of a bitch old Uncle Lester really was.

Chapter 21

THOS AND JOE WERE both heartsick over their strawberry picking debacle, and Joe was also discouraged about his attempt to provide nesting sites for song birds. A pair of English sparrows had moved into his ramshackle bird house.

Patricia, who was given to clever, if sometimes cutting remarks, said, "Maybe if you built a nicer looking place, you'd get classier tenants."

Joe felt the same way about English sparrows as he did about starlings: they were non-native birds that drove away "good birds" who were better at insect control, in addition to singing better and being more attractive. He thought seriously of using his air rifle on the foreigners, but gave it up as a hopeless project.

The boys decided to head for the woods. There, they knew, the world always looked like a better place. During the school year, it was very difficult to find the time to go into the woods, but now that summer had come, they felt it was high time to go. As they went by Rover's house, their old wandering companion knew instantly what was up. He became so excited, he lost a little of his usual dignity and let out a few wild yelps. It had been many months since they had walked in the woods, so Joe decided he'd better ask permission from Rover's owner before they took him with them.

Mrs. Parsons smiled and said she was sure Rover was eager to go. Once more she asked them to bring him back safely. Then she looked at the boys silently for a moment. Then she looked at Rover and said," You watch over these two boys, won't you?"

Rover looked at her and then at the two boys. Thos was sure that Rover understood every word she said.

The woods had been freshened and re-decorated by the long winter and miracle of spring, and they were as "lovely, dark and deep," as ever, and all the frustrations and heartbreaks of the town were put behind them as the shade and silence of the woods enveloped them.

When they came to the stream, they drank deeply and then pushed their way through the undergrowth to Harry and Armand's spring. They had never told anyone about this pool, for they both felt there was something sacred about it. Thos followed Joe's example when he, without a word, knelt down and made the sign of the cross. They stayed only briefly, then continued on their way.

When they got to Martel's swimming place where the old log bridged the river, they were pleased with how much water there was flowing by. Joe dipped his hand in and decided it was too chilly yet to go in. Rover slurped up some of the water, but did not go in either.

"Why don't we go up the river to the blueberry patch?" Thos asked."

"That's quite a walk," Joe said, "And I don't think they'll be any berries yet."

"We can check it out anyway," Thos said. "Besides, I always like to see the old mill."

"Okay," Joe said, "let's go."

They traveled north along a narrow path beneath a canopy of large trees, with Rover doing his usual thing of scouting ahead. How the dog ever figured out what direction they wanted to go was a mystery, but he always managed to be ahead of them.

Finally they reached a place where blueberry bushes grew everywhere. They were still blooming, and Joe said it would be several weeks before there were any berries, but he said it looked like there might be a good crop that year.

Then they came to an old dirt road near which was the remains of an old water mill. The great wheel and the machinery that had once powered it were long gone, and the stone foundation and the stout oak timbers were all that was that was left of what had once been a thriving lumber mill. The ruins still managed to stir the imaginations of the boys. They ate their lunch of raisin biscuits, and each boy broke one of his biscuits in half and shared it with the grateful Rover.

"This is the life!" Joe exclaimed. "To heck with starlings, English sparrows, rats, and Uncle Lester!"

Thos picked up a stone and threw it in the river. "This is even better than going to a picture show," he said.

Thos scooped up some water from the river to take a drink, but Joe stopped him. "We'll have to wait 'til we get back to Harry's brook before we drink," he said. "No telling what kind of crud might be in the river here."

On their way back they went by Martel's swimming hole again. By this time the day had become much warmer: and even though they knew the water was still chilly, they decided to take a dip to refresh themselves. Rover took another drink of the water but evidently figured it was still too chilly for him. He explored the area for a few minutes, then he lay down near the boys' clothes.

Once they got used to the water, it was wonderful and they were both having a great time when they heard the voices of some guys coming from the direction where city kids usually came.

"I think we better get out of the water," Joe said.

They got out of the water and were standing there letting the sun dry their naked bodies, when three boys, about the age of James, came out of the woods. Thos could tell immediately that they were not from Anneville.

The largest of the newcomers, a tall, heavy-browed lad wearing a striped polo shirt, was staring at Thos and Joe in a way that was very strange: he was staring at their genitals. Never before in their skinny-dipping days had this happened. There was an unwritten, but inviolate law among Anneville boys that one should totally ignore the fact that most of the kids who swam at Martel's or any of the other swimming holes swam in the nude.

"Well, would you look at them two little guys," said the tall boy. "Naked as jay-birds!"

Meanwhile, Rover, still lying by the boys' clothes, had begun to eye the strangers warily. Thos and Joe, feeling very uncomfortable now, tried to move towards their overalls, but the big boys blocked their way.

"Look," said the tall boy. "Will you look at them little wienies? Whdddda' ya' say we pull their little peckers off and feed them to the fishes?"

The boy was probably joking -- maybe he thought it was fun to terrorize little kids; but whatever he thought he was doing, it was a big mistake.

And whether Rover understood every word the boy was saying (as Thos devoutly believed), or if the dog just simply felt the fear that gripped Thos and Joe -- no one knows. But Rover moved like lightning. In an instant he had placed himself between his young friends and the strangers.

Rover had become a fiend out of hell--a blur of fur -- all snarls, all growls, all fangs, all wild eyes. His border collie instincts had kicked in. He was now protecting his wooly flock, or herding rutting rams into a fold.

His jaws snapped and nipped but drew no blood. The startled city boys, helpless with fear, moved obediently in the direction Rover directed them, and he quickly drove them into the water, clothes and all.

Joe and Thos hurriedly pulled on their overalls, jammed their feet into their shoes and headed into the pathless deep woods while Rover kept his captives standing in knee deep water trembling with terror.

As soon as the boys had disappeared into the woods, Rover whirled and followed after them.

The city kids, making sure the demi-wolf had left, moved out of the chilly water -- their wet pants sticking to their legs, their sodden shoes making squishing sounds as they stepped onto the bank.

Joe and Thos made sure they had placed some distance between them and the "city bums," before they crouched down in a thicket; and when Rover joined them they sat down and hugged him enthusiastically. The fierce border collie had once more become the gentle, dignified Rover, Man's best friend. As they heaped praises on him in their hushed voices, Rover's tail wagged vigorously, and he seemed to smile with satisfaction. It appeared to Thos as though Rover were saying, "Man! That was really fun!"

After a while Joe crept, Indian style, close to the swimming place, and made sure the big kids had gone: then he let Thos and Rover know that they could come back to the path. They walked home with Rover staying very close to them. He was enjoying the petting and praising he was getting, but he was also making sure that no more harm would come to his charges that day.

Patricia was waiting for them when they got home, and she was very worried. I'm glad you're here, Joe. Regis put a bean up his nose and I don't know how to get it out."

"Cripes!" Joe said. "How did it happen?"

"He and Rosebud were playing with some dried beans. They dared one another to do it. Rosebud got hers out easily, but it's stuck up Regis's nose, and he screams every time I try to get it out."

Joe and Thos went in to see Regis who was sitting on the kitchen floor looking miserable.

"What's up, Chief?" Joe asked cheerfully.

"Don't try to get it out! It hurts when you try to get it out," Regis sniffled.

"Can you feel it when you stick your finger up there?" Joe asked.

"No, but it hurts when I poke around."

"I won't stick my finger up there, Chief. Just sit there and take it easy. I'll be back in a minute."

He went into the living room to talk to Patricia, who was reading *Anne of Green Gables*.

"I don't know what to do," Patricia said, putting down her book. "I've tried to get him to blow his nose -- everything. It won't come out."

"We'll just have to keep him calmed down until Mother gets home," Joe said.

"She'll kill me," Patricia said. "She told me to keep a close eye on the two of them."

In about an hour Mother came home. At first she was angry at Patricia; and then when she had no luck trying to get the bean out, she became worried about Regis. "This is my seventh child and I thought I'd seen everything, but this is something new. You all keep and eye on things. I'm going up to Bonard's and use his phone to call the County nurse, Miss Summers."

She was gone about fifteen minutes, and when she returned she said that Miss Summers was going to come by.

Miss Summers arrived in a Ford coupe. She was a heavy set jovial woman with her brown hair tied back with a blue ribbon, and a mole on her lower right cheek. She wore wire rimmed glasses, but her eyes were alert and merry.

"Well, what have we here?" she said, as she fixed Regis with a friendly smile. "A handsome red-headed little man! My! my! I bet he's very brave! Now, I'm just going to shine my flashlight up your nose and check. It won't hurt a bit."

She had Mother hold him and tilt his head back while she searched both of his nostrils. "Hmm," was all she said.

Then she took a cotton swab and gently probed his nasal cavities.

"Hmm," she said again. Then her voice became that of a health professional: commanding, and assertive. "Regis, this will not hurt, but I want you to do exactly what I tell you to do. Do you understand me?"

"Yes, Miss Summers," Regis said.

"I'm going to pick you up and hold you upside down. I want you to hold your hand over your mouth, like this," she said, demonstrating the procedure with her fleshy red hand. "Now for practice, you do it, Regis."

Regis, as always, did exactly what he was told.

"That's good!" Miss Summers said." Then she gently took both of his skinny little ankles in one hand, lifted him aloft and thumped on his back with her other large paw. Air exploded out of his nose, and then out of his mouth when his hand let go; but there still was no sight of the bean.

"I'll have to take him up to the hospital," Miss Summers said.

Mother held Regis in her arms as they drove off to the Anneville hospital.

"What'll happen if they can't get the bean out?" Thos said.

"Don't worry, the doctor will get it out," Patricia said, and then, doing an impression of Lizzie Horton, she added, "But if they can't get the bean out, it will grow; and Regis will sure look cute with that red hair and green bean stalks growing out of his ears!"

Thos, who could not remember ever riding in any motor-driven vehicle, looked longingly after Miss Summers's Ford as it drove away. "Regis is sure lucky. I wish I could get to ride in a car," he said.

"Don't say that, Thos!" Patricia, the most superstitious of the children, warned. "Remember what Mother always says: 'Be careful of what you wish for!'"

Patricia's warning would prove to be prophetic.

The doctor was able to get the bean out and Regis was none the worse for the ordeal. Mother, however, was concerned about having to leave her children in the care of a twelve-year-old girl. Mother had only made a few dollars after several weeks of hard work. Was it worth it to risk her children's safety?

Less than two weeks later and incident happened to Thos that made Mother determined to quit her job as a silk stocking salesperson and stay home to watch her kids.

It was a rainy day, and Thos, Joe, and Bobby Ellison were playing in the basement. This was not a great place to play. The center of the place was dominated by the furnace, and the walls were lined with stacked wood, and various things like a broom, a rake, an ax, and a buck saw. The buck saw was a saw blade about one and a half inches wide and two feet long that was stretched on a wooden and steel frame. There was a turnbuckle that allowed the band saw to be stretched tight, and a handle which was held by two hands when logs, held in a saw horse, were cut. Prudent people would normally keep the buck saw hung up on the wall of the garage or barn when it was not in use. The Robinsons simply kept it leaning against the cellar wall.

The boys were playing tag-- a "no-no" when Mother was home, but she had not come home from her job of selling stockings. She probably was waiting until the rain stopped before giving up for the day. Bobby was hot on the trail of Thos, who was racing around the furnace, dodging out of Bobby's grasp whenever he got close. As they passed the buck saw, Thos tripped. The soft skin of the underside of his right forearm raked across the sharp teeth of the saw blade as he fell. They tore three deep furrows in his flesh from his elbow to his wrist. At first there were only three ugly red lines, then as the blood gushed out, his whole forearm was soaked in blood.

Thos gritted his teeth against the pain as all Anneville tough guys were supposed to do, but Joe and Bobby yelled for Patricia. She came quickly, and trying desperately not to panic, she sent Joe to Bonard's to call the nurse. She told Bobby to watch Thos while she ran upstairs to get a freshly laundered pillow case. She inserted Thos's arm in the pillow case, tied her handkerchief around his upper arm to keep the makeshift bandage from coming off. Then she and Bobby helped Thos up the cellar stairs to the kitchen. They had to lay him down on the linoleum for now shock was beginning to make Thos very weak. As the blood began to soak the whole pillow case, Bobby had to grab the counter with both hands to keep from fainting. "Oh, my gosh!!" he said.

By the time Miss Summers arrived the bleeding had slowed considerably. Luckily no arteries or veins had been cut. Miss Summers took one look at the bloody mess. She did not even bother to remove the pillow case. Taking a large roll of gauze, she wrapped it quickly along the length of the arm, fastened it with adhesive tape, and said, "We'll have to take him to the hospital. You can come with me," she said, pointing to Joe. Then she turned to Patricia. "Where's your mother, child?"

"She's out working," Patricia said.

"Well, as soon as she gets back, tell her what happened. Tell her he'll be okay. As soon as we know what the situation is, I'll send word back with this lad here."

She looked at the worried faces of Patricia, Bobby, and Rosebud. "Don't worry, we'll fix this little guy up. What's his name?"

"Thos," Joe said.

The rain had stopped, and the reassurances of Miss Summers, plus the idea of getting to ride in her coupe, had made Thos feel a little better. He remembered Patricia's warning about, "Be careful of what you wish for," and wondered about whether there were something to this superstition business.

Then he almost forgot about his arm as he watched Miss Summers turn the key, step on the starter, stepping on the clutch, shifting the gears, and all the other marvelous actions that went into the driving of an automobile. "Imagine what it must be like to own your own car, and be able to drive it around!" he thought.

The ride to the Anneville Hospital was all too short for Thos: he could have ridden in that car for hours. He comforted himself by remembering that he probably would get another ride back home.

Dr. Simpson went to work quickly and gently. "This isn't as bad as it looks," he told Miss Summers after he had cleaned and examined the wounds. "He's a lucky boy that nothing critical was cut. If it doesn't get infected, he'll be as good as new in a week or two. He'll have some great scars, though." He looked closely at Thos. "How old are you, son?"

"Seven," said Thos.

"Your name's Thos?"

"Yes, Doctor."

"Well, Thos, you're quite a tough little guy, isn't he, Nurse Summers?"

Getting to ride in the coupe and being called a "tough little guy," was more than worth getting his arm torn up, Thos thought.

When he got back home, with his arm all bandaged and in a sling, Thos felt almost like a hero.

But Mother did not treat him like a hero. "How many times did I tell you not to play in the cellar?" she said severely. "If you weren't bandaged up so much, I'd give you a good thrashing! This is the final straw! I can't leave you kids for a minute before you try to kill yourselves. First Joe gets sunstroke, then Regis gets a bean stuck up his nose, and now this!"

Patricia began to cry. "Oh, it's not your fault, Patricia. You're just too young to have that much responsibility. Don't worry, I've learned my lesson. From now on I'm staying home and taking care of my children. The few dollars I've made is not enough to take such a chance."

Then she went to Thos and carefully hugged him and gave him a kiss on the cheek. "Thank God, you're okay, Dear," she said.

Thos had to wear his arm in the sling for four days, and he was unable to play, and he certainly was not able to go to the woods. He spent the time reading books by Albert Payson Terhune about heroic collie dogs who saved their masters from danger and death.

Miss Summers came after four days to change the bandage. "Oh my," she said, "It's looking just fine! Just keep taking good care of it like you've been doing, and you'll be as good as new soon. If you promise to be careful, you don't have to wear the sling anymore."

Thos was almost disappointed. The sling had brought him so much attention and sympathy, he would miss it. He also had nurtured a small hope that Miss summers would take him for another ride in her car -- no such luck!

All the kids were happy that Mother would not be going to work any more, but no one was happier than Patricia. Looking at Thos's bandaged arm, she said: "I'm sorry you hurt your poor arm, Thos, but remember, "It is an ill wind that blows no one good.""

Thos didn't understand this, and he didn't ask for an explanation , so he never really figured out exactly what the heck it meant.

It would be some time before Thos could go back to his usual activities. At first he moped around the house and felt sorry for himself that he couldn't go to the woods. Then he made the mistake of trying to amuse himself by teasing and sometimes tormenting Rosebud and Regis. He discovered Rosebud was terrified of bugs, so he would scare her with grasshoppers or sow bugs.

He also discovered that Regis had a very active imagination and could easily be spooked with any horror tale. Thos at first tried his hand at doing impressions of Keats Gidney doing impressions of King Kong or Dracula. Then he would try to do Keats's "trance" thing, where he would cover his face with his hands, and then slowly uncover what he thought was a scary visage. This stuff scared the bejabbers out of the little red head, but what really petrified him was talk of "The Black Legion." Thos had seen pictures of this American fascist organization which professed love of Adolph Hitler and hatred of Jews, Blacks, union organizers, and Roosevelts. They wore black hoods with white skull and crossbones emblazoned on them. After Thos showed Regis a picture he had found in an old magazine, and described what horrors they inflicted on their victims, he had only to say, "The Black Legion will get you," and poor Regis would start shaking. Whatever possessed Thos to do such things is unknowable, but this sort of behavior soon got him in serious trouble with Mother. She first warned him when Regis awoke in the night screaming with a nightmare, and when Mother comforted him, Regis told her what Thos had been doing.

Then an incident occurred with Rosebud that got Thos a thrashing he would long remember: He had discovered a large spider web in a bush in the back yard of their home. A very large, yellow and black garden spider had made the web, and Thos had watched with horror when a fly had been trapped, and the spider had scuttled quickly out and finished his victim off.

Somehow Thos had talked Rosebud into coming out to watch while he captured a fly and tossed it into the horrible web. He thought she would run screaming when the spider appeared, but instead she just crouched there completely transfixed, watching the spider do his thing.

Thos might have survived his cruel joke without being punished, if he hadn't gone one step too far. While poor Rosebud crouched watching, hypnotized by the horror show unfolding before her, Thos captured a grasshopper and tossed it down the back of her dress.

Her hysterical screams rent the air and Mother and Patricia came flying out of the house. As soon as Mother had calmed down Rosebud and found out what had happened, she grabbed a hair brush and went after Thos. Never before had he seen mother so angry. He tried desperately to be tough and not cry out, but this just made her whack him even harder. Her blows were painful and her anger frightened him; but what hurt even more was the tongue lashing she was giving him: "You mean little bugger! I'll teach you how to be cruel!" And with each cutting word would lay a few extra blows on his backside. When she was finally exhausted, she ordered him to his room. "And you better stay there, you little devil, 'til I let you out, if you know what's good for you!"

Thos had learned his lesson: there would be no more tormenting little kids from now on. But his reputation for being "a mean little bugger" stayed with him for a long time.

Patricia, perhaps to give him something to do while his arm was healing besides being mean to Regis and Rosebud, took him to the Russell Memorial Library to get a library card and introduce him to the joys of reading. He first read *Pinocchio*, which he enjoyed very much, but it set him to thinking about "bad little boys," and wondering what had led him to become one of them. He resolved that when his arm got better, he would have to do something to prove that he wasn't totally rotten.

Then he got hooked on reading books by Albert Payson Terhune about heroic collie dogs, and he almost was able to forget the guilt he felt about terrorizing his younger siblings. Then he got in trouble again.

It was now August and the days were long. He was still not allowed to go out and roughhouse with Joe and his pals, so after supper he would go upstairs, sit with his back against the headboard of his bed and read his books. Mother had told him not to do so much reading, so when it finally began to get dark, he stuck the book under the covers and pushed it down near the foot of the bed. In the summer Mother sent Rosebud and Regis to bed as soon as it was dark, but let the older kids stay up for a few hours more. Regis shared Thos's bed, and Thos wanted to be out of there before he crawled in. Mother had strictly forbidden him to tell Regis any more stories.

Thos had gone out on the back porch to watch the fire flies blinking out in the grass of the common ground, when suddenly he heard a blood-curdling scream coming from his bedroom. He ran into the house and saw Regis, screaming with terror, coming down the stairs two at a time. Mother ran to meet him and cradle him in her arms. She tried to get him to tell her what happened, but all he could mumble was something about the "Black Legion." When she finally got him calmed down, the first thing she said was, "Thos! You come here! I thought you had learned your lesson the last time! I'll beat that meanness out of you, if it's the last thing I do!" This time the beating was even worse than the first one, but somehow it wasn't as painful; for now he was playing the martyr--the innocent victim being punished for something he didn't do. Soon, however, she added a new punishment more dreadful than the beating: "Thos, you march up there to your bedroom, close the door, and I don't want to hear another peep out of you for the rest of the night. Regis will sleep in my bed."

"What kind of a monster had scared the wits out of poor Regis? Was it still in the room? Would it get me?" Thos thought.

"Mother!" He pleaded, but all he got was a slap across the head. There was no sympathy from Patricia or Joe either. Whatever it was that frightened Regis was still in the room, and his only help now lay in prayer. Muttering Hail Marys and begging his Guardian Angel for help, he went up the stairs and entered the room. He quickly jumped into bed and pulled the covers over his head. As he straightened his leg, he stifled a scream. For a brief, heart-stopping moment he thought the monster had him, but then he realized that he had simply pushed his foot between the pages of *Lad: A Dog*, one of Albert Payson Terhune's best books.

He tried to explain that he was not guilty of scaring Regis this time, and that he had been unjustly punished, but it was no use. The family still believed that he had a mean streak in him. He became determined to redeem himself in the family's eyes as soon as he could.

By the time his arm finally healed well enough to where he could go into the woods, there were only three weeks of vacation left.

The scars on his arm attracted much attention, and he grew pretty good at making up tall tales about how he got them: He had fought off an angry bear. He had been attacked by a tiger; He had fought a duel with a wild Indian -- nobody, of course believed a word of these yarns, but he did get some good laughs with them. The best laugh came, though, when Joe told the boys that Thos had received the wounds trying to fight off a beautiful girl who was trying to kiss him.

While his arm was healing, Joe had helped him make a sling-shot, and as soon as the arm was healed, Joe taught Thos how to use the weapon properly. Bobby Ellison said that having Joe teach you how to use a sling-shot was like having Robin Hood show you how to use a bow and arrow.

When they went into the woods now, Joe and Thos always took their sling-shots and a pocket full of stones with them just in case they ran into anyone who gave them a bad time. They felt safe with Rover, but they didn't want him to have to do all the fighting for them. Joe could not use his air rifle because he didn't have the money to buy any more **B B's**.

Money! It seemed that no matter how much they tried to forget their poverty, something would always remind them how scarce money was. They knew that they could get along without BB's, but there were many other things that were absolute necessities. With Mother not being able to work it was quite possible that their family would not have enough money to last the winter. Certainly they would not have enough to get the electricity hooked up again. Lorraine and James were doing their best to see that this would not happen, and Mother had tried her best. Maybe it was time for Joe and Thos to try to make a few bucks to throw into the kitty. Maybe this would be the way Thos could show that he was not such a "mean little bugger" after all.

They decided they would try picking blueberries, and then try to sell them door to door.

Joe felt that the blueberries should finally be ripe, so they hiked up river to the old mill. Mother had let them take two of her old stew pots with them. They were old and leaky, but they were clean; and they had bucket handles on them which made them ideal to use for berry picking.

The bushes were heavy with large, gorgeous blueberries.

"Pick them gently and don't squeeze them. Try not to get any twigs or leaves in our buckets," Joe said. "Be careful where you step. I've never seen a copperhead here, but you never know."

They picked steadily, but their pots filled very slowly. It seemed to Thos that it took an awfully long time before even the bottom of his pot was fully covered.

Joe could tell time by the position of the sun, so when he thought they were halfway to lunch, he said they could take a short break.

They plucked some berries from the bushes and ate them with some of their raisin biscuits. They both shared their biscuits with Rover again.

"How much to you think we've picked so far?" Thos asked. "Think we've got a quart?"

"Not much more than a pint, I think," Joe said. "It takes a lot of blueberries to make a quart. I know it's hard work, but keep thinking of the money we'll make."

"How much do you think we've made?" Thos asked.

"We haven't made much -- maybe ten cents each. These are good berries. We can probably sell them for ten cents a pint."

They went back to work refreshed, and by noon Joe figured they had close to a quart each.

They were definitely getting tired, though, and by early afternoon they decided to quit and start the long walk back home.

Mother was very happy with the beautiful berries. "I could make some wonderful pies with those. Thanks to Roosevelt's agricultural surplus program we've got plenty of flour, lard, and sugar."

Joe and Thos looked at each other.

"We want to sell them and make some money for the winter," Joe said.

"Where will you sell them?"

"We'll go around knocking on doors," Thos said proudly.

"Oh, my! We can certainly use the money. But do you realize how hard that is?"

"These are good berries," Thos pointed out.

"Okay, I'm really proud that you want to make money for us. Maybe, after you sell these, you could go and pick some for making pies later in the week."

"There's plenty more there, Mother," Joe said.

The next day Mother made them wait until about ten o'clock before she let them head out on their sales campaign. First she had them wash the berries and put them into pint mason jars. They each had two pint jars, and they set out with high hopes. Mother had told them that most people would not have the money to spend ten cents for a luxury like blueberries. She told them to start up North Main street where the well-to-do people lived.

They began their sales campaign with high hopes. Joe told Thos to work the east side of the street while he would work the west. Thos soon found out that selling freshly picked blueberries was not any easier than selling packets of seeds. Mostly they met with dirty looks from the people, and snarls and growls from their dogs. After two hours of hard work neither one of them had sold one blueberry.

"Maybe we should lower the price," Thos suggested.

"Naw," Joe said, "We just gotta keep at it. We'll . . ."

"What you guys doing?" The voice came from one of three boys standing near a shed behind some elm trees. The three boys started walking towards them.

"Hi!" Joe said. "It's Skinny, Fat, and Robert. Right?"

"Right, Robert said. "You're the guy with the slingshot we saw at Martel's."

Joe turned to Thos. "This is my kid brother Thos. He's the one with the scars I told you about. Show them your scars, Thos."

Thos turned his arm so they could get a view of his wounds.

"Jeez?!" the one called Fat, said; and the one called Skinny, whistled softly.

Thos liked the looks of these three. They obviously liked Joe; and even though they lived in a neighborhood where the kids had bikes and sleds and ice skates and their parents owned cars, they seemed to accept Joe and Thos as equals. There was none of this: "Oh, you're on the town," kind of look.

Thos noticed that the shed they had been standing near had "S S S" painted on its side. He pointed to the crude lettering. "What's that mean?"

Skinny looked at his two pals. "It's a secret," he said. Then he looked at their berries. "What's with those?" he asked.

"We're trying to sell them," Joe said.

"Robert walked closer to examine the berries, and for the first time Thos noticed that he walked with a pronounced limp. "Those are good looking berries," he said, "But you'll have a rough time selling 'em around here. I deliver papers around here, and I can tell you most people are tighter than the bark on a hickory tree."

"Where should we go?" Joe asked.

"Not everybody's a tightwad," Robert said. "There are a couple of ladies who are real sweethearts - they love kids. Mrs. Hartin's a peach. She lives in that house, there, the one with the stone chimney. Then, if you go up Pequod street, that's the one up there to the right - 57 Pequod Street -- that's Mrs. Pagoska: she's not only a saint, she's pretty too. If they don't buy your berries, I know a couple of other people too."

Joe was almost dumbfounded. "You're not trying to set us up?"

Robert was hurt. "Do I look like that kind of rat?"

"No! No, I'm sorry, Robert. I was just surprised, that's all." Then Joe turned to the other two. "I know you said you were Fat, and you were Skinny, but I don't feel right calling you those names. Neither one of you is really fat or skinny. What's your real names?"

The one called Fat stuck out his hand and grinned. I'm Larry," he said, "And this is my kid brother Pete."

Joe told Thos to go to Mrs. Pagoska's house, and he went to Mrs. Hartin's. Robert was right. Mrs. Pagoska was a sweetheart. He left her house with two shiny dimes in his pocket and the memory of a smile that would probably keep him warm all winter.

Joe was equally successful with Mrs. Hartin. After thanking Robert and his pals they hurried back to tell the good news to Mother. As they walked along, Thos said to Joe, "What's wrong with Robert's leg?"

"Polio," Joe answered. "But it doesn't bother him. You ought to see him swim. All three of them are like fish -- underwater or whatever. The three of them can walk on their hands like crazy, but Robert's the best. They usually swim in a pond in the pine woods, but the Boy Scouts are draining that pond now to dig out some of the mud, so they came to swim at Martel's. They all have swimming trunks."

"They're sure swell guys," Thos said. "wouldn't it be great to live in that neighborhood?"

"Forget about it," Joe said. "Just 'cause we made forty cents doesn't mean we're off the town yet. But I agree, they're neat guys."

Mother was happily surprised with the money . "I wish I could use half of this to let you go to the movies, but I'll need every cent if we want to get the electricity turned on." She looked at Thos. "You're not really a mean little bugger, are you Dear?" and she gave him a hug.

This incident was the crowning glory of an all too short summer. Suddenly it was Labor Day and time to go back to School.

Chapter 22

Thos and Joe hated to see the summer end, but there were some advantages to the coming of the new school year. For one thing Lorraine and James were now back with the family, and their presence made Thos feel more secure and comfortable. Their stories about their summer adventures kept the Robinsons entertained and fascinated for many happy hours.

Lorraine had had an especially great summer. She had worked for a rich lady as a house maid; but, as Lorraine said, "She treated me more like a friend and a family member than a servant."

The woman's name was Russell, and she was very involved in women's rights: she loved Eleanor Roosevelt, and told Lorraine that Eleanor was even a greater person than Franklin Delano Roosevelt. Mrs. Russell said that she didn't believe in "The brotherhood of Man," she believed, "in the brotherhood and sisterhood of humanity." She believed in tolerance and religious freedom, and when she found out that Lorraine was a Catholic, she saw to it that Lorraine could get to Mass on Sundays, even though Mrs. Russell herself was Methodist. When Lorraine spoke so glowingly of Mrs. Russell, Thos could detect just a little bit of jealousy on the part of Mother.

James had worked at a summer resort in Hyannis. He worked hard, but had had fun playing baseball with some of the other guys who worked there. Mother decided that, unfortunately, Lorraine and James had not made enough money to pay for the electricity for the winter. The money they had made was much needed, but it would have to be used for shoes for Rosebud, who would now be going to school, and for mittens for all the kids, whose old mittens were all in deplorable condition.

All the children were disappointed because this meant that the Robinsons would have to spend another winter without electric lights or radio, and that Mother would have to continue to do her ironing with flat irons heated on the stovetop.

Thos's new teacher at Parting Ways School, Miss Kiezera, was another wonderful woman. She was gentle and loving, and she kept the classroom a friendly, well organized place for all of her students.

Parting Ways School, Thos was beginning to realize, was like the woods, a place in Anneville where the oppressive shadow of the Great Depression was not as omnipresent as it was in his home and on the streets of the town. This sense of security applied only to those areas of the school that were under the control of the teachers and the other staff members of the school. This did not include the schoolyard.

Thos had now gotten to know some of the kids in his class very well, and he still had a very special relationship with lovely Heather. She continued to give him much needed help with his drawing and his penmanship drills, and neither one of them gave any thought to the fact that there was a difference in the color of their skins or their economic situation. In a word they became good friends. Sometimes things would happen that would remind Thos that he and Heather were different in some ways. Heather was always perfectly dressed and groomed: it was obvious that she was cared for with loving attention to her appearance. Her pigtails were always meticulously fashioned, and the ribbons that tied off the ends of those braids were always color coordinated with her pretty clothes. No seven year old little girl ever looked any more fetching than did little Heather Kingston.

When Heather stood next to Thos, he would become conscious of how bedraggled he usually looked in comparison to her.

One day during recess Thos sought Heather out to ask her a question about the coming geography test; he had forgotten the capital of Maine and was sure it would be one of the test questions. He found her sitting by herself on a bench watching the other kids playing volleyball. Whether they had excluded her from the game or whether she just did not want to play was not clear.

He sat down and started talking to her. He noticed that the other kids were staring at the both of them, and he could tell that Heather was uneasy about the situation. He became so angry he wanted to jump up and shout, "What the heck is wrong with you people?" And he resisted the temptation to yell out an overused expression of the day, "Now that you're eyes are full, fill your pockets." He ignored the rest of the kids, however, and concentrated on letting Heather know that he appreciated her help. He braced himself to receive gibes from some of the boys, and he was ready to challenge any of them who gave him a bad time, but no one ever mentioned it.

When he asked James about this incident later, Thos could tell that his brother was considering carefully what he was about to say. "Look, Thos," he began, "it is good that you are concerned that Heather is being treated unfairly, but you will find that there is much greater unfairness going on in this country and the world. It is not only happening to Heather's people, but to many others. What to do? Do what you can -- don't ignore it or don't forget it. Remember that there are a lot of other people who are disturbed about it too. Maybe you and I can help to change things for the better in the future. It seems that there has always been a struggle going on between those who want to make the world a better place for everyone, and those who only want to make it a better place for themselves. I know whose side I'm on in this struggle, and I hope you will always be on that side too, Thos."

Now that Thos was in the third grade he was allowed to participate in one of the roughest but most beloved of the schoolyard games. It is probably called by many different names, but in Anneville it was called "cock a' rooster." The rules were simple. To begin with, all the participants gather at one end of the playing field. The dimensions of the field depend on whatever is available, but generally it is in the shape of a soccer field. At a signal all the kids race to the opposite end of the field to a pre-arranged goal line. The last kid to reach that goal line is assigned to be "it." This means he must stand in the center of the field, and as the whole gang of kids run back to the original goal line, the "It" kid must try to tackle as many of the "thundering herd" as he can. The tackled kids then become part of the "It" team and the process is repeated until all the kids on the field have been tackled. Eventually even the most powerful and quickest of the participants becomes part of the "It" team and the game is over.

The first time Thos played the game he dreaded the thought of being one of the first kids tackled, but he found out that, though he was probably the skinniest kid on the field, he could run pretty fast, and he managed to make several trips up and down the field before he was tackled. The greatest part of the game came near the end when the quickest and the strongest of the kids still remained un-tackled, and all the rest of the gang tried to bring them down. It was during one of these melees that Thos had one of his bottom teeth broken, and it gave him pain for a long time afterwards. But it didn't bother him too much, for a broken tooth was a badge of honor in the woods and fields and streets of Anneville.

Cock a' rooster was popular in the schoolyard because it was a game any number could play if they were crazy enough to enjoy it, but football was the game of choice at that time of the year everywhere else in Anneville. Touch football was very common, but, if a guy really wanted respect, he played tackle football. No one could afford helmets or pads, and injuries were common -- mostly bruises, "charley-horses," or various types of sprains and strains.

James was now attending Melville Junior High in New Bradford, and he quickly made friends with many of the city kids who constituted the main part of the student body there. He got along especially well with the athletes on the campus, and he discovered that some of them had formed a sandlot football team, and felt they were pretty good. They called themselves "The North Enders," and were eager to test their mettle against some of the guys in Anneville. James said the would see if he could try to get some of his pals together. "I don't know," he said with good-natured sarcasm, "Whether they've got the guts to play against you New Bradford guys, but I'll see what I can do."

When James told his pals about the idea of playing the North Enders, they were very excited. They would call themselves The Anneville Tough Guys, and they were convinced that they would have no trouble at all beating any team composed of only city bums.

James pronounced that while most football plays of the day amounted to "three yards and a cloud of dust," The Anneville eleven would turn that strategy into "one yard and a pool of blood."

A game between the Anneville Tough Guys and the North Enders was scheduled at Brooklawn Park on the following Saturday, and Thos and Joe were looking forward to seeing the city bums getting slaughtered.

Unfortunately for James and his pals, though, The north end of New Bradford was made up almost entirely of French Canadians, and to put "tough" before their name was a foolish redundancy.

Late Saturday afternoon Thos and Joe watched the limping and bone-weary Anneville Tough Guys straggling up Maine Street from the river. "They whipped us 18-0," James said grimly. "They taught us some lessons in single wing football. We've got a re-match next Saturday." He looked around at his dejected pals. "What do you say, guys? Are we gonna show them how fast we can learn, or what?"

"You damned right!" they all grunted hoarsely.

Every night after school James and his pals met on Taber's Field, and James's voice could be heard shouting, "Point of attack! Weak side Buck! Get at least three blockers ahead of the ball carrier on every play. Statue of Liberty! Flying wedge! Move to the ball! Move to the freaking ball!"

Corny as it sounds, after every practice they huddled, shouted, "Anneville! Anneville!" and broke for home.

The next Saturday Joe and Thos were asked to do the chain gang work at the game. "Watch yourselves," James said, "but whatever you do, keep a sharp eye on where the ball is spotted and what down it is!"

The day was overcast and drizzly. Working the chains was wearisome, and would have been boring had not the game meant so much to them.

At half-time the game was 0-0 and the players, who, of course, all played offense and defense, were exhausted. The second half became an endurance contest, and by this measure they were dead even. Bud LePierre, though, was easily the fastest and most powerful runner on the field; and in the fourth quarter, behind the blocking of Moose Boudreau, Ziggy Janowski, and Manny Souza, Bud had given his team a first and goal on the three yard line. Two plunges later they scored, and things looked good for Anneville.

With three minutes left in the game though, the North Enders had a first down on the one yard line.

Both teams were so tired now they could hardly walk, but neither would take their last time out for fear they might need it in the last seconds of the game.

Kicking a field goal was not an option; neither team had a kicker who had any accuracy at all.

On the second plunge the North Enders were only two feet from the goal line. In the horrible collision that was the third plunge, Pee-pee Pelletier managed to recover a fumble. The North Enders were forced to take their last time-out, and Anneville was able to run out the clock.

The game ended Anneville Tough Guys 6, North Enders 0.

Thos and Joe got to share just a little in the glory, for they were allowed to march in the triumphant procession which made its way across the bridge and up the hill to Anneville. Just before they reached the town hall, they assumed their offensive formation, taking up the whole street, and forcing the few cars that were on the road at that time to drive slowly behind them. Pee-pee was allowed to carry the ball, and Bud proudly wore his helmet, the only one the team had.

The word had spread throughout the town, and small clusters of townsfolk applauded as they strutted by. Joe and Thos marched a modest distance behind, carrying their sticks and chain.

The names of that proud eleven was an interesting example of the polyglot composition of the United States of America.

The game between the Anneville Tough Guys and the North Enders was just one small example of the kind of rough house play that was common in towns and cites throughout America in the thirties. Many of these boys and boys like them would, in a few years, be fighting in World War II. One likes to imagine that if Imperial Japan and Nazi Germany had known more about what was happening on the playing fields of America, they would have been less likely to think of The United States as a "decadent democracy."

So far the school year of 1934- 35 was going pretty well for the Robinsons. Rosebud was surviving her first year at Parting Ways School without any serious trouble: she had the advantage of advice from her five older siblings, and the teachers had come to have a favorable attitude toward all of the Robinson children.

James had already established himself at Melville Junior High as a good guy to get to know, and Lorraine had quickly become one of the most popular sophomores on the campus.

The real problems of the family were still unsolved, though: there still was not enough nourishing food to eat, suitable clothing was still scarce, and with the winter approaching there was still no fuel to keep them warm when the fierce New England weather blew in.

Perhaps not as critical, but still very inconvenient, was the lack of electricity; but all the family knew that this was just one of the things they would have to put up with for a while. The evening prayers always included a petition to Heaven to "Grant us an independent income that will at least allow us to keep body and soul together."

Mother was able to again have a huge load of firewood dumped into their front yard. At least this time the firewood arrived before the serious cold weather, and the Robinson boys were able to take a couple of after-school sessions to get it stacked away in the cellar. It was tough work and Thos was relieved when it was done, and they wouldn't have to do it for another year.

As the weeks dragged on the monotonous routine began to sap Thos's spirits. Try as he would he could not dispel his negative thoughts, and give in to a feeling that James had warned him to avoid: "Whatever you do," James had said, "never get to feeling sorry for yourself -- that is only for sissies. What happens--happens. Grin and bear it."

But Thos couldn't help himself from thinking about how some kids had lots of fresh fruit, fresh milk, and plenty of food to eat, while day after day his family had the same thing: oatmeal with canned milk in the morning, watery soup with cabbage and carrots for lunch, and whatever Mother could scrape up for supper.

He didn't dwell on this, but such thoughts plagued him frequently, especially when he was walking home from school.

Then one day in mid-October as he neared his house, he saw a car parked in front of it. This was a nice car -- a late model Ford V8 that looked like it was well taken care of.

He hurried to the house, and when he opened the door, he saw a very pretty dark-haired woman, and a prosperous looking middle-aged man in a suit and tie.

"Thos," Mother said, "This is your Aunt Emily and your Uncle Lloyd."

Before the tongue-tied Thos could speak, Aunt Emily had gathered him in her arms and planted a soft cool kiss on his cheek. Her eyes were blue and kind like Miss Moore's, and she smelled of summer flowers fresh from the fields."

"My goodness, Thos! The last time I saw you, you were just a little adorable infant! You looked like your father then, and now you're the spitting image of him!"

She caught herself, and looked apologetically at Mother. Aunt Emily was Daddy's younger sister. she had won beauty contests as a teenager and married Uncle Lloyd, a man who owned a clothing store in Florida. Thos could not remember ever seeing either of them before.

The visit from Aunt Emily and Uncle Lloyd was a red letter day in the lives of the Robinsons. They only stayed until about ten o'clock that night. Mother tried very hard to get them to stay the night, but Uncle Lloyd, who had looked unhappily at the soup and stale bread for supper, and was totally astonished at the kerosene lamps the family had to use for lighting, insisted that, "he and Emily had to move on." He pointed out that, "At times like these a business man cannot stay away from his business very long, and he needed to visit Boston before he headed back to Orlando.

Before he left he looked quizzically around at the kerosene lamps. "Has there been a power failure around here?"

Aunt Emily quickly interrupted, him. "Lloyd, dear, have you forgotten? The Depression is here. Lot's of people can't afford electricity."

"I apologize for my stupidity, Mrs. Robinson," Uncle Lloyd said, with obvious embarrassment.

Before they left he had found out how much the monthly electric bill would be, and wrote out a check for fifty dollars and slipped it to Mother. "This should give you lights for a year. I truly wish I could do more."

Aunt Emily, for her part, gave each of the Robinson kids a dime, a deed that would live in the memory of each of the kids for the rest of their lives.

As the visitors drove off into the night to the waves of Mother and her seven happy kids , Mother said, "Children! We'll have electricity and radio for a whole year!" She looked skyward. "Thank you, Dear God!" Then she turned to her children. " We're adding Aunt Emily and Uncle Lloyd to our prayer list tonight, and we'll pray for them from now on."–

CHAPTER 23

ONE PIECE OF ADVICE that people like to give to those who live miserable lives is: "If you want to forget about your own troubles, think of those whose troubles are worse than yours." This advice, like most advice, is easy to give and hard to take.

Mother tried earnestly to consider the woes of others. She was able to scrape up the eighteen cents a week for the *New Bradford Times* which kept her abreast of the national and international news.

Friends would give her second hand copies of some of the popular magazines of the day: *Liberty, Saturday Evening Post*, and her favorite: *Good Housekeeping*.

As long as she had electricity, she had her radio back; and she could listen to late-breaking news, and to pundits and commentators.

From these sources Mother and her older children discovered that many groups of people were a lot worse off than the Robinson family. Mother would grow angry when she would read about the violent treatment visited upon blacks and union organizers; and her heart ached when she read of the suffering of the dust bowl victims, the wretched condition of the coal miners in Appalachia, the grinding poverty of the rural South, and the desperate plight of the ethnic communities in urban America.

There was little Mother could do about these matters,, but she was registered to vote; and in the November, 1934 election she voted for any candidates who backed Roosevelt, for she was convinced that he was the great hope of the little people in her country.

She also made up her mind that she would do whatever she could do to help miserable people in her own community. This attitude led her to become involved in a situation that became one of the most sensational events of the year in the town of Anneville.

Mother knew there were many poor souls in town who were more miserable than she was, and the most unhappy of these, she found out, was Cecile Laval. Hector Laval was able to find work on the farms sporadically. Sometimes, especially in the winter, he could find no work at all, and would mope bitterly around the house making life miserable for his family, particularly Cecile.

Sometimes Mother would hear Hector screaming and cursing at Cecile, and occasionally Mother could tell from the pleading and sobbing of Cecile's voice, that he was abusing her unmercifully.

One day Cecile appeared at the door bruised, battered, and crying pitifully.

"Can I come in, Mary?"

Mother hugged her and brought her into the parlor. "Sit down in the Morris chair, Dear, and I'll fix you a nice cup of tea."

"I'm afraid, Mary, He might come over here after me, and he might hurt you too."

Mother's Irish flared up. "If that big rat come in this house, he'll leave on a slab! No man on this earth is ever going to push me around again!"

Cecile began to weep. "What can I do, Mary? I'd leave him in a minute, but how can I live? I don't have a cent. I couldn't get to my folks in Montreal, and even if I could, they're as poor as I am. Besides, there's the children. Yvonne, Theresa, and Francois are old enough to take care of themselves, but poor little Gilbert needs a mother."

"Cecile, I'm not the one to tell you how to deal with problem husbands. I haven't done too well at that myself. In my case I think I'm better off without a man who only added to my miseries, but I can't tell you what to do. All I know is that you can't give up. Fight back! You won't always win, but you'll feel better if you fight back. That's about all I can tell you. If things get too bad, you can always come here. We'll have a cup of tea together and cry on one another's shoulders." Then Mother smiled bitterly "that bugger won't dare come here. If he does, by St Patrick! I'll let him have it with one of the shillelaghs my boys made." Her eyes twinkled. "You ought to see those little war clubs! There are two of them--one for each of us. If he comes over here, we could give that big rat what he deserves!"

Cecile finally smiled. "I sure wish I had your spunk, Mary," she said.

During the dreary winter that followed, Mother and Cecile had many cups of tea together, but the subject of Hector's abuse was not discussed again. The sound of Cecile and Hector quarreling was still heard too frequently, but there evidently were no more violent episodes, and Cecile never again brought up the subject of how miserable she was. Mother wondered about this, but was not about to bring up the subject herself.

Shortly after St. Patrick's Day, though, Cecile came over for another cup of tea. Mother knew immediately that Cecile had not come to simply sip tea. There was a strange look in her pretty eyes -- not the usual look of misery -- it was almost a glow. It was a look of desperate longing -- the look, Mother thought, of someone hopelessly in love.

"I've gotten myself in such a mess, Mary. I have no idea what I can do!" and she buried her face in her hands, and her shoulders shook with sobs.

Mother found a clean handkerchief and handed it to her. "There, there, dear. Go ahead and cry. sometimes it helps." she said.

Cecile cried for a while, then sniffled and blew her nose. "I hate to burden you with this, Mary, but I've got to tell somebody."

"Whatever it is, Cecile, I don't want to hear it. You must have somebody else . . ."

"Please, Mary! You're the only one who might understand. Maybe even you will think I'm dirt and won't let me in your house again."

At this, Mother prepared herself for a shock, but she wasn't prepared for the outburst that followed.

Cecile again put her hands over her face, and sobbed as she tried to talk: "I'm having an affair, Mary! I've got five kids, I've been married for fifteen years, and I'm having an affair! I'm so ashamed!"

Mother stared at Cecile in stunned silence.

"No," Cecile continued. "I take that back. I'm not ashamed! I'm in love! I've never been in love before. What I had for Hector -- there's a name for it, but it wasn't love -- no excuses -- when he lost the farm -- Gilbert is three years only, Mary -- Hector can't----. He made me swear I'd never tell anybody -- what happened isn't what you think, Mary. I'm in love -- he loves me, he wants me to divorce Hector. Oh God! Mary, What a mess!"

She stopped, waiting to see if Mother would say something, but Mother, for once in her life, had lost her gift of gab. All she could manage to say was, "Who in the hell is this man?"

Cecile took a deep breath. "It was like lightning. It was in Gabrowski's grocery. I saw him looking at me.

He smiled and said, 'I saw you at Mrs. Robinson's. Your husband was helping clean up the dump.'

That's all he said. But the way he was looking at me! And, God help me, the way I looked right back at him -- it was like an explosion that starts a wildfire that nobody can put out!"

Mother interrupted. "Cecile! Who is it?"

"Giles Brewster!" Cecile said, and when she said his name, her face lit up like a high school girl telling her classmate about her new boyfriend.

"Oh Dear God!" was all Mother could say.

"I know it's crazy -- I know I'm terrible -- I know the people of Anneville will tar and feather us or make me wear a big scarlet "A" or something -- I don't care! And Giles doesn't care either."

Mother looked at her friend and said, as kindly as she could. "Cecile, dear. What about your children?"

Cecile's exuberance faded, and she began to weep again. "I don't know what to do, Mary, I just don't know."

"Do you think I'm a tramp, Mary?"

"No, dear. Even the vilest hypocrite wouldn't call you that. But sometimes you do sound like a starry-eyed flibbertigibbet. You say that Giles says he wants you to divorce Hector and marry him. Did he actually say that?"

"He did, Mary, We've been talking about it for weeks. That's why I had to talk to you. I know you're a good Catholic and all. You probably think that divorce is sinful and immoral."

"I'm not going to talk to you about religion. My religion teaches me to 'judge not lest you be judged.' If you insist, I'll talk to you the way I'd talk to my daughters if they were in your situation. Okay?"

"Please, that's what I need. Help me, Mary."

"I don't think I can help you, Cecile, but I can try to make you see this thing more clearly."

Cecile put her hand on Mother's. "Thank you," she said. "I was so afraid you'd . . ."

Mother patted Cecile's hand. "Now, have you any idea how much legal rigmarole a divorce causes in this state? "

"Giles talked to me about that. We both realize it's going to be a mess."

Mother took a sip of tea, then offered Cecile a raisin biscuit, which she waved off.

"What about Hector? From what I've heard, he can get violent."

"Poor Hector," Cecile said, and her lake-blue eyes were genuinely sad. "You don't really know what a tortured soul he is. I can't help him. He's even told me he'd be better off without me. Losing his farm, not being able to find work, having to ask for and accept hand-outs -- all of that has broken him -- taken his manhood away in more ways than one."

"That's happened to a lot of men. It's just one more horror of these horrible times. But that doesn't give him the right to take out his misery on you," Mother said.

"Even so, I don't want to hurt him, but he wants to keep custody of the children, and I can't let him do that. The three older ones might be able to get along if we had divided custody, but I must have Gilbert. That's my big problem: I can't live without Giles now, and I can't leave Gilbert."

Mother was silent at this. She looked up at a crucifix that hung above the door to the parlor.

"Cecile, dear Cecile, I can't help you there. Have you talked to your minister about this?"

"I've never talked to him about anything personal. I don't even go to services very often. I guess I don't want to hear what he would tell me."

"What does Giles say about all this?"

"He says our immediate problem is a legal one, and that's what he wants to concentrate on. He said I could probably get custody of the kids. There would be an ugly court battle, but he thinks I would win. He said he can tell me exactly what to do legally, but he can't tell me

211

what to do morally. He's the one who suggested I talk it over with you. He said you're the only really

moral person he knows."

Mother became flustered, then sardonic. "Your Giles is in trouble if he really believes that."

"You're the strongest person I know, Please help me, Mary."

"I'm really sorry, Cecile. You have to make this decision for yourself -- only you can decide. I know if I were you I'd have to think of the welfare of my children first-- especially little Gilbert. You know enough about Hector to know whether the older kids would be okay with him. It isn't like you'll never see them again. when they're a little older they can decide for themselves who they want to live with. That's all I can tell you. I'll do anything else I can to help, but I can't be your conscience." Mother got up and hugged Cecile. "I'm very flattered that you trust me, but I'm afraid that all I can give you is tea and sympathy."

But it turned out that Cecile and Giles needed more than tea and sympathy from Mother. Hector sued for divorce on the grounds of infidelity, and demanded custody of the children, alleging that Cecile was an unfit mother.

Giles asked Mother if she would testify that Hector had abused Cecile, and at least in one instance, had abused Gilbert -- the time he draped Gilbert's wet pants over the poor child's head. The last thing Mother needed was to get involved in this mess, but she felt that she had no choice. Giles had been her only advocate on the board of selectmen, and Cecile was a neighbor and good friend: Mother agreed to testify.

Anneville was no worse than any other town in its appetite for gossip and salacious details about an adulterous affair, but it certainly was relishing every bit of news about this case; and people were choosing up sides as to whether they sympathized with the lovers or were outraged at the scandalous behavior of one of their selectman and his adulterous paramour.

The trial began in the early summer of 1935. The Robinson family had once more survived a long dreary winter -- in fact things had not gone too badly: Lorraine and James had done very well in the New Bradford schools, and Rosebud had quietly and stoically endured her first year at Parting Ways. All the family was looking forward to summer, despite the fact that they were worried about Mother having to testify publicly in the sensational Brewster-Laval case.

Of course none of them was allowed to attend the trial; however, a vivid account of Mother's brief testimony appeared in the *New Bradford Times* the day after she testified:

"Mrs. Mary Robinson, an attractive blue-eyed beauty, testified that Laval had abused his wife and their child. Her testimony appeared to have had a telling effect on the jury, so when Mr. Evans, the plaintiff's lawyer cross-examined the Robinson woman, he tried desperately to shake her testimony. His attempts failed to pierce the calm, earnest demeanor of his witness until, in apparent desperation, he fired a bombshell: "Mrs. Robinson, you are a very attractive woman. I remind you that you are under oath when you answer this question:" his voice rose dramatically as he shouted, "Have you, yourself, ever had an affair with our local Casanova, Mr. Giles Brewster?"

Amidst the shouts of 'Objection! Objection!' and the pounding of the judge's gavel, Mrs. Robinson rose from the witness chair, her blue eyes blazing with indignation, "Never! Never!" she shrieked.

When the trial was finally over, Cecile was granted custody of Gilbert and visiting rights to her other children. During the trial Giles, who had resigned his position as Selectman, lived in his summer home at Mattapoisett, and Cecile lived at Giles's mother's home in Fairhaven. After the divorce was final, they drove to Elkton, Maryland, and were quietly married. Then they moved into Giles' Mattapoisett home with little Gilbert.

Most people agreed that Mother's dramatic performance on the witness stand had won the case for the Brewsters, and most people admired her for her willingness to stand by her friends in their time of need.

Cecile and Giles were very grateful to Mother, and as soon as they got settled, they invited Mother and her five youngest children (James and Lorraine were away working on Cape Cod) to their home for a memorable day at their beach front home.

Giles picked them all up in his wooden station wagon (known then as a "beach wagon"), and drove them the twenty miles to his place.

Just the long ride in the beach wagon alone would have been enough to make Thos totally happy, but the whole experience was almost as wonderful as Christmas Day itself. He had never seen the ocean before. Actually, Mattapoisett is on Buzzards Bay, but to Thos and the rest of the kids, this was the Atlantic Ocean. The food and hospitality lavished on them was something they had never experienced before in their lives, and nothing could have pleased Mother more than to see her children so happy. It also gave Mother much pleasure to see her friends Cecile and Giles so deliriously in love.

As Giles drove Mother and her kids back to Anneville, Mother thought: "Maybe there is much truth in the old bromide that says, " The best way to be happy is to try to make others happy."

CHAPTER 24

Respect is as essential to the health of the human spirit as vitamins are to the health of the body.
-Harry Hopkins-

SOME PEOPLE IN AMERICA, even during The Depression, had contempt for poor folks, especially those wretches who accepted public assistance. It was believed that anyone who takes hand-outs is somehow morally deficient and is responsible in some way for his own plight. This attitude was widespread in Western culture, and it was believed by many that those who accepted public charity should be made to feel ashamed of themselves. Thus they would not come to expect such assistance and take it for granted.

James once talked about why people acted this way. At a family gathering he said that he believed that there is an innate need in the darker regions of the human soul to have some people to pity and look down upon. He said that this feeling often degenerates into hate. Evil men sometimes turned this need to hate into powerful political movements; and he gave the examples of Adolph Hitler's Nazis, and the Ku Klux Klan in America. He also cited Robert Frost's poem, "Fire and Ice," in which the poet predicts that the world might someday be destroyed by hate.

James said facetiously that he believed that if the world ever got to a place where everybody was really equal in the eyes of their fellow man, many people would be very unhappy because they would have no one to look down upon. Therefore, in that event, we could hire people to go around pretending they were inferior. They could shuffle about the community with hang-dog looks, and act as though they wanted people to forgive them for being alive. These actors would be well paid, and when they were off duty they could get pleasure out of lording it over the other "inferiors" who were on duty.

Both James and Lorraine were now attending New Bradford High School and were respected and popular. Their classmates could tell that James and Lorraine were not very well off: this was obvious from their clothes and their meager stock of school supplies -- notebooks, pencils, pens and such. Since this was very common among most students, no one paid much attention to this, but occasionally something would happen that reminded James or Lorraine of the dire state of their finances.

Soon after James started at New Bradford High, one of the coaches approached James and asked him to "go out" for football. James, who knew that this would require ten dollars to pay for the health insurance needed for any student who wanted to play on a school team, simply said that he couldn't go out for any team because family obligations made it necessary for him to go directly home after classes were finished. A kid named Steve Simpson overheard this exchange, and confronted James in the boys' rest room. "Hey Robinson! I know why you don't want to go out for football: you're afraid of getting hurt -- you're nothing but a pantywaist."

James's temper flared, and he grabbed Steve, lifted him off the ground and held him aloft a few inches from a brick wall. "Look, you little jerk! The only reason I'm not slamming you against this freaking wall is that I don't want the wall to get all covered with crap! If you want to find out who's the panty-waist here, meet me any place off the school grounds at any time! I'll show you "pantywaist!"

James set the kid down, and Steve skulked away with one of his pals telling him, "Jeez! You damned fool! Didn't you know that guy's from Anneville?"

* * *

Christmas vacation began that year on Saturday. James took Thos and Joe to go hunting for the Christmas tree. Patricia was over at Lizzie Horton's house. She and Lizzie were both working on their Dionne Quintuplet scrapbooks; and Regis and Rosebud were playing in the dining room, so Mother and Lorraine were able to chat privately in the parlor.

"It's going to be a great Christmas this year; we might even get snow" Mother said.

Lorraine spoke in a half-whisper, so Rosebud and Regis wouldn't hear. "That would be great. This is the first time since we left Pennsylvania that we'll have a sled under the tree for the kids, and to have a white Christmas would be a miracle. You have it hidden where they can't find it I hope?"

"It's covered with an old blanket up in the attic, so even if they go up there, and they won't go up there if they know what's good for them, they won't see it. You understand that it's not a new one, but the American Legion men painted it up and it looks and smells like new."

"Those men are very kind," Lorraine said, "but I wish we could, just once, get something nice without depending on charity."

"Now, Dear, let's not go into that again. We wouldn't have much of a Christmas without help from kind people. After all, everyone is dependent on the charity of God for everything they have."

"You're right, of course, and I am grateful for everything. I've really had a great year so far."

"You love that school, don't you dear?"

"I do, Mother, I really do. When I'm there I feel -- I feel almost like I'm not on the town anymore. The kids don't have any idea of how poor we are: most of my friends are very well off -- they live in nice homes and have cars and everything. Elaine--she's one of the best-looking girls on campus--keeps asking me to stay overnight at her house. It's a great feeling to be treated like -- well like I'm just as good as they—"

"That's foolishness, Lorraine! I don't want to hear any more of that! You're not only as good as they are: you're better! Our family in Ireland was descended from royalty!"

"Mother! Please don't keep saying that! I don't care who we're descended from, we're still dirt poor, and we have to live on hand-outs! And I hate it!"

"Let's change the subject, Dear." Mother said gently. "This is going to be a great Christmas. Even better than usual. They're finally going to let me sing a solo: 'Oh Holy Night.' Do you remember how I used to sing that at Midnight Mass in the Church of the Resurrection? The organist, Leonard, would get tears in his eyes when he accompanied me. Those were happy days. Were you happy then too, Dear?"

"Yes, I was happy then, but I'm mostly happy now, too. I'm sorry if I sounded like I wasn't. I'm glad you're going to sing 'O Holy Night.' Wait 'til they hear you sing that one, there'll be a lot of teary eyes in St. Francis Xavier's this Christmas morning too, Mother!"

Monday December 23, was "Get the house cleaned up for Christmas" day. Mother was directing all seven of her children in cleaning every square inch of the house with the exception of the attic which was strictly off-limits for Joe, Thos, Rosebud, and Regis. Thos, now 8, was well aware that the attic was where the Christmas presents were stored. Both he and Joe had known for several years that the idea that Santa brought the gifts on Christmas Eve was only a pleasant fiction. When Lizzie Horton had told them two years before, she warned them that they were never to let the grown-ups know that they no longer believed in Santa Claus, for once the parents found out, there would be very few, if any, Christmas presents from then on.

Thos liked the presents, but that was only one of the many reasons why he loved the whole celebration of the holiday. Even the work of cleaning the basement, his chore on clean-up day -- and a dirty, dusty, and tiring chore it was -- failed to dampen his Christmas spirit. The house was filled with the smell of the fresh pine tree that he and his brothers had found in the woods, he had seen baskets of food delivered to the house by the American Legion, The Salvation Army and other kindly organizations. And, Alleluia!, they were now on vacation from school!

Then, in the early afternoon, disaster struck! Just after Thos had finished drying the dishes from lunch, a shiny, splendid Packard pulled up in front of the Robinsons' house. The driver, a distinguished, white-haired gentleman, stepped out, went around to the passenger's side and helped out an attractive, well-dressed woman. Then, from the back seat of the car emerged two very pretty teen-aged girls. The gentleman opened the trunk, and he and the two girls each picked up a cardboard box and began carrying them to the house. The gentleman knocked on the front door, and when Mother opened it, the gentleman stepped aside, and let the prettiest of the two girls, who had evidently been elected to be the spokesperson, say, in a very lovely voice: "Good afternoon! My name is

Elaine Harwood. These are my parents, Dr. and Mrs. Harwood, and this is my friend, Beverly Blaine. Beverly and I are Rainbow Girls, and on behalf of our club we would like to wish you and all of your seven children a very Merry Christmas. Is it all right if we put these gifts inside your house, or, if you prefer, on the porch?"

Mother was surprised, but she maintained her dignity. "Oh, my gracious! How nice of you all to come! Thank you very, very much, and a Merry Christmas to all of you! Come on in! Come on in, please!"

They came in and set the cardboard boxes where Mother directed them, and for a moment stood awkwardly around and surveyed the Robinsons' living room. For a moment the only sound was the gurgle of the kerosene bottle as it fed some of the fuel to the stove. Then Elaine gasped. "Oh, Lorraine! For goodness sake! What are you doing here? Are you helping these people out too? What club are you with?" Then, suddenly, she stopped and put her hand over her mouth. " Oh, my gosh! Robinson! Are they, like, relatives of yours? Oh . . ."

Lorraine's face was pale and drawn, but she retained her composure. "Yes, Elaine, they are my relatives -- this is my home -- this is my Mother, these are my brothers and sisters. We -- we want to thank you for your kindness. It is very nice to meet you, Doctor and Mrs. Harwood. Mother, this is Elaine Harwood; and these are her parents, Dr Harwood, and Mrs. Harwood. This is Beverly. Elaine and Beverly are the good friends at school I've been telling you about."

"How do you all do?" Mother said graciously. "Welcome to our home, and let me fix you all a nice cup of tea."

Elaine's father had quickly grasped the situation. He had heard much about this Lorraine. Evidently she was a very clever girl who had passed herself off as someone belonging to the same social class as his daughter and Beverly Hutchinson. Now she had been found out. Now, at least, Elaine knows what kind of trash this Lorraine really was. Well, he would straighten this mess out with his wife as soon as they got out of this dreadful neighborhood.

"Thank you very much, Mrs. Robinson," Dr. Harwood said icily. "But we know that this is a very busy time of the year. We must apologize for barging in on you like this, and we must be moving along. It's been a great pleasure meeting all of you." He shook Mother's hand, bowed, and hurriedly shepherded his small flock out the door.

Mother stood on the front porch and waved goodbye as the Packard pulled away.

When they were well out of sight, Mother hurried inside the house. "James, you get the rest of the kids bundled up warmly and take them out in the back yard. Don't come back in until I call you. I want to talk to Lorraine. By the time the kids had got their warm clothes on, they could hear Lorraine crying in the bathroom. solemnly they trooped out and left the house to Mother and her first born child.

"Please, Dear," she said, "Come out. We've got to talk. James has taken all the other kids out. Come out, please, Honey, I need someone to hug."

Lorraine came out, and the two women clung to each other and wept silently for a while.

Then Lorraine stopped crying, gently moved away and dried her eyes with her handkerchief. "That's enough weeping," she said: "Let's bring the kids in; it's cold out there."

"I just checked them through the window; they're okay. James has them playing ball -- you know him. He's even got Regis and Rosebud in the game. They're all having fun. We have plenty of time for a cup of tea. If I know Patricia, she won't be back from Lizzie's for at least another hour."

Mother quickly filled the kettle and set the tea things on the table.

"Sit down, and we'll have a good chat." While she was preparing the tea, she talked about the weather and the Christmas preparations, but when she had finally poured the tea, she became serious, "I can only guess how much pain you feel right now, but you don't know what real pain is until you have a child of your own that's in pain and you can't do anything to take the pain away. It may not be as bad as you think: Elaine and Beverly seem like very nice girls . . ."

"Mother," Lorraine broke in, "I'm not going back to that school; I can't."

"You can and you will. I won't let you quit school and that's final! I don't want to hear anymore of this foolishness. If you know what's good for you, you won't bring it up again!"

Lorraine set her cup down firmly. "No, Mother! I'm never going to set foot in that school again! I'm quitting school and I'm getting a job. And, if you know what's good for you, Mother, you won't try to stop me!"

"Please don't mock me, Dear," Mother ordered, then her voice became softer. "But you said you loved school! Elaine and Beverly -- and the other girls! What about your boy friends -- Don and Lawrence? And Richard? Lorraine, Dear, I know you have a crush on him. You should see how your eyes light up when you talk about Richard."

"All that is over, Mother. It ended when Elaine and Beverly walked through that door. I know it sounds melodramatic, and you think I'm playing the martyr; but I was living a lie, and now I see the truth. I hate having to accept charity. I know you hate it too, but you're helpless because of those kids out there. But I'm not a kid anymore and I'm not helpless. And as soon as I can, I'm taking you all out of this – this pit we're in. God willing, I'm getting us off the town and out of Anneville forever."

Mother wept. "But it'll break my heart if you quit school!"

But nothing Mother could say would change Lorraine's mind. Finally, the two of them agreed not to talk about this matter until after Christmas -- "We'll at least make sure that the kids have another wonderful Christmas, then we'll discuss your future," Mother said.

It was another very Merry Christmas. The sled was, all the kids agreed, the best present of all. The snow started to fly the day after Christmas, and the sled was soon put to very good use. The fact that there was only one sled for the seven children was no problem -- maybe one of the few good things about poverty is that one learns to share willingly and cheerfully.

Lorraine never set foot on the New Bradford High campus again. She had James notify the registrar that she was quitting school, and wrote a letter to her summer employer, Abigail Russell, asking her if she could send her a recommendation, and if she had any friends who needed a live-in house maid.

Mrs. Russell immediately replied and offered Lorraine a job in her Sudbury home. She said she would be very happy to have her come to work for her, and if Lorraine agreed, she would drive down to Anneville to pick her up. She said that Lorraine and Mother and she could negotiate the wages, the hours, and the working conditions at that time.

Lorraine was ecstatic. Mother was still reluctant, but she now realized that it was useless to try to change Lorraine's mind.

After the meeting with Mrs. Russell, Mother was much less opposed to Lorraine's plans.

Mrs. Russell was very sensitive to the situation. She made it seem as though getting Lorraine to work for her was the nicest thing that had happened to her in a long time. Without making it appear as though she were being charitable, she offered Lorraine a very generous deal – forty-eight dollars a month, a forty hour week, board and room; and she would see that Lorraine could get to Mass every Sunday.

Luckily, Mrs. Russell had come down on a Wednesday, when all the kids except Regis were in school. Regis watched sadly while Lorraine loaded her things into Mrs. Russell's La Salle. Lorraine tried to keep her eyes dry as she hugged him, then, leaving Mrs. Russell standing by the car, she went in and said goodbye to Mother. "It's going to be fine, Mother, you wait and see."

Mother managed to remain calm. "God be with you, Dear. Now get out of here quickly, before we both . . . Mrs. Russell is waiting for you, darling. Don't forget to write!"

Lorraine hurried out and climbed into the car. Mother waited until the car was gone, then she went into her room, fell on the bed. She wept silently for a few minutes, dried her eyes, and went out to check on Regis and start on the ironing.

Chapter 25

After Lorraine left, Mother lost much of her fire. The January cold clamped its icy fingers all over New England, and even though the financial condition of the Robinsons had been improved because of Lorraine's employment, an air of gloom settled over their house on Hill Street. Mother was so depressed she seldom left her bed: and Patricia had to shoulder most of the command of the house. Patricia, and sometimes James, were allowed to consult Mother about household matters, but none of the other kids were allowed to disturb Mother when she was in bed. James found out from Regis that Mother would come out of the bedroom when the kids were at school, and that she made sure that he was taken care of. Once Regis asked James, "What's wrong with Mother?"

"She misses Lorraine, and she just can't stand the cold anymore." James said.

"I miss Lorraine, too," Regis said.

James had managed to get an after-school job with a woodcutter who ran a miserable little business when the weather was cold. During the day he went into the woods and gathered dead trees and fallen branches, and piled them into an old model A truck he would park as close to the woods as possible. He dumped this wood in front of his ramshackle hut on the edge of town. He offered James fifteen cents an hour to work after school cutting up the wood into bundles. At night he and James would drive into New Bradford and try to sell the wood to passers-by for ten cents a bundle. If business was bad, they would have to resort to door-to-door peddling.

It was cold and dirty work, but that wasn't the worst of it. Occasionally Thos and Joe would walk out to where James and Mr.

Portier were working. Portier had rigged up a large buzz saw to a table. He would jack up the back wheels of his truck and run a belt from the drive wheel to the saw. Once the 36 inch blade was spinning, it could cut through the thickest logs with ease. there was no shield on the blade, and the only way it could be stopped was by shutting off the engine -- there was no switch near the saw, there were no brakes. A safety inspector would have turned pale at the sight of it.

The thought of James working with this dangerous contraption was so frightening to Thos he had a nightmare about it, and that Sunday he offered up his Mass for the safety of his big brother.

If the weather were cold enough, James could make as much as three dollars, which could be put to good use buying groceries. Now, though, he had little time or energy for schoolwork, so his grades suffered considerably. He was no longer able to earn all "A's" and be a candidate for "top of the class."

Life was very dull for Thos and Joe while the snow was heavy. Their sled had broken down under its continuous use: a bolt holding the runners to the wooden frame had worked loose and become lost in the snow. No amount of searching did any good. Once again the Robinsons were without a sled.

But one incident happened in January that livened things up a little.

On a bitterly cold afternoon Robert Aumont was delivering newspapers in the neighborhood. Because of the snow, he was unable to ride his bike, and had to trudge around his route by foot.

As he neared the Robinson house, he took a short cut across the common land. The swampy ground was frozen solid and he would have had no trouble if a gang of Anneville street rats had not decided to attack him. They were like a pack of wolves attacking a lone caribou floundering through the arctic snow. Robert was a tough kid, and with well-aimed snowballs he was able to keep them at bay. But the kids were not just content with pelting him with snowballs and keeping him from his route; they were taunting him about his polio damaged leg with cries of "hop-a-long!" and "Gimpy!"

Joe spotted the situation from the Robinsons' back window, and he and Thos threw on their outdoor clothes and ran to the rescue. Between

Robert, Joe, and Thos, they quickly routed the attackers and scored some pretty good snowball hits on the cowards as they scurried away.

Joe invited Robert in for a cup of hot cocoa, but he thanked them and said he didn't have time because he had to finish his route. "You guys saved my bacon out there, though, and I won't forget it," he said.

"Joe and I haven't forgotten how you helped us sell our blueberries that time near your house, either," Thos told him as he left.

Evidently Robert Aumont's mother was very impressed with Joe and Thos's "rescue" of her son. She had known James because he played baseball and football with her son Jerry, and she had heard about some of Mother's exploits, but she was too busy trying to raise her own brood of seven kids to pay much attention to the Robinson clan. A few days after the snowball fight, however, while the kids were in school, Mrs. Aumont paid a visit to Mother.

Florence Aumont was the kind of woman that kids would automatically recognize as a mother figure -- a woman who loved them all, and who would like nothing better than to scoop them up in her arms and hug them to her ample bosom. Adults too would usually succumb to her smile and kindly eyes. Mother, though she had just got out of bed, and was fixing lunch for Regis, was genuinely happy to see Florence.

"Mrs. Robinson, I hope I'm not disturbing you," Mrs. Aumont began.

"Of course not! I'm so happy to see you! And, please call me Mary."

"I'm Florence. It's too bad we can't visit more often, but, you know probably better than I that being the mother of seven kids doesn't give one time to do much visiting."

"Truer words were never spoken, Florence, but I hope you have time for a cup of tea. We can sit in the parlor while Regis finishes his breakfast."

After the tea was served, Florence got down to the purpose of her visit. "I need to ask you a favor, Mary."

"Go right ahead!" Mother said eagerly. "If it's at all possible, Ill be glad to do it."

"As you know," Florence said, "I'm the Anneville representative for the circulation department of the *New Bradford Times*. My son Robert has a huge route and I've been thinking for some time that I would divide it in half and let Robert have an easier time of it. I need an honest, hard-working boy to take over half the route, and I was wondering if I could ask your son Joe if he would be interested in the job."

Mother was flabbergasted. She wanted to jump up and hug Mrs. Aumont. The kind way in which this wonderful offer was proffered did not disguise the generosity of it. A paper route! A chance for a poor kid to earn some cash in those hard times was something that only a boy with either very important connections or extraordinary luck could ever hope for.

Joe would not earn much, of course, but the little bit he did earn would be enough to make a big difference in the family budget. Mother hugged Florence Aumont as she left, and thanked her warmly. The good news about the paper route was the spark she needed to snap her out of her personal depression.

By the time the kids came home from school, Mother was her old self again.

Joe was even happier than Mother was about the paper route. It meant that he would have to walk many a weary mile toting his bag of newspapers (a bicycle was out of the question), and that he would have to brave all kinds of weather (it was unthinkable that any kind of weather could prevent a paper boy from making his accustomed rounds). He would have to fend off some of the most vicious dogs that any man would dare to own, and that he would do all this for a very small percentage of the eighteen cents a week each customer paid to have the paper delivered to his house six times a week. The paper had to be placed carefully at each house between the doorknob and the door frame; if it were left on the porch, or, heaven forbid, thrown on the driveway or lawn, the paper boy would be fired. Despite all this Joe was delighted to have the job. He quickly learned the route, and then taught it to Thos who would take care of the route if Joe got sick or was unable to service the route for any other reason.

The coming of spring in Anneville was perfectly glorious that year of 1936. But in the rest of the world things were still far from being perfect. Hitler had consolidated his diabolical grip on Germany, Japan was gradually devouring what was left of China, Mussolini's air force was bombing and slaughtering thousands of spear-carrying

Ethiopian natives in order to bring the blessings of Italian fascism to that unfortunate country, and The Great Depression, despite all of Roosevelt's efforts, had still left "one third of the Nation ill-fed, ill-clothed, and ill-housed."

But for the Robinson family, at least, things were finally beginning to look a little better. By the time St. Patrick's Day came Mother was brimming with enthusiasm. Lorraine had been sending frequent letters telling of how happy she was, working for Mrs. Russell. Lorraine sent almost all of her salary to Mother, and this, along with what James and Joe were contributing, was making life a lot easier for all the family.

As Easter approached, the kids could tell that Mother was planning something big. Lorraine would be arriving home on Holy Thursday and be staying until the Monday after Easter. Mrs. Russell would drive her to Boston's South Station. Lorraine would board the train there; and when she arrived at the New Bradford station, James would meet her and escort her home to Anneville. They would have to walk from the end of the trolley line to home; but James would carry her suitcase, and the walk up the hill, which they had made so many times before, would be a very happy one.

Mother had prepared a wonderful Easter dinner -- baked Virginia ham, green peas, roasted yams, mashed potatoes, and for dessert, Lorraine's favorite: apple-brown-betty with whipped cream.

She had bought a bottle of cranberry juice which she mysteriously said was for a "toast" celebrating a big surprise. she said she would save the toast for the very end of the Easter feast.

The meal was so delicious and plentiful, the conversation so lively and full of laughter, the dessert so unbelievably scrumptious, that most of the kids forgot all about the cranberry juice toast and the surprise that Mother had planned.

Mother finally brought out the cranberry juice and the glasses for the toast: she, Lorraine and James used the last three wine glasses left from the "good old days," and the rest of the kids had to drink from salvaged jelly jars. When all the glasses were filled, Mother told everyone not to drink any of the juice until she gave them the signal. Then she went into her room and came out with a mysterious letter.

Standing at the head of the table, she began the ceremony: "This letter, my darlings, is a copy of one I have just sent to the Board of Selectmen. Listen carefully as I read it:

Gentlemen,

For some time, as all of you know, my family has had to beg the taxpayers of this town through you to provide us with cash assistance in order for us to keep body and soul together. All of us would like to thank you for your generosity, and we will never forget what you have done for us. However, we have finally arrived at the point where we can survive without your help. As of this date you may cease to send us the weekly seven dollar check which has meant so much to us over the last few years. You have my permission to tell one and all that the Robinson family is no longer, 'on the town.'

Thank you, and may God bless you all,

Sincerely,

Mary Kathleen Robinson."

All of the children applauded. Then Mother proposed a toast: "To Lorraine, and all of our family! *Erin go braugh!*"

They all solemnly lifted their glasses and downed their cranberry juice. Then, in the brief silence that followed, and for the first time in the history of the family, the voice of little Regis was heard at the dining room table. Pointing to the letter, he said excitedly: "Read it again, Mother! Read it again!"

Epilogue:

AT A PARTY IN honor of her eightieth birthday, which all of her seven children attended, Mother bragged that all four of her sons had served their country honorably during wartime – James, Joe, and Thos during World War II, and Regis during the Korean war.

James added that none of her children had ever been arrested, never been on public welfare, never smoked or abused alcohol or drugs, and that none of them had ever knowingly been unkind to any of God's creatures. At this Mother looked around at all seven of her brood and said firmly,, "And they darn well better keep on doing the right thing, if they know what's good for them!"

The Robinsons circa 1931, just before the family was devastated by The Great Depression
Top row: L. to R.   Lorraine, Patricia, James.   Front row: L.to R.   Thos, Rosebud, Joe
Regis is absent--he was too young to be out in the cold.

The Robinsons, Thanksgiving Day, 1944
L. to R. Lorraine, Patricia, Mother, James, Thos, Regis, Rosebud, Joe

Lightning Source UK Ltd.
Milton Keynes UK
UKOW02f2249100816

280404UK00002B/142/P